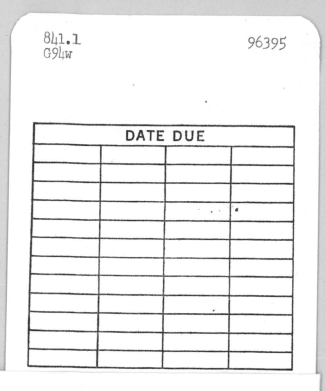

DATE DUE			

William, Count of Orange

FOUR OLD FRENCH EPICS

Edited by
Glanville Price,
with an introduction by
Lynette Muir
Translated by
Glanville Price, Lynette Muir
and David Hoggan

Dent, London
Rowman and Littlefield, Totowa, N.J.

Made in Great Britain
at the Aldine Press   Letchworth   Herts
for J. M. DENT & SONS LTD
Aldine House   Albemarle Street   London
First published 1975
First published in the United States 1975
by ROWMAN AND LITTLEFIELD, Totowa, New Jersey

This book is set in 10 on 11 point Baskerville 169

Dent edition
Hardback ISBN: 0 460 10367 9
Paperback ISBN: 0 460 11367 4

Rowman and Littlefield edition
Library of Congress Cataloging in Publication Data

Guillaume d'Orange (Chansons de geste).   English.
  William, Count of Orange: four Old French epics.

  (Rowman and Littlefield university library)
  CONTENTS: The crowning of Louis.—The waggon-train.
—The capture of Orange. [etc.]
  Bibliography: p.
  Includes index.
    1. Guillaume, Saint, Duc de Toulouse, d. ca. 812—
Romances. I. Price, Glanville, ed.   II. Title.
PQ1481.A3P75   1975   841'.1   74-23825
ISBN 0-87471-608-x
ISBN 0-87471-609-8 pbk.

Contents

Introduction

William, Count of Orange, the principal character in the poems translated in this volume, was one of the best-known heroes of the medieval French epics or *chansons de geste*—so called because they sang of the *gesta* or deeds of the peers of Charlemagne and other Frankish warriors. In the Middle Ages, William's fame was surpassed only by that of Roland, Oliver and Ogier the Dane. Indeed, for one writer, at least, he eclipsed all these save Roland; in Dante's vision of Paradise, William (Guglielmo) appeared in the Heaven of Jupiter, the paradise of the warriors, accompanied by Rainouart (Rinoardo), immediately after Charlemagne and Roland. No other hero from the *chansons de geste* appears in the *Divine Comedy*.

The stories of William were constantly retold, in verse and prose, in France. There were three poems of *Willehalm* and *Rennewart*, as well as a prose text, in Middle High German, and a cyclic compilation in Italian, *I Nerbonesi*. In England, however, William seems to have been virtually unknown in the Middle Ages and the situation has scarcely altered since; of all the collections of medieval tales of Charlemagne and his peers, written in the last hundred years or so, only one, Andrew Lang's *Book of Romance*, contains a story of William and Rainouart and the battle of Aliscans. Why is this? One possible reason is the comparatively minor role played by Charlemagne in the William cycle: most of the poems tell rather of the count's services to Charlemagne's weak and vacillating son, Louis the Pious. Another reason may be the absence of any reference to William in such influential works as Ariosto's *Orlando Furioso* and the other important Renaissance romances. In addition, the location of the poems in Southern France and Provence may have made them less attractive to English minstrels after the break-up of the Norman empire. It is even possible that the humour which is such an important feature of the cycle offended the sense of propriety of some of the nineteenth-century medievalists. Whatever the cause, the fact is indisputable; and it is hoped that this volume of translations of the four major adventures of the Count of Orange may do something to atone for this neglect and introduce to a much wider audience the adventures, heroic, pathetic and often comic, of William Shortnose and his numerous kinsmen.

The *chansons de geste* were divided by a thirteenth-century poet into three groups; the *gestes* of the King of France (Charlemagne), of Doon of Mayence and of Garin of Monglane. The first cycle mentioned includes the most famous of all the *chansons*, the *Song of Roland*. The second tells of the revolt of Doon and his family against the Emperor Charlemagne, and the tragic, internecine warfare that results. The third *geste* deals with the family to which William belongs. Garin of Monglane, William's great-grandfather, is the founder of the lineage whose exploits are recorded in the twenty-four poems of the cycle. Many of the manuscripts in which these poems are preserved are cyclic: that is, they contain a sequence of the poems arranged as a continuous narrative. Within this large *geste* is a smaller one, the cycle of William of Orange, second son of Aymeri of Narbonne, who had in all seven sons and five daughters so that the childless William was plentifully supplied with nephews to accompany him in his many and varied adventures.

The core of the *geste* of William of Orange consists of six poems in which he plays the major role:

1. *The Youthful Exploits of William* (*Les Enfances Guillaume*). William sets off for the court of Charlemagne to be knighted. On the way he routs a Saracen army with the aid of a club, not being qualified to use the knightly sword. He distinguishes himself at the court and when he finally receives the order of knighthood, Charlemagne gives him his own sword, Joyous. Thus armed, William embarks on his long career as the loyal and intrepid defender of the emperor and his son.

2. *The Crowning of Louis* (*Le Couronnement de Louis*) tells of William's battles in France and Italy against the traitors and pagans who, in turn, threaten the young, vacillating and cowardly king, Louis, son of Charlemagne.

3. *The Waggon-train* (*Le Charroi de Nîmes*) follows immediately on the preceding poem and tells how William, disgusted at the king's failure to reward his services with a fief, sets out to win lands for himself from the pagans who have overrun Southern France. By a trick which recalls the Wooden Horse of Troy he obtains entry to the city of Nîmes, which he then seizes from the pagan kings who had been ruling it.

4. *The Capture of Orange* (*La Prise d'Orange*) continues the story and tells how William visits Orange, in disguise, to woo the beautiful pagan queen, Orable, with whom he has fallen in love. After desperate adventures, he wins both the city and the lady for Christendom and himself.

5. *The Song of William* (*La Chanson de Guillaume*) is an older version of the poem known in the cyclic manuscripts as the battle of *Aliscans*. The first part of the *Song* describes the defeat in the Archamp of Vivien, William's nephew, by an overwhelming force of pagan invaders, and William's vain attempts to avenge him. In the second part of the poem (which is a discordant and probably much re-written continuation), William acquires the services of Rainouart, a gigantic folk-hero, who, armed with a great club (*tinel*), finally brings about a French victory in the Archamp. He is then revealed as the pagan brother of William's wife, Guibourg (the name taken by Orable at her baptism).

6. The last poem in the sequence, *William the Monk* (*Le Moniage Guillaume*), tells how, after Guibourg's death, William retires from the world and becomes a monk, but is too quick-tempered and ready with his fists to fit into a religious community. After many brawls and adventures, he becomes a hermit, wrestles against and defeats the devil and finally expires in the odour of sanctity.

Heroes of romance who lived long enough to reach 'retiring age' often ended their days in religious houses. William's life as a monk has a more historical basis, however, for the epic William is here iden-tified with the historical Count William of Toulouse, Charle-magne's nephew, who renounced the world in 804 to become a Benedictine monk. According to the *Chronicles of Aniane*, he went first to the monastery founded, near Montpellier, by the great reformer St Benedict of Aniane. Subsequently William withdrew to a separate house in the 'desert' at Gellone, about five miles from the mother-house of Aniane. He died at Gellone about 812 and was canonized in 1066 as St Guillaume du Désert with his feast day on 28th May. For many years, in the eleventh and twelfth centuries, Aniane and Gellone fought over their claims to the relics and prestige of St Guillaume. Aniane claimed that Gellone was only a dependent 'cell' of Aniane; while Gellone counterclaimed that it was a separate foundation, established by William, and their *Chronicles* carefully expunged any references to William's prior entry into the religious life at Aniane. The situation was further complicated by the tradition that William brought with him into the religious life a precious frag-ment of the True Cross, given him by the Emperor Charlemagne. This relic was obviously another important source of prestige and wealth and both houses claimed they possessed it. As part of their 'battle of charters', Aniane and Gellone produced accounts of William's deeds of piety and sanctity in religion and also in the world. These references, especially those in the Latin Life of the saint, the *Vita Sancti Wilhelmi*, composed at Gellone in the early twelfth century, provide a number of details which make it clear that this St William was, for the monks, not merely the historical Count William who had served Charlemagne, but also the epic hero, William of Orange. Probably the most significant passage in the *Vita* is that which describes how Count William defeated the Saracen King Tibalt (Theobaldus) outside the city of Orange, and subsequently held the town itself for many years against all counter-attacks. Now this story is completely fictitious. There were no pagans and no King Tibalt anywhere near Orange in the early ninth century, nor any Count William, either. On the other hand, the *Capture of Orange* is one of the best-known incidents in the poetic biography of the epic William, son of Aymeri of Narbonne. The earliest version we possess of the *Capture of Orange* was written considerably later than the *Vita*; so we must either accept that the monk who wrote the *Vita* made the story up and was copied by the minstrel who write the poem, which is so unlikely as to be quite unacceptable, or assume that an earlier version of the poem existed, together with a tradition of the exploits of the epic William sufficiently well established to be 'borrowed' by the monks of Gellone. In support of this, we have the evidence of Ordericus Vitalis, who in his *Ecclesiastical History*, composed between 1130 and 1140, prefaces an extract from the *Vita* with the following anecdote. Hugh d'Avranches, count of Chester, had a chaplain, Gerald, who used to tell stories of warrior saints as examples to the barons. Among them he spoke of William, the holy champion of God, who became a monk and lived as a knight of Christ. 'People sing songs of William,' says Ordericus, 'but the true tale is as follows,' and he goes on to quote the *Vita*. Obviously, then, by 1130 the monk, William of Gellone, and the epic hero, William of Orange, were thought of as one person. Furthermore, just as in English tradition all outlaw stories became attached to Robin Hood, so the adventures and exploits of many other Williams (Bédier mentions sixteen) were absorbed into the growing legend. It abounds in contradictions and inconsistencies. Yet it reveals also a remarkable inner cohesion and unity, due almost entirely to the very human, consistent and attractive portrayal of the central figure, William the short-nosed marquis.

The nick-name *court nez* or 'short-nose' is attached to William in all the poems of the cyclic manuscripts and its origin is explained in the *Crowning of Louis*. William fights a single combat against the pagan champion, Corsolt, one of whose blows glances off William's helmet, down the *nasel* or nose piece and slices off the unprotected end of the nose. William is furious, foreseeing the mockery he will have to endure, and redoubles his blows, finally slaying Corsolt with a mighty stroke. 'God!' cried William, 'what a vengeance for my nose!'

(*Crowning*, line 1122). It is obvious that this incident was invented to explain a nick-name which may originally have been *courb nez* 'hook-nose', the form found regularly in the *Song of William*, which preserves an earlier tradition than the cyclic manuscripts. 'Hook-nose' is also attested by the Latin fragment known as the *Nota Emilianense* which was discovered in 1953 and has been ascribed to the third quarter of the eleventh century at the latest. The *Nota* tells briefly of Charlemagne's expedition to Spain and the disaster which befell the army on its return through the Pyrenees—an obvious reference to the battle of Rencesvals, immortalized in the *Song of Roland*. A list is given of Charlemagne's peers which includes 'rodlane, bertlane, oggero spata curta, ghigelmo alcorbitanas'. Under their bastardized Latin forms we can recognize here the names of Roland, Bertrand, Ogier Short-sword and *Guillaume al courb nez*—William Hooknose.

The picture of William in the poems translated in this volume is remarkably consistent. He is valiant and quick-tempered, loyal to the king despite the latter's many failings, and a devout son of the church, although his ethos may sometimes appear a trifle eccentric for a budding saint; his mood varies between fits of depression caused by the number of valiant men he has killed in the king's service (*Waggon-train*, line 70) or his fear that he may have behaved disloyally to the king (*Waggon-train*, lines 790–800), and exuberant cheerfulness as he hoodwinks the Saracens in Nîmes with his preposterous tales as the disguised merchant with eighteen children or in the wooing of Orable in Orange under the very nose of her pagan stepson. This gaiety and vitality infuse the whole cycle; whenever William holds the stage there is an undercurrent of humour and the joy of living. The only exception to this, rendered the more noticeable by its rarity, is the first part of the *Song of William*. After an opening which includes some humour in the drunken vainglory of Thibaut and his ignominious flight from the field, there follows a long section recounting Vivien's lonely and protracted martyrdom and William's two vain attempts to avenge him. Even here, however, flashes of humour break through, notably in the character of little Guy and the gentle mockery of Guibourg, William's wife, who serves him a copious repast when he returns defeated from the Archamp, and then remarks that a man who can consume a great haunch of pork, a roast peacock, two loaves of bread and a gallon of wine cannot really be so hopeless as he claimed. The sombre tones of the first part of the *Song of William* are, however, more than compensated by the fantastic humour of the Rainouart episodes in which the gigantic scullion slaughters his foes with reckless abandon. In this sequence, too, there is a good deal of gentle mockery—for example when Rainouart tries to win horses for the French prisoners he has released but kills the horses with their riders every time, because he cannot control the force of his blows; only when Bertrand suggests that he try a thrust not a bash does he succeed in killing the rider without also cutting the horse in half (*Song*, lines 170–1).

This recurring comedy of situation and incident, where the basic humour is reinforced by the mockery of the characters themselves, is an important feature of the whole cycle of William of Orange, and distinguishes it from the other *chansons de geste* and from most European epic. For it is not parody; we laugh with the characters, not at them. Even the fantastic Rainouart is given a genuine, human character. He is gluttonous and a winebibber, quick-tempered and easily offended, but he has also a softer side and a certain naïve simplicity: his delight and surprise when he discovers that the sword Guibourg has given him can kill a man as easily as his cudgel—'This is wonderful, that so small a weapon should cut so sweetly' (*Song*, line 3330)— reveal a childlike quality like that of the young Perceval, who, on being shown the use of protective armour, remarks that it is a good thing the deer he hunts do not have mail-coats. The nearest the cycle comes to parody, in fact, is in the *Capture of Orange* when William sets out like any romantic hero to win the unknown lady of whose beauty he has become enamoured. But even here the astringent is not far to seek; the consequences of William's amorous adventures are stressed not by the writer from outside the story but by William's own nephew, Guielin, who nearly drives William mad by his mocking comments: 'You used to be called William Strongarm, now they will call you William Sweetheart' (*Capture*, lines 1562–3).

The importance of the nephews of William is another feature of the cycle, which is intensely clannish in its formation: a medieval *Forsyte Saga*. This is to some extent true of all the *chansons de geste* but it is particularly stressed in this cycle; the childless William is never lacking a nephew to accompany him and be at his right hand. The most important is Bertrand who is with William in three of these poems, the *Crowning of Louis*, the *Waggon-train* and the *Capture of Orange*. Indeed, Bertrand has little existence away from William. He is a foil, a lieutenant, a companion; and although he is a rounded, developed person, he rarely plays a solo part. Vivien, on the other hand, is one of the most important figures in the whole cycle of Garin de Monglane, and has several poems of which he is the hero, culminating in his tragic and heroic end at the Archamp. It is certain that this first part of the *Song of William* was originally a separate poem, relating the martyrdom of a heroic saint, for Vivien is a Christ figure, almost an anti-hero: as he staggers bleeding and faint across the wastes of the Archamp, tortured by thirst and heat, he presents a marked contrast to the heroic serenity of the death of Roland at Rencesvals, attended by angels and assured of Paradise. Until the manuscript of the *Song of William* was discovered at the beginning of this century, the story of William's early defeat and final victory over the Saracens with the aid of Rainouart was preserved in two separate poems. The first, the *Knightly deeds of Vivien* (*La Chevalerie Vivien*, sometimes called the *Covenant Vivien*) told of the Saracen invasion, the first battle, with Vivien's loss of his men and refusal to flee, followed by William's arrival on the battlefield. The end of the battle, with William's defeat and the death of Vivien, then the Siege of Orange, William's appeal to Louis and the coming of Rainouart were told in a longer sequel called *Aliscans*.

Only two women play a part in the cycle, William's sister Blanche-fleur who makes a brief, inglorious appearance in the *Song of William*, and his wife Guibourg, or Orable, who is probably the most important female character in the whole corpus of *chansons de geste*. Her role in the *Capture of Orange* is important but fairly conventional. The *Song of William*, however, presents a delightful portrait of a gracious châtelaine and a wise, witty and loving wife. We would have to search far to find her equal in medieval French literature: perhaps the nearest would be Nicolette in the thirteenth-century song-story of *Aucassin and Nicolette*.

Not all the Christians are shown in a favourable light. Thibaut and Esturmi at the beginning of the *Song of William* are drunken cowards, but the most elaborately drawn 'villain' is certainly Louis, the king. Unlike his father, Charlemagne, who with all his faults was a strong and vigorous leader of men, Louis the Pious appears throughout the cycle as weak, cowardly, treacherous, grasping and, eventually, hen-pecked. It is the unattractive character of the king that brings out so strongly the genuineness of William's loyalty. Despite everything, he never seriously considers rebellion, although on a number of occasions he comes close to renouncing his allegiance. This behaviour is the more marked if we remember that the *geste* of Doon of Mayence deals with just this theme: the revolt of the family of Doon against Charlemagne and the tragic consequences of the resulting warfare.

The concept of loyalty to the king and to France runs as a leit-motiv through the cycle, with the other, perhaps even more important, theme of the defence of Christendom. William and his kin share the crusading spirit of the *Song of Roland* and could truly claim the title of Defenders of the Faith. At the very beginning of the *Waggon-train* we are reminded that William of Orange is also St William, who 'exalted holy Christianity' (line 12). It is significant that these expeditions, to Nîmes and to Orange, are seen as incursions into

Saracen lands not merely in order to enlarge the national boundaries of France but to win back Christian territory that should never have been lost. After Orange has been captured, we are told that William never held it a day without fighting, a conclusion that recalls the weariness of Charlemagne at the end of the *Song of Roland* when told by the Angel he must go and fight again: 'God,' said the king, 'my life is full of toil.'

The struggle between Christian and infidel forms the theme of the *Song of Roland* but is not otherwise predominant in the *gestes* of Charlemagne and of Doon. It is fundamental, however, to the whole cycle of Garin of Monglane and especially to the story of William of Orange, so that the development of the epic hero from the historical warrior-turned-monk seems not unreasonable. We have seen that the monks of Gellone who wrote the *Vita*, and the *jongleurs* or minstrels who composed the early poems, must have known and used each other's work; but it is not easy to determine how this two-way traffic arose. For Bédier, the meeting ground was the pilgrim routes to St James of Compostella; pilgrims travelling across southern France to this celebrated shrine would have stopped at Gellone to honour the relics of St William and the True Cross, and the *jongleurs* would have found in them a profitable audience for their songs. The theory is not implausible but aspects of it have been severely criticized by other scholars and the question will remain open so long as the whole problem of the sources and origins of the *chansons de geste* remains the subject of vexed and apparently insoluble debate. As Frappier has very pertinently pointed out, it would be a pity to allow the argument about sources to distract us from the more important study of the literary and aesthetic merits of the texts as we have them.

The style of the poems is as varied as the mood, passing from the heights of elegiac lament through an earthy humour to the depths of bathos. One of the difficulties in translating such works is the need to vary rapidly, often from one sentence to the next, the tone and mood of the language. An accurate rendering inevitably gives the reader an impression of very uneven writing in the original, especially in the *Song of William* which is a corrupt manuscript, many of the lines being defective in both length and assonance.[1] The verse structure of all four poems is the same; they are divided into *laisses* or sections of anything from three to over a hundred and fifty decasyllabic assonanced lines. The change from one *laisse* and assonance to the next is at the complete discretion of the poets who display very varied degrees of skill in handling this verse form. At best, each *laisse* is a coherent unit

[1] Assonance is a rhyme on the vowels only, which is used in the *chansons de geste* and other Old French poems.

of both sense and sound, often ending with a single-line sentence which provides a crisp conclusion. Considerable use is made of repetition, especially at the beginning of two or more consecutive *laisses*; but throughout the poems phrases and sometimes whole sentences are repeated in similar or identical words. This technique can be a great aid to comprehension in an oral text, and it is worth remembering that the *chansons de geste* were originally designed for reciting aloud. It could be confusing, however, and in the *Capture of Orange* for example it is abused to the extent of making it difficult on occasions to be certain whether the incident described is the same one told in two different ways, or two different incidents. Repetition of epic formulae is common in battle sequences and the personal descriptions are almost exclusively of this stock variety. The *Song of William* has a strange refrain, 'Monday in the evening' (occasionally varied to Wednesday or Thursday), which occurs in a separate half line and is found, usually at the end, in over half the *laisses*. No one has yet succeeded in explaining this refrain satisfactorily. It is peculiar to this manuscript, nor is anything comparable known in any other medieval work, although the inexplicable word AOI is found spasmodically, at the end of some lines, in the Oxford manuscript of the *Song of Roland*.

The legendary, heroic qualities of the William poems are carefully 'earthed' by a spatial, temporal location in central and southern France in the ninth century. Much of the history is inaccurate, and the geographical distances are often unrealistic, but the people and places described are more often than not recognizably authentic. There is no element of fairy-tale or magic, such as is found in the romances, not even the Christian supernatural of the *Song of Roland* and scriptural or hagiographical tales. The heroes eat and drink and fight with rumbustious humour and almost Rabelaisian gusto, against a background of cities that we can still visit today. Laon and Bourges are now famous for their cathedrals rather than their palaces, but the great market of Orange has a whole row of stalls selling olives and quantities of exotic fruits and spices so that it may still 'smell very sweet for there is an abundance of peppers and cinnamon there' (*Capture*, lines 250–1). The Roman theatre of Orange, like the amphitheatres of Nîmes and Arles, was a medieval fortress. It is almost certainly the palace Gloriette which figures so prominently in the *Capture of Orange*. At Gellone, which is now called St Guilhem-le-Désert, there are still the ruins of a tiny chapel on the hill and the bridge traditionally built by the devil under William's orders. Many tourists visit the village, and its romanesque church still possesses the famous relic of the True Cross and the sarcophagus which is supposed to have contained the relics of St William, although most of the bones were scattered and lost at the time of the Revolution. Visiting St Guilhem today, we can see the final victory of the monks of Gellone over their rivals at Aniane, for the crowded streets and numerous visitors of the former are in marked contrast to the sleepy emptiness of Aniane, whose church is a second-rate eighteenth-century basilica. In the latest edition of the Guide Michelin to the Gorges du Tarn, St Guilhem rates one and a half columns and two stars. Aniane is not even mentioned.

Select Bibliography

J. Bédier, *Les Légendes épiques. Recherches sur la formation des chansons de geste. I. Le Cycle de Guillaume d'Orange*, 3rd edition, Paris (Champion), 1926.

J. Frappier, *Les Chansons de geste du cycle de Guillaume d'Orange*, 2 vols, Paris (SEDES), 1955–65. (*The Song of William* is discussed in Vol. 1, our other three texts in Vol. 2.)

Madeleine Tyssens, *La Geste de Guillaume d'Orange dans les manuscrits cycliques*, Paris (Belles Lettres), 1967. (A study of the relationship of the various manuscripts that include our texts.)

Editor's Foreword

These versions of four medieval French epics are the work of three different translators. Our general policy has been to provide, in readable modern English, a translation that as far as possible renders faithfully the sense of the original without being slavishly literal. Within these limits, there has been no attempt to impose uniformity of style on the three translators. In general, where the text is uncertain or ambiguous, we have not drawn attention to this but have selected one acceptable rendering on the basis of the notes, glossary and critical apparatus provided in the editions used.

As Dr Muir points out in her Introduction, the poems are 'divided into *laisses* or sections of anything from three to over a hundred and fifty decasyllabic assonanced lines'. In our prose translations, we have kept the division into *laisses*, giving at the end of each *laisse* and occasionally elsewhere, where we have divided a long *laisse* into paragraphs, the reference to the closing line as numbered in the editions used.

Where the name of the same character occurs in somewhat different forms in different texts (or sometimes within the same text), we have adopted one standardized form throughout. Where there is an obvious English equivalent (e.g. 'William' for *Guillaume*, etc., 'Walter' for *Gautier*, etc.), this has been adopted. Otherwise we have either adopted a modern French version or, where no such form exists (for example, in the case of exotic Saracen names), we have retained one or other of the medieval forms. An index of proper names will be found at the end of the volume. The family relationship between William and other characters mentioned in the epics is set out in a genealogical table on p. xviii.

The translation of each of the four poems is followed by references to the editions used and a minimum of explanatory notes. Bibliographies of studies relating to each particular poem will be found in Langlois's edition of the *Crowning of Louis*, McMillan's editions of *The Waggon-train* and *The Song of William*, and Régnier's edition of *The Capture of Orange*. A brief bibliography of more general works is given on p. xvi.

G. P.

LEGENDARY GENEALOGICAL TABLE OF WILLIAM'S FAMILY *

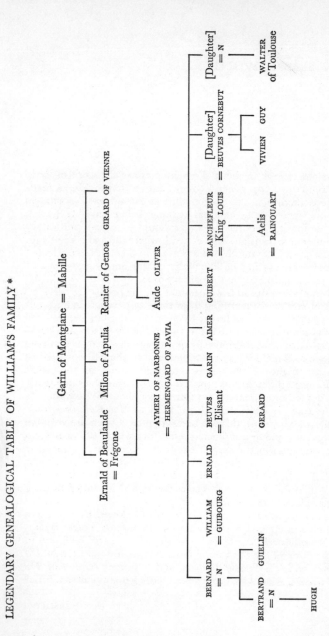

* Names of characters who appear in the poems of this volume are indicated in capitals. Some of the information incorporated in this Table is derived from later poems, but secondary traditions which contradict the data of our texts are omitted. '=' signifies 'married to'. 'N' indicates that the name of the spouse is unknown.

The Crowning of Louis

1. Listen, my lords, may God be your constant help! Would it please you to hear a fine song, courtly and comely, that tells of valiant deeds? I do not see why any lowborn songster should make bold to tell a word of it unless he is ordered. But I mean to sing to you now of Louis and of William Shortnose, the valiant, who endured so much at the hand of the Saracens. No one could sing to you of a better man.   [9]

2. Noble barons, would it please you to hear a story with a moral, told in a well-made and comely song? When God chose to Himself nine and ninety kingdoms, the best one of all was the one that became sweet France. The best of all kings was the one called Charlemagne; it was he who delighted in exalting sweet France. There was not a land God made that did not come under his sway: Bavaria and Alemannia belonged to him, and Normandy, Anjou and Brittany, Lombardy, Tuscany and Navarre.   [19]

3. The king who wears the golden crown of France must be an upright man and valiant in his body. If there is any man who does him a wrong, he must leave him no peace in plain or in forest until he has overpowered him or killed him. If he does not do this, France loses her glory; then, history says, he was wrongfully crowned.   [26]

4. When the Chapel at Aix was consecrated and the abbey [1] was set up and dedicated, there was a great assembly of the court, such as will never be seen again; fourteen counts mounted guard on the palace. The poor people came there to seek justice: no man put forward a plea without receiving a very fair judgement. In those days, justice was done, but things are no longer the same, for wicked men have made justice a

I

mask for covetousness and because of bribery fair hearings are
no longer given. God is righteous, He who governs and feeds
us, so such men will be consigned to the stench of Hell, the evil
pit from which they will never return.   [38]

5. That day eighteen bishops or more were present, and eighteen
archbishops. The Pope of Rome himself sang the mass.   [41]

6. That day the offertory was most generous; since that time
there has never been a better one in France. He who received
it made great rejoicing.   [44]

7. That day twenty-six abbots or more were present, and four
crowned kings. That day Louis was exalted before them and
the crown was placed on the altar; his father the king had
named this day for him. An archbishop went up to the pulpit
and addressed the Christian people: 'Barons,' he said, 'listen
to my words. Charles the Great is nearing the end of his days.
He can no longer live the same life as before; he is no longer
able to wear the crown, but he has a son to whom he wishes to
pass it.' When they heard this, they showed signs of great joy,
stretching up their hands to God: 'Glorious Father, receive our
thanks that no stranger has been given us as a king.'   [60]

Our emperor addressed his son and said: 'Fair son, hear
what I have to say. Look at the crown over there on the altar;
I am willing to give it to you on this condition: that you com-
mit no wrong nor live in lust or sin nor act treacherously
towards any man nor deprive any orphan of his fief. If you are
willing to do this, I shall praise God for it; take the crown and
you shall be crowned king. But if you refuse, my son, let it stay
where it is; I forbid you to lay a finger on it.   [71]

8. 'Louis, my son, you see the crown here by me. If you accept
it, you will be Emperor of Rome. You will be able to lead a
good hundred thousand men in your army and cross in
strength the waters of the Gironde to destroy and confound the
pagan nation and unite their lands to ours, as is your duty. If
you are willing to do this, I give you the crown; but if not,
then never dare to accept it.   [79]

9. 'If you are going to take bribes, fair son, or encourage and
promote excess or commit lechery or glorify evil, or deprive

any young orphan of his fief or any widow of as much as four pence, then in Jesus' name I forbid you, Louis my son, to accept this crown.' When the youth heard this, he made no move to come forward. Then many a valiant knight wept for him and the Emperor was greatly aggrieved and angered. 'Alas!' he said, 'how wickedly I have been deceived! Some worthless rascal has slept with my wife and bred me this cowardly heir. Never in all his life shall he get advancement from me. If he were ever made king, it would be a great wrong. Let us cut off all his hair and put him into this monastery; he can pull the bell ropes and be the sacristan, so he will have a pittance to keep him from beggary.'   [98]

Beside the king sat Arneïs of Orleans, he who was so proud and haughty. Full of treachery, he began to speak to the king: 'Rightful Emperor, restrain yourself and listen to me. My lord is young, he is only just fifteen; if he were made a knight now, he would soon be a dead man. I beg you, entrust this burden to me for three years, until we see how matters develop. If he shows himself brave and a worthy heir, then I shall restore it to him gladly and willingly and extend his lands and his fiefs.' And the king replied: 'This request should be granted.'—'Our hearty thanks, sire,' said all the courtiers who were relatives of Arneïs of Orleans. He was just about to be made king when William arrived, returning from hunting in the forest.   [114]

His nephew Bertrand ran to his stirrup and William asked him: 'Where have you been, fair nephew?'—'In God's name, sir, inside the abbey church, where I heard a great wrong and a great evil. Arneïs wants to betray his rightful lord and is to be made king straight away, for so the Frenchmen have decided.' —'Perish the thought!' said William the proud. With his sword girt at his side he entered the church, pushed through the throng of knights and came up to Arneïs, standing there all finely arrayed. His first thought was to strike off his head, then he remembered the glorious Lord of Heaven, for to kill a man is a grievous mortal sin. Clasping his sword, he returned it to its sheath, then he stepped forward and, throwing up his sleeves, he grabbed him by the hair with his left fist. He raised his right and brought it down on his neck, broke his neckbone through the middle and toppled him dead at his feet.[2] Seeing him dead, he began to reprimand him: 'Ah, scoundrel!' he said, 'God give you grief! Why did you try to betray your rightful lord? You ought to have loved him and held him dear, extending his lands and favouring his fiefs. But guile will profit you no longer. I only intended to chastize you a little but now you are dead and I do not give a halfpenny.'   [141]

Seeing the crown sitting there on the altar, the count seized it without delay, came up to the youth and set it on his head. 'Receive this, fair lord, in the name of the King of Heaven; may He give you the strength to be a just ruler!' When the father saw this, he was glad on his son's account: 'Lord William,' he said, 'accept my hearty thanks. It is your lineage that has raised up mine.'   [149]

10. 'Ah, Louis,' said Charles, 'noble son, now you will have my kingdom to govern. May you preserve it in such a manner that you never deprive any young orphan of his rights nor any widow woman of as much as a shilling. And take care to serve Holy Church well, so that no devil may ever bring you to shame. Take care to treat your knights with esteem, then you will be honoured and well served by them and loved and held dear in all lands.'   [159]

11. After Louis had been made king that day, the court dispersed and the hearings were adjourned. Each Frenchman returned to his lodgings. [Charlemagne lived no more than five years longer.] [3] Charles the king went back up into the palace and, seeing his son, addressed him straight away: [165]

12. 'Louis, my son, I shall not hide this from you: now you will have possession of my whole kingdom after my death, as surely as I pray God to bless me. I know well that any man who wars against me also defies you and that the man who hates me shows you no love either. If I can capture such a man, by God the Son of Mary, I swear I will take no ransom for him, but will have him hacked to pieces and killed.   [173]

13. 'Louis, my son, I do not seek to hide this from you. When God created kings to govern nations, He did not do it so that they might give false judgements or commit lechery or pro-

mote evil or deprive a young orphan of his fief or a widow
woman of as much as four pence. On the contrary, a king must
strike down wrongs under his feet and trample on them and
stamp them out. Towards the poor man, you must humble
yourself and, if he has a plea, it should not vex you; rather you
should help him and succour him and for love of God restore
him to his rights. Towards the proud man, you must show
yourself as fierce as a man-eating leopard and, if he tries to
make war on you, summon throughout France all the noble
knights until you have up to thirty thousand, have him
besieged in his strongest fortress and all his land laid waste and
devastated. If you can capture him or have him delivered into
your hands, show him neither mercy nor pity but have all his
limbs cut off or let him be burnt in a fire or drowned in water.
For, if ever the French see you trampled under foot, the
Normans will say by way of reproach: "We have little need of
a king like that! A curse be on the head of any man who goes
to fight in his army again or ever goes to serve at his court! We
can easily help ourselves to his possessions." [203]

   'And another thing I want to tell you about, my son, that will
be very important to you, if you live: not to take a lowborn
man as your counsellor, the son of a lord's agent or of a bailiff.
These would betray their trust in a minute for money. Choose
rather William, the noble warrior, the son of proud Aymeri of
Narbonne and brother of Bernard of Brubant, the warrior; if
these men are willing to support and aid you, you can com-
pletely rely on their service.' The youth replied: 'By my head,
you speak the truth.' He went to the count and threw himself
at his feet. Count William rushed to raise him up and asked:
'Young lord, what do you want of me?'—'In God's name, sir,
succour and pity. My father says you are a fine knight, that
there is no greater warrior under the vault of heaven. I wish to
entrust to you my lands and my fiefs so that you may protect
them for me, noble knight, until I can bear arms myself.' The
count replied: 'By my faith, willingly.' He swore to him on the
relics of the abbey that he would never possess anything worth
as much as four pence unless Louis gave it to him gladly and
willingly. [227]

   Then he came up to Charlemagne, for he had no wish to

delay, and knelt down before the king. 'Rightful Emperor,' he
said, 'I beg to take my leave, for I am obliged to go riding off
and travel straight to Rome to pray to St Peter. I do not seek to
hide that I made this promise fifteen years ago and have not
yet been able to carry it out. But now I do not wish to put off
this journey any longer.' The king granted his permission, sad
and vexed at heart, and put in his charge a band of sixty
knights and thirty pack-horses loaded with gold and silver. At
the moment of separation, they rushed into each other's arms
and exchanged kisses. As it happened, the warrior was setting
out on a journey from which he would not come back before
facing great hardships and Charles would be dead before he
returned and Louis left as his heir. Then, before William could
take any action or arrive back in France, Louis would be
wrongfully locked up and hidden away, expecting nothing
better than to have all his limbs cut off, and William could
easily have arrived too late.   [248]

14. William Strongarm was in the abbey church, asking leave
to depart from the Emperor Charles, and he entrusted him
with sixty men-at-arms and gave him thirty pack-horses laden
with gold and silver. The count rode off, making no delay, and
Louis accompanied him a good distance on his way. In tears he
called out to William Strongarm: 'Ah, noble count, by God
who is a spirit, you see that my father is passing away from the
things of this world. He is old and frail and will never again
bear arms, and I am young and of tender years. If I do not
have help, everything will go to ruin.' The count replied: 'Do
not be uneasy about that, for, by the apostle men visit [4] at the
Ark, when I have completed this pilgrimage, if ever you
summon me by letter under your seal or by any man worthy of
your trust, then for no man on earth will I fail to come to your
help with all my powerful warriors.' The count rode off,
making no delay. Of his journeying, I have little to tell: he
crossed the Great St Bernard which caused him great fatigue,
and all the way to Rome Strongarm travelled without a
break.   [271]

*   *   *

15. William the noble warrior rode off on his journey, and

with him went Guielin and the renowned Bertrand. Under
their cloaks they bore their inscribed swords but they had
packed in the baggage their fine hauberks and their gilded
helms. The squires laboured under the weight of their stout
shields and their spears. Of their journeying, I have little to
relate: they crossed the St Bernard which caused them great
fatigue and made their way through the Romagna and
travelled all the way to Rome without a break. The squires
found lodgings for them; the name of their host was Ciquaire
and William entrusted all his possessions to him. That night
the count was well provided for and after the meal they all
went to bed; the count soon fell asleep for he was utterly
exhausted. [288]

He dreamt a dream which terrified him greatly. From the
direction of Russia there came a blazing fire which set light to
Rome on all sides; a huge hound came rushing up at full speed,
leaving the rest of the pack behind; William was under a
spreading tree and was extremely frightened by this beast, for
it gave him such a blow with its paw that it bent him right over
towards the ground. The count woke up and commended him-
self to God. Never was there a dream that came true so com-
pletely, for the Saracens were already on their way. King
Galafre and King Tenebré, King Cremu and the Emir
Corsolt had already taken the main strongholds of Capua;
King Guaifier had been captured there, along with his
daughter and his very beautiful wife and thirty thousand
wretched prisoners who were all to have their heads severed
from their trunks. But such was God's love for the judicious
William that all would be freed from their captivity because of
his stand against Corsolt from beyond the Red Sea, the
strongest man you have ever heard of. It was he who cut off
William's nose, as you will hear before it gets dark, if you pay
me enough to make me go on singing. [314]

At this point in the story, day began to break. Count
William got up early in the morning and went to the church to
hear the service; he had all his arms placed on the altar,
intending to ransom them with Arabian gold. The Pope, a
most noble and valiant man, put on his vestments to sing the
mass. When the service was over and fully said, suddenly two

messengers came rushing up post haste. They had such news to
tell as would cause great fear that day to many a freeborn
man.   [325]

16. William Strongarm was in the abbey church and mass had
been sung by the wise Pope. When it was over, two messengers
arrived bringing him bitter news: that the Saracens were doing
him a very great harm; they had taken by storm the great city
of Capua and led off thirty thousand prisoners, one and all due,
unless they were rescued, to die by the sword. The Pope was
greatly dismayed at this and went looking for William Strong-
arm. Someone pointed him out, kneeling down below on the
marble floor, praying to God our spiritual Father to give him
strength, honour and courage and the like to his lord, Louis the
son of Charles. The Pope did not hold back at all; he took a
rod and struck him on the shoulder. The count raised his head
and turned his face towards him.   [342]

17. Count William rose up to his feet and the Pope began to
speak to him: 'Ah, noble lord, for the sake of God the just, tell
me I beg you if you can help me. The pagans our adversaries
are attacking us, led by King Galafre who is first among their
kings; and he who used to protect us in distress, the mighty
King Guaifier, has been captured by force, along with his
daughter and his highborn wife and thirty thousand wretched
prisoners who will all lose their heads, unless they are rescued.'
—'Ah! God help us!' said the count with the proud coun-
tenance, and he began to cross himself at the thought of so
many kings. His nephew Bertrand rebuked him for this:
'Uncle William, have you gone mad, then? Never before have
I seen you afraid of any man.' William replied: 'Spare me, for
God's sake, fair nephew. Our force is useless against their
numbers; we had better find a messenger for we must send to
Louis to get him to come and bring us help and support, while
Charlemagne stays behind to administer justice; he is old and
frail and can no longer ride a horse.' And Bertrand said: 'May
the just God confound and drive mad and bring to death any
man who goes to deliver that message; may his shield be
pierced with holes and the mesh of his hauberk torn apart and
unravelled and may he himself be struck with a great spear, so

that everyone can see he is a messenger! The pagans are attacking us in their hundreds and their thousands. To arms straight away! We have no time to lose. Let us defend ourselves and not waste time.' But among the men of Rome there was only dismay; they had few fighting men, less than a hundred thousand. [377]

18. The count with the proud countenance was in the abbey church; the Pope, a courteous and wise man, said to him: 'Noble lord, for the sake of God the Spirit I beg you, rescue us from the savage race!'—'Ah! God help us!' said Count Strongarm. 'I came here on a pilgrimage, so I brought only a small band of warriors; I have only sixty knights in arms, I could never fight against so many kings.'—'Ah! God help us!' said the wise Pope. 'Look, here is St Peter, the guardian of souls; if you undertake this feat of arms today on his account, my lord, then you may eat meat every single day for the rest of your life and take as many wives as you have a mind to. You will never commit any sin however wicked (so long as you avoid any act of treason) that will not be discounted, all the days of your life, and you shall have your lodging in paradise, the place Our Lord keeps for His best friends; St Gabriel himself will show you the way.' [5]—'Ah! God help us!' said Count Strongarm, 'never was there a more generous-hearted cleric! Now I will not fail, for any man alive or for any pagan however foul or wicked, to go out and fight against these scoundrels. Fair nephew Bertrand, go and fetch your arms, you and Guielin and the other warriors.' [404]

William Strongarm called for his arms; they were brought before him where he stood. He pulled on his hauberk and laced his green helm; he girded on his sword by its baldric of silk brocade. They led up his piebald horse and the count leapt on its back without using the stirrup. A vermilion buckler hung from his neck; between his fists he held a stout sharp spear and attached his banner to it with five golden nails. 'My lord Pope,' said the wise William, 'how many fighting men have you here in your march?' The Pope replied: 'I can tell you that for sure: we have three thousand men, all of them with a chin-piece of mail, a stout spear and a sharp-edged sword.'

The count replied: 'That is a good beginning! Let them all be armed and the foot soldiers too, so that they can defend the gates and the barricades.' And the Pope replied: 'Yes, that is the right thing to do.'   [422]

Throughout all Rome the warriors formed up their companies and when they were armed they assembled in that place. The Pope made the sign of the cross over them. 'Noble warriors,' said the wise Pope, 'any man who dies in battle this day will have his lodging in paradise, the place Our Lord keeps for His best friends; St Gabriel himself will show him the way.' Then they rose up to their feet and each one seized his arms to face the proud savage race. When they reached the main gate, which was far from low, they beat violently on it in their fine mettle. 'Noble warriors,' said the wise Pope, 'you will remain here with those armed men while I go and parley with the Emir Galafre. If for any wealth that I can promise him he consents to turn back his ships and his barges, and his great armies that are installed here, I will give him the great treasure of the Ark; not a chalice or cope will be spared, nor gold or silver nor anything worth a penny piece, rather than have so many noble and wise men die.' And they replied: 'It is right that this should be known.'   [445]

At this he set off, accompanied by an abbot, and went without delay to the tents. There he met the mighty King Galafre; he did not greet him, it would not have been right for him to do so. The mighty king looked at him proudly; the Pope addressed him straight away: 'Sire,' he said, 'I have come here as a messenger on behalf of God and St Peter, the guardian of souls. I have a message for you from him, to tell you that if you turn back your ships and your barges and your great armies that are installed here, I shall give you the great treasure of the Ark; not a chalice or cope will be spared, nor gold or silver worth a single penny, rather than have so many noble men-at-arms die. Take counsel, then, noble and highborn king.' The king replied: 'You cannot have much reason in your head. I have come here into my rightful inheritance, established by my grandfather and great-grandfather and before them by Romulus and by Julius Caesar who built these walls and bridges and defences. If by force I can topple down these pillars, I shall wreck everything that belongs to God and reduce all the clerics that serve Him to suffering and degradation.' The Pope was much dismayed at this; he would not have chosen to be there for all the gold of Carthage. [471]

He asked for a safe-conduct from the Emir Galafre and he gave him three Saracens as surety. King Galafre addressed him once again: 'Listen to me, lord with the broad-brimmed hat! Never let it be said that I am doing you a wrong with regard to this city which is part of my inheritance. Choose a man with his arms all at the ready and I shall take one from my powerful family: we will have them brought face to face as champions. If your God has any power to do so, let my warrior be defeated by yours; then you will have free possession of Rome as a heritage and for the rest of your life no one will deprive you of as much as a cheese. Lest I should break my word to you over this, take both my sons as hostages and accept not a penny of ransom money for them, but have them both hanged on a tree!' When the Pope heard this wise proposal, he could not have been more glad for all the gold of Carthage; he remembered Count Strongarm standing there all ready for battle in the church before the Ark and knew that no better warrior ever bore arms. [494]

19. The Pope was a very learned man; he saw clearly that God was willing to help him, now that his rights could be defended by a single champion. He stated his rights clearly to his challenger: 'Sire,' he said, 'let me speak frankly. Since we are to reach a settlement by means of a single combat, I should be glad to see this champion of yours who is ready to challenge God's rights in Rome.' The king replied: 'I am happy to grant it.' King Corsolt was brought before him and stood there, ugly and squint-eyed, as hideous as a devil. His eyes were red like coals in a blazing fire; his head was broad with bristling hair; the distance between his eyes was half a foot and from his shoulders to his waist was a good two yards. A more hideous man never ate bread. He began rolling his eyes at the Pope and shouted at him: 'Little man, what do you want here? Is it because of your orders that you have that shaven crown?—'Sire,' replied the Pope, 'I serve God in His church, God and

St Peter who is our leader. On his behalf I should like to beg
you to turn back your armies; I will give you the great
treasure of his church, not a chalice or censer will be left, nor
gold or silver worth a single penny, but I will have it all spread
out here before you.' The king replied: 'You are not very
well-informed, if you dare come pleading for God to me! He is
the man who has angered me more than anyone else on earth:
my father was killed by a thunderbolt from heaven, he was all
burnt up and no one could do anything to save him. When
God had killed him, He acted very cleverly! He went up to
heaven and refused to come back down here again! I never
was able to chase and pursue Him, but since then I have
avenged myself on His men: of those who belong to Him by
water and baptism, I have destroyed more than thirty thou-
sand, burning them with fire and drowning them in water.
Since I cannot go and make war against God up there, I will
spare not a single one of His men here below! So God and I
have no further quarrel: the earth is for me and He can have
heaven! If I can capture this territory here, I shall lay waste
all that belongs to God; I shall have the clerics that serve Him
flayed with knives and, as for you, who are lord of this church,
I shall have you roasted on the coals of a hearth until your liver
drops out into the embers!'   [543]

When the Pope heard him speaking like this, it is not sur-
prising that he was terrified. He and the abbot began to
whisper about it: 'By St Denis, this Turk is raving mad! It is a
great wonder he is still standing here with his feet on the earth
and that God has not dispatched him to the fires of Hell. Alas!
William, marquis with the proud countenance, may He
protect you who was raised on the Cross! Your strength is of no
avail against such a man.'   [552]

He asked for a safe-conduct from proud Galafre, who gave
him his sons by his own wife as hostages; they led him on foot
as far as Rome. Count William was the first to come towards
him, seized his stirrup-iron and asked: 'My lord, what
success have you had? Tell me, did you see the enemy who is
trying to dispute God's right to Rome? Noble lord, did you
manage to do that?'—'Yes, fair sir, and I shall be frank with
you: he is not a man but a devil! If Roland and Oliver were

still alive, and Yves and Yvoire, Haton and Béranger, and the
Archbishop and the youth Manessier, Estolt of Langres and the
courtly Walter and along with them Gerin and Engelier,[6] all
the twelve peers who were mown down, and even if your noble
father Aymeri the warrior, so worthy of esteem, and all your
brothers who are such fine knights were here, they would never
dare to meet him in battle.'—'God!' said William, 'tell me
who that can be! Now I see clearly that the clergy has turned
false! You are always saying that God is of such great worth
that anyone He is willing to sustain and help can never be
brought to shame or disgrace or burnt in fire or drowned in
water. But, by the apostle men come to seek in Rome, I swear
that even if this man stood up forty yards into the sky I would
still fight him with my iron and my steel. If God wishes to lay
low our faith, I may well be killed and hacked to pieces. But if
He is willing to sustain and aid me, there is no man under
heaven who can do me harm, burn me in fire or drown me in
water!' [587]

When the Pope heard him talking in this way, he cried:
'Ah! noble knight, may He protect you who was raised on the
Cross! Never did a knight speak such brave words! May Jesus
aid you wherever you go, since your thoughts and desires are
all set on Him!' They brought out the arm of St Peter from the
church; they had all the gold and silver stripped from it and
let the count kiss its major joint; then they made the sign of the
cross with it on his steel helm, against his heart and before and
behind. He had great need that day of such an exceptional
ceremony: after that, no man could do him any injury, except
indeed for one the width of two pennies, which later caused the
freeborn man great reproach. He mounted then on his fiery
steed; around his neck he hung his quartered shield, in his fist
he held a stout sharp spear. From there to the mound he rode
without delay. The pagan enemies studied him closely and said
to one another: 'That is a fine looking knight and a bold and
wise one, courtly and well schooled; if he were coming to fight
against an equal, we would have a fierce engagement today
from the very beginning. But his strength is of no avail against
Corsolt; he would not give a penny for fourteen men like that!'
[613]

20. King Galafre had come out of his tent all dressed and
shod in a manner fitting for a king. He looked towards the
mound and the man who was on it and said to his men: 'The
Frenchman has arrived; I see him on the mound and he holds
his shield well. It is he who is to fight against mighty-limbed
Corsolt, but in comparison with him he is feeble and small. It
will be small glory to Mahomet and Cahu if he is not quickly
overcome by King Corsolt.' The king summoned his cham-
pion, who came before him and he went to meet him with out-
stretched arms: 'Welcome, fair nephew!' he said, 'You see
the Frenchman there on the flattened top of the mound: if he
is attacked, he has no intention of giving ground.' Corsolt
replied: 'He is as good as dead and vanquished! Now that I
see him there, I have no need to wait any longer. Bring me my
arms at once; why should I waste time?' Seven kings and
fifteen dukes rushed to fetch his armour and bring it to him
under a spreading tree. Armour like that is never seen nowa-
days: if any other man had put it on his back, he would not
have been able to move from the spot for all the gold that ever
was! [635]

21. Fourteen kings helped arm the adversary. On his back
they placed a steel-clad byrnie and over this a white, double-
mesh hauberk. Then he girded on his sword with its sharp-
cutting blade: it was six feet long and half a foot in width. He
took his bow and strapped on his quiver and his cross-bow and
steel arrows and javelins sharpened all ready for throwing.
They brought before him his charger Alion, a horse that was
extremely fierce and so unruly, I have heard say, that no one
could approach it by a good six feet except those it was
accustomed to. He had four javelins attached to his saddle and
his iron mace loaded on the hind-bow behind him. King
Corsolt mounted by the stirrup; around his neck he hung a
shield embossed with pure gold. His quartered shield was a
good six feet wide, but he did not deign to take a lance. He was
all finely decked out with twice the usual equipment. God!
what a horse that was for the man who could master it! In
spite of everything, that charger could gallop so fast that no
hare or greyhound could keep up with it! [658]

Corsolt turned back towards his uncle and shouted at the top of his voice: 'Be silent and listen to me! Let the seneschals come out, let the tables be set up and the meal be got ready! There is no need to delay it because of this Frenchman; I shall have finished killing and hacking him up before you could walk thirty paces. I do not intend to touch him with my sword, if I can give him a blow with my mace. If that does not bring him to the ground and his charger along with him, may no freeborn man ever serve me a meal again!' The pagans shouted: 'Mahomet aid you!' He spurred his horse and rode out through the middle of the army and the pagans commended him to Mahomet. [672]

Count William saw his opponent approaching, ugly and hideous and all weighed down by his armour; if he felt afraid of him, it would be no wonder. He called upon God, the just Father: 'Holy Mary!' he exclaimed, 'what a fine charger that is! He would serve a worthy man so well that I must take care to spare him with my weapons. May God who governs all things protect him and prevent me from harming him with my sword!' Those were not the words of a coward. [682]

22. William had gone up on to the top of the mound, equipped with his fine arms and armour. He saw the pagan approaching, all fearsome; if he felt afraid of him, he could not be blamed for that. He dismounted from his well-rested steed and turned his face towards the East. He said a very fine prayer; there is no man on earth, born of woman, who, if he said this prayer in good faith in the morning when he got up, could ever after that be troubled by any devil. He called upon God with great humility: [7] 'Glorious God who made me at my birth, who made the earth all according to your will and enclosed it around by the sea; who formed first Adam and then his wife Eve and brought them into Paradise to dwell there; who gave them to eat the fruits of all the trees except for one apple-tree that was forbidden them. But they ate of it and that was a great folly; a great shame came upon them when it could not be concealed. They were forced to leave Paradise and come to earth, to dig and plough and suffer and endure a mortal life. Then Cain killed Abel with great cruelty; the earth itself had

to groan and cry out. A cruel recompense was given to him that day: nothing else would grow and he was forced to wander off.[8] Lord God! those who were born of that race were never willing to serve and honour you again; you brought them all to an end in the Flood. Not one escaped except Noah and his three sons, each of them with his wife; of all the beasts, to restore life in the world, he caused a male and a female to be placed in the ark. [717]

'Lord God! from that new world that was born of them there issued the Virgin who was of such virtue that you deigned to conceal your own body in her. In her your body was formed of flesh and bone, and of the holy blood which became the blood of martyrdom. In Bethlehem the admirable city it pleased you, true God, to be born and truly that was on the night of Christmas; you caused St Anastasia to be raised up then: she had no hands to honour your infant body with, but you restored them to their full powers for her. Then you were visited by the Three Kings and honoured with gold and myrrh and incense and you caused them to return by another way because of Herod who was so cruel that he wanted to have them killed and dismembered. The Innocents were beheaded at that time, three thousand of them, as learned clerks have discovered. [735]

'For thirty-two years you walked about on earth like any other man of flesh, teaching the people, and you went into the desert and fasted there until forty full days had passed and you let yourself be carried off by the Devil. On the Sunday before Easter when we should bear palm branches, it pleased you, Very God, to go into Jerusalem, the admirable city, by the Golden Gates which were opened up for you. You left aside the rich and acted with great simplicity for your heart was turned towards the poor. You went to lodge in the house of Simon the leper.[9] The twelve apostles were gathered there and Mary Magdalene came quietly and secretly below the table, not daring to say a word, and with her bright tears she washed your feet and afterwards dried them with her hair: immediately her sins were forgiven her. [753]

'Then Judas acted towards you with great cruelty: in his great madness he sold you for thirty silver pennies of the days of Methuselah; by a kiss you were betrayed and handed over to the false Jews and bound to the pillar and maltreated until the next morning. Then when it was daylight you were led out to a hill called Mount Calvary; they made you carry your great cross on your shoulder and deck yourself in a most hideous mantle. Indeed, you could not go forward one step without being struck or buffeted. On the Holy Cross your body was made to suffer, your precious limbs were tortured and strained. Longinus came there, to his great good fortune; he could not see you but he heard you speaking and pierced you through the side with his lance: blood and water flowed down all clear on to his hand. Then he wiped his eyes with it and saw the light of day; he confessed his sins with great humility and immediately they were all forgiven him. Nicodemus and along with him Joseph came to you like thieves in the night and took down your body from the Cross and laid you to rest in the sepulchre, and on the third day you rose from the dead. Straight away you descended into Hell; you went there to set free all those who were your friends and who had languished there for a long time. As all this is true, fair King of Majesty, protect my body that I may not be wounded. I must fight here against this evil spirit who is so huge and overgrown and mighty-limbed. Holy Mary, be pleased to help me so that I commit no cowardly act from faint-heartedness that could ever be held as a reproach against my lineage.' [789]

He crossed himself and rose to his feet. The Saracen came towards him, all fearsome, and addressed William: 'Tell me, Frenchman, and hide nothing from me! Who were you talking to all that long time?'—'Indeed,' said William, 'I shall tell you the truth: I was talking to the glorious God, the King of Majesty, asking Him in His goodness to lend me His help so that I may cut all your limbs off and defeat you in this combat.' The pagan said: 'That was a mad idea! Do you really think your God has such power that he could defend you against me in a fight?'—'Scoundrel!' said William, 'God bring you to harm! If He is willing to sustain and aid me, your great pride will soon be laid low!'—'Indeed,' said the Turk, 'your thoughts are very bold! If you were willing to adore Mahomet and reject and defy your own god, I would give you honour and riches far greater than ever your family had before.'—

'Scoundrel!' said William, 'God bring you to harm! for never will God be defied by me!'—'Indeed,' said the Turk, 'you are a very bold man, since I cannot persuade you to give up the battle. What is your name? Do not try to hide it from me!'— 'Indeed,' said William, 'I shall tell you the truth for I have never hidden my name for fear of any man. In God's name, I am called the marquis William, son of Aymeri, the old man with the hoary beard, and of Hermengard, my mother with the fresh complexion; brother of Bernard of the city of Brubant, and of Ernald of Gironde; brother of Garin who is worthy of praise, of Beuves of Commarchis, the dreaded; brother of Guibert of Andernas, the youngest of the family; noble Aïmer is also my brother,[10] he who never enters a lodging nor goes under a pointed roof, but spends all his days in the wind and the gale hewing down Saracens and Slavs; he has no love at all for your people!' When the pagan heard this he almost went out of his mind; he rolled his eyes and raised his eyebrows high: 'Cowardly Frenchman! you have lived too long then, for your lineage has slaughtered my kindred!' [834]

23. The Saracen called out to him scornfully: 'Come now, William, you are quite wrong in the head if you believe in someone who does you no good at all. God is up above, high on the firmament; He never possessed an acre of land down here, for all that belongs to Mahomet and is at his command. All your masses and all your sacraments, your marriages and your wedding ceremonies are no more to me than a breath of wind. Christianity is nothing but ravings!'—'Scoundrel!' said William, 'may God Himself crush you! It is your faith that is worth nothing at all, for, as everybody knows, Mahomet was only a prophet of omnipotent Jesus and went around preaching when he was in the world. He came to Mecca first of all and drank too much in his drunken way and then he was disgustingly eaten up by pigs.[11] Anyone who believes in him has no fine feelings at all!' The pagan answered: 'Those are foul lies! If you are ready to do what I say and believe sincerely in Mahomet, I shall give you honours and a fief far greater than even the best of your relatives ever had, for your lineage is of

the noblest stock and I have often heard tell of your own deeds
of prowess. It would be a great shame if you were to die vilely
here. If you agree, tell me so at once, for if not, you will soon
die in torment!'—'Scoundrel!' said William, 'may God
Himself crush you! Now I think even less of you than at the
beginning: the brave man is not the one who offers threats!'
With fine agility, William sprang into the saddle; he did not
touch the stirrup or hold on to the saddle-bow. He caught up
his shield and hung it at his neck, brandished his spear fiercely
in his anger, his pennon floating from the end of his lance. The
Saracen boldly watched him, saying under his breath so that
no one could hear him: 'By Mahomet to whom my soul
belongs, this man is full of the fiercest bravery!' If William had
but known his thoughts and been willing to come to an agree-
ment, the matter could easily have been settled peaceably.
[878]

24. 'Come now, Frenchman,' said the savage Corsolt, 'in the
name of your God for whose sake you fight, do you lay claim to
Rome as your rightful inheritance?'—'I shall tell you straight,'
said Count Strongarm, 'I have come to fight with my horse
and my arms in the name of God the Father who is a spirit. By
right Rome belongs to our Emperor Charles, and all the
Romagna, Tuscany and Calabria besides; all the offerings
and the treasure of the Ark belong to St Peter and under him
to the Pope who guards it for him.' The king replied: 'All that
is nonsense! If you want to take this heritage by force, then in
justice and reason you must attack me. I shall give you a very
fine advantage to start with: take your spear and hold fast to
your arms; strike me on the shield, I shall make no move. I
want to see something of your mettle and how a small man like
you can strike in a battle.' And William said: 'I would be a fool
to wait any longer!'   [896]

He spurred his horse and charged a full fifty yards from the
hill which was so high and broad; he held all his weapons
tight and the Saracen did not stir from the spot. The Pope said:
'Now we shall have the fight. On your knees, every one of you,
and let every man pray God with a fervent heart to bring back
William Strongarm safe and sound to mighty Rome!' The

noble count saw all the warriors praying for him; he would
have been a fool to wait any longer. He pricked his horse and
loosed the two reins, brandished his lance with its silken
pennon and struck the pagan on his vermilion shield. It
pierced the coloured and polished surface and the wood behind
it, it tore and unravelled the mesh of his white hauberk. His
old-fashioned byrnie served him not at all: William's stout
spear passed right through his body, so that anyone who looked
carefully could have seen the broad pennon showing, hanging
from the blade on the other side. Count William charged so
violently that he tore his good spear right out of him again. Yet
the pagan did not lose heart for that, but said softly, so that no
one could hear him: 'By Mahomet, to whom I have given my
allegiance, it is only a fool who mocks a small man when he
sees him going into a great battle. When I first saw him this
morning in this meadow, I thought very little of him or of his
valour and besides I acted like a fool when I gave him an
advantage over me, for never did I suffer such harm from any
man before.' He felt such pain that he all but fainted. Count
William rushed in to strike again.   [931]

25. William was very powerful and strong; he struck the pagan
right through the body and pulled his spear out again so wildly
that he broke the shield-straps around his neck and the gold-
embossed shield fell to the ground. All the men of Rome
called out loudly: 'Strike again, noble knight, and may God
keep up your strength! St Peter, lord, be the protector of our
side!' Count William heard these words; he spurred his
charger, which leapt forward at once, brandished his shaft,
unfurling his banner, and struck the pagan in the back on his
hauberk, which tore apart and unravelled and ripped open.
His old-fashioned byrnie was no use to him at all; William's
spear went right through the middle of his body and the blade
showed on the other side. Any other man would have been
killed by far less a wound. The Saracen did not flinch at all;
he took a javelin from his saddle-bow and threw it at William
with such force that it came whistling down like a thunderbolt.
The count ducked down, fearing a mortal blow, and it passed
through the armour on his back. God prevented the weapon

from touching his flesh. 'God,' said the count, 'you who created St Lot, protect me, Lord, from meeting an unjust death here today!' [957]

26. The Saracen felt himself deeply wounded: the burnished spear was lying against his lung and his blood was flowing right down to his stirrup. He said softly, so that no-one could hear: 'By Mahomet, whose forgiveness I count on, never have I suffered such damage from any man before! Besides, I consider myself an idiot for letting him have a free blow at me.' He took a sharpened javelin from his saddle-bow and threw it at William with such violence that it whistled in its flight like an eagle. The count swung aside, fearing a foul blow, and the weapon pierced his shield with the lion emblem; his old-fashioned byrnie gave him no protection: the blade passed his side with such force that it flew on and sank two feet into the sand. [973]

When William saw this, he lowered his head and called upon God by His most Holy Name: 'Glorious Father, who formed the whole world, who built up the earth on blocks of marble and girt it all around with the salt sea; who created Adam from earth and slime and also Eve his wife, as we know for sure; who gave them possession of Paradise, making them free of the fruit of all the trees except for one apple-tree which you forbade them. They ate of it and did nothing but ill and afterwards suffered a bitter reward for this, for they were sent to Hell, to the pit of Baratron, and there served Beelzebub and Nero. And once at Easter-time you went in procession, riding on the foal of an ass with all the little children following you, and because of this nowadays on Palm Sunday all the priests and altar-boys make a procession. And you went to lodge with Simon the leper and granted forgiveness to the Magdalen who placed her eyes against your feet without restraint and wept over them out of the goodness of her heart; you raised her up to her feet, taking her by the chin, and granted her forgiveness of all her sins. There Judas betrayed you; he sold you for money and was ill-rewarded for his pains, for the villain received only thirty pence and you were delivered up to the Cross. The Jews acted in this like the most villainous criminals;

they would not believe in your resurrection. You went up to
Heaven on the day of the Ascension and because of this, Lord,
will come the great redemption on the Day of Judgement when
we are all gathered together. On that day, no father will be a
mite of help to his son; the priest will not come before the
altar-boy nor the archbishop before his small server; the king
will not come before the duke nor the count before the stable-
boy, and no man who is a traitor will be saved. You gave the
confession of faith to the apostles; you installed St Peter at the
head of Nero's Meadow and converted St Paul his companion;
you protected Jonah in the belly of the fish and preserved from
hunger the body of St Simeon; you preserved Daniel in the
den of the lion and struck down the villainous Simon the
Magician; Moses saw the flame burning in the bush which did
not consume the wood nor reduce it to ashes. As all this is true
and it is our duty to believe it, protect my body from death and
from prison and let me not be killed by this Saracen villain. He
carries so many weapons that no one can get near him, for his
cross-bow is hanging in his lap and an iron mace is hanging on
his saddle-bow. If He who pardoned Longinus does not see to
it, he will never be overcome, he has far too many weapons!'
[1029]

Corsolt spoke a couple of words in reproach: 'Ah! William,
you have the heart of a brigand; indeed, you seem to be a
wonderful champion and you look no fool when it comes to
hand-to-hand fighting! But you will never escape alive from
weapons like these.' Then he turned his Aragonese charger and
drew his sword which hung at his side and struck William in
such a way that he cut through the nose-piece of his helm,
slashed the hood of his shimmering hauberk, cut off his hair
along his forehead and sliced the tip off his nose. Many a time
the noble knight was to suffer mockery because of this. The
blow glanced off the saddle-bow and cut the charger clean in
two. So fierce was the blow and struck with such violence that
three hundred links of chain-mail were scattered on the sand;
but the sword flew out of the scoundrel's hand.   [1047]

Count William leapt up from the ground on to his feet and
drew Joyous, which was hanging at his side; he wanted to
strike his opponent on the top of his helm, but he was so huge

and overgrown and tall that he could never have reached so
high for all the gold in the world. The blow came down on his
shimmering hauberk so that three hundred links were scattered
on the sand. The Turk's old-fashioned byrnie stood him in
good stead and the blow did not harm him in the least. Corsolt
said a couple of words to him, quarrelsomely: 'Ah! William,
you have the heart of a brigand! But your blows are not worth
a fly!' All the men of Rome cried out with a single voice and
the Pope as well, trembling with fright: 'St Peter, lord, save
your champion, for, if he dies, it will be a shameful reproach to
you; as long as we live no mass will be said nor any lesson read
in your church!'   [1065]

27. Count William with the judicious look stood fully armed
on the broad hilltop, watching the pagan who had lost his
sword after he had cut right through the horse's backbone.
The Turk rode off more than a bowshot then turned and came
spurring back towards William, brandishing his mace, open-
mouthed and foaming like a wild beast in the heat of the chase,
pursued by the hounds through the thick-grown forest. The
count saw him coming and raised his targe. The Turk struck
it with such violence that he split it from top to bottom; he cut
it right open alongside the boss so that a sparrow-hawk in flight
could have passed without touching through the hole. The
mace flew down past his helm and the count lowered his head
at that moment. Had it not been for God and the Blessed
Virgin, never would Rome have been delivered by him. All
the men of Rome cried out at the tops of their voices and the
Pope said: 'What are you doing, then, St Peter? If he dies out
there, it will be unlucky for you: as long as I live and draw
breath, there will never be any mass sung in your church!'
[1089]

28. Count William was badly stunned and laboured under the
blow. He found one thing very surprising: that the Turk had
stayed so long on his charger after bleeding so much. If he had
wanted to, William could easily have brought him to the
ground, but he was trying as much as he could to spare the
charger, thinking that if he could capture it, it would serve him
very well. The Saracen rode towards him with reins loosed

and mocked at William standing there: 'Cowardly French-
man, now you are badly out-witted, for you have lost the half
of your nose; from now on you will be Louis's almsman and
your family will be reproached because of it. You can see there
is nothing you can do to save yourself and I have to be getting
back now with your body, for the emir is waiting for me to
have dinner; he must be wondering why I am so long.'
[1108]

He leant down over his saddle-bow for he wanted to load
him fully armed on the neck of his charger. When William saw
this, his mood changed: now he had a chance to deliver his
blow and, with no thought of sparing him, he struck the king in
the middle of his helm inlaid with gold, so that the flowers and
precious stones tumbled down, and cut off his main headpiece
of mail. He had to get rid of the trusty hood so that he could
strike his skull and split it open a handsbreadth. The pagan
was bent right down on the neck of his horse; his armour
weighed him down and he could not straighten up again.
'God!' cried William, 'what a vengeance for my nose! Now I
shall never be Louis's almsman and my family will never be
reproached because of it!' He pulled his arm out of the loops of
his shield and threw it away out over the empty field. No
knight ever acted so bravely. If the Turk had been whole and
sound and healthy, it would have a bad beginning, but by
God's will he was no longer able to do anything to help him-
self. Count William lost no more time; with his two fists he
seized his steel sword and struck the king with no thought of
sparing him right on the laces of his inlaid helm. The helm with
the head inside it flew four feet away; the body tottered and
the Saracen fell.   [1136]

Count William wasted no time; he wanted to gird on the
fine sword that cut off his nose, but it was too long for him; he
took it and hung it to the saddle-bow. The stirrups were too
long for him by a foot and a half; he shortened them by a good
half-foot. Count William mounted by the stirrup; he had
drawn his spear out of the Saracen's body where he had
driven it and the blood was all congealed round the shaft.
'God!' said William, 'what hearty thanks I owe you for this
horse that I have taken here! I would not give it up for all the

gold of Montpellier; there was a time today when I desired
nothing so much as to have it.' [1151]

From there back to Rome he did not linger. The Pope was
the first to come towards him and kissed him when he had
unlaced his helm. What tears were shed by his nephew
Bertrand and Guielin and the courtly Walter! They had never
been so afraid before in all their lives. 'Uncle,' said Bertrand,
'are you sound and well?'—'Yes,' said he, 'thanks be to God
in Heaven, except that my nose has been shortened a little, but
I know my name will be lengthened because of that.' The
count re-baptized himself on the spot: 'From now on let all
who love me and hold me dear, the men of France and the
men of Berry, always call me Count William Shortnose, the
warrior!' Never from that moment could this name be
changed. Then they went without any pause to the main church
and it was a great joy to the man who held his stirrup. That
night they made merry for the noble knight's sake until the
next morning when it grew light and then they had another
matter to deal with. Bertrand said: 'To arms, knights! Since
my uncle has won the combat against the strongest of the
enemy who was so much dreaded, we can surely face up to the
weaklings. Uncle William, take your ease now, for you have
suffered great stress and strain.' When William heard this, he
gave a hollow laugh: 'Ah, Bertrand, my lord, enough of
quarrelling! This attempt to thwart me will do you no good,
for, by the apostle that palmers go to visit, not all the gold of
Montpellier would keep me from going out in the first rank
and striking with my steel sword.' When the men of Rome
heard him speaking in this way, the most cowardly among
them became bold and light-hearted. Then the villainous
traitors had better beware: already they had lingered too long
in those parts and the men of Rome were preparing for battle.
[1188]

29. King Galafre had come out of his tent all dressed and shod
in a manner fitting for a king. He addressed his men: 'Now I
have suffered a terrible loss, since Corsolt has been defeated by
such a man. The god they believe in is indeed worthy of trust.
See to it that my tent is struck for me at once; let us take to

flight, for why should we stay longer? If the men of Rome have
seen how things are, not a single man of our army will escape.'
And they replied: 'We shall do as you say!' They sounded
fourteen bugles all together; the whole army heard the alert
and mounted. William heard this tumult and said to his men:
'We have waited too long; the pagans are fleeing, those
villainous infidels. After them at once, for our God, King Jesus'
sake!' All the men of Rome rushed out with a single cry, with
William the noble count, exhausted as he was, holding his
place in the first rank. He pricked Alion with his sharp spurs;
the horse reared up so that he could scarcely be held back,
finding the man on his back very light.   [1210]

They overtook the pagans between two hills. There you
could have seen a sustained battle, so many feet cut off, so
many heads, so many trunks! Count Bertrand did not spare
himself at all: after using his lance, he drew his sharp blade;
the man he struck was split open right down to the chest, his
hauberk was not worth a bean to him. Bertrand received many
blows, but gave more in return. And Guielin struck many a
blow there and Walter of Toulouse; but above all others, it was
William who was feared. King Galafre was picked out in the
battle; William spurred towards him, his shield at his neck.
When King Galafre saw him, he called on Mahomet and Cahu
with all his heart: 'Mahomet, lord, what misfortune is upon
me! I beg you, show your might and let me capture William.'
He pricked his charger with his pointed spurs; Count William
was not at all dismayed. They exchanged fierce blows on their
shields and about the bosses these were broken and split; their
white hauberks were torn and unravelled; they felt the sharp
blades passing along their sides. God sustained the redoubtable
William, He and St Peter whose champion he was, preventing
him from being wounded in the flesh by the king. The noble
count gave him such a blow in exchange that he made him
lose his stirrups on both sides. The horse lowered its back when
it felt the blow and the king fell to the ground. The point of his
helm was driven into the ground so violently that two of the
laces snapped. Count William halted over him and drew his
sword with its sharp blade. He was on the point of striking his
head from his body when God showed His power and per-

formed a miracle thanks to which many a woeful and sorrowing captive was freed that day from imprisonment.   [1249]

30. Count William was a very fine knight. He saw before him the king with his head held down and could already have struck off his head if he had wished, when he called out for mercy and pity: 'Baron, do not kill me, if you really are William, but take me alive; you have much to gain by it. I shall restore to you the powerful king Guaifier, along with his daughter and his high-born wife and thirty thousand wretched prisoners, who are all sure to lose their heads if I die.'—'By St Denis,' said the count with the proud face, 'for a reason like that you should certainly be spared.' Count William steadied himself in his stirrups; the king handed over to him his fine steel sword. William sent him off to the Pope at the head of three hundred other prisoners.   [1265]

When the Saracens, those faithless traitors, saw their rightful lord brought low in that way, they took to flight along the roads and the lanes and rode without stopping as far as the Tiber, where they found their ships which they needed so urgently. They went aboard at once and drew out from the shore. Count William turned back and left them. The king was disarmed under an olive-tree; the noble count began to speak to him: 'Ah! noble king, by God the just, how can we get back those wretched prisoners who are confined and bound in your barges?' The king replied: 'You are foolish to talk about that, for, by the Cross that palmers go to see, you shall have nothing of them worth a penny-piece until I am raised up from the font and baptized, for Mahomet can help me no longer.'—'God,' exclaimed William, 'receive my hearty thanks for this!' The Pope lost no time, but had the font prepared at once, then they raised up the king from the water and baptized him. William the warrior was his godfather and so were Guielin and the courtly Walter and fully thirty other valiant knights besides, all of them freeborn men. They did not change the name he had but confirmed it as a Christian name. [1292]

They called for water and sat down to eat. When they had all eaten sufficiently, Count William leapt to his feet: 'Ah! noble king,' he said, 'by God the just, step forward now, fair godson! How can we get back those wretched prisoners who are confined and bound in your barges?' The king replied: 'I must think carefully about that, for, if the Saracens and pagans know that I have been baptized, they would sooner have me flayed alive than hand over as much as a penny-piece. But now let me be stripped of all my clothes and put on a broken-down pack-horse and sent in a group of four knights down to the Tiber, near enough to shout to the boats. Let all your men be in readiness behind that wall, in that grove of olive-trees. If the Saracens make an attempt to come out to help and rescue me, you must all be ready to lower your lances.'—'God,' said William, 'by your holy pity, no better convert ever ate bread!' They did all that he asked them to do, except that they spared him a beating; instead they daubed him with the blood of a greyhound. From there to the Tiber they made no delay. Then King Galafre began shouting at the top of his voice: 'Nephew Champion, lord and son of a baron, come to my rescue! Have the wretched prisoners sent out, for I tell you, in return I shall be freed from captivity.' Champion said: 'Mahomet has stood by you well, since your life is to be spared in exchange for a ransom.' They had the galley drawn in to the shore; they brought out the wretched prisoners. But those faithless brutes had beaten them so much because they themselves were defeated and routed that there was not one among them that was not bleeding at the waist and on the shoulders, the trunk and the head as well. Out of pity, the warlike William wept. [1333]

31. When they freed the captives out of the barges, there was not one among them that was not bleeding in the face and on the shoulders and the whole chest as well. Out of pity, William Strongarm wept. He turned to the Pope and drew him aside to talk: 'My lord,' he said, 'by God who is a spirit, many a noble man there is naked to the waist; let us give them clothes and furs and cloaks and let each of them have gold and silver on the spot, so that they can get back to their own lands.' The Pope said: 'Honourable and noble man, everyone should be generous in doing honour. It is very proper that this advice of

yours should be followed.' From there to Rome they returned without delay; they opened their clothes-chests for the captives and gave them clothes and furs and cloaks. Each one received gold and silver on the spot so that they had no trouble getting back to their own lands. [1351]

32. While this was being done and everyone was back in Rome, Count William sat on a mounting-block. The mighty King Guaifier came up and at once fell on his knees at his feet. 'Noble knight, lord,' he said, 'you have done me a great service. You have rescued me from the hands of the enemy who would have carried me off in bonds to their own countries; never would I have seen my domains and my fiefs again. I have a daughter, there is no fairer under Heaven; I shall give her to you gladly and willingly if you care to receive and take her, and you shall have half my kingdom and at my death you will be my heir.' The count replied: 'I must take advice about that.' He turned to the Pope and drew him aside. 'My lord,' he said, 'should I accept this wife?'—'Yes, indeed, fair sir, gladly and willingly. You are a young knight; you need to acquire land.' The count replied: 'It shall be agreed, then.' They brought out the bride to let him see her. No man of flesh, no pilgrim nor palmer, could ever travel or ride so far afield that he would meet a more beautiful lady. This is the one that William the warrior would have taken as his wife, if he had not been forced by a grave circumstance to put off the whole matter, as you will hear before the sun sets. [1377]

33. Would it please you to hear of the lady's beauty? No man of flesh could travel so far that he would ever come across a more beautiful lady. This is the one William Shortnose would have taken as his wife, if he had not been forced by a grave circumstance to give it all up, as you will hear before it grows dark. Suddenly two messengers arrived, spurring post haste. They had come from France and wearied their horses, yes, worn them out, broken them with fatigue and ruined them. They enquired after William and searched for him until they found him in the church where he was about to marry his bride. The Pope, that noble and valiant man, was all vested to sing the mass and William had taken the ring to marry the lady

when the messengers arrived and threw themselves at his feet.
[1393]

'Have pity, William, for the sake of holy charity!' they
cried. 'You have had little thought of Louis, for the noble and
valiant Charles is dead and the great inheritance has passed to
Louis. The traitors want to cast him out of it and crown
another man king, the son of Richard of the city of Rouen.
They will bring the whole country to sorrow, noble lord, unless
you come to the rescue.' When William heard this, he hung his
head. Then he turned to the Pope and drew him aside. 'My
lord,' he said, 'what advice do you give me?' The Pope replied:
'God be praised! He who seeks advice should always receive it.
I should like to advise that, like a penitent, you go to the rescue
of your lord Louis. It would be a great misfortune if he were
disinherited.' The count replied: 'I shall do as you say; your
advice will never be rejected.' William kissed the lady with the
fresh complexion and she kissed him too; she could not leave
off weeping. And this parting between them was such, as it
transpired, that they were never to see each other again in
their whole lives.   [1416]

'Lord William,' said the valiant Pope, 'you must go off now,
back to sweet France. The Emir Galafre will remain here; he
will take charge of Rome on your behalf.' The count replied:
'You are talking madness! I have never been accused of
treason [12] and from now on I must be very careful to avoid it.'
—'Lord William,' said the valiant Pope, 'you must go off now,
back to sweet France. You will go at the head of a thousand
knights and with thirty pack-horses laden with gold and silver.
You have captured them all, so it is right you should take them
with you.' The count replied: 'I accept that with thanks.'
[1429]

*   *   *

34. One Sunday, a fortnight after Easter, William Strongarm
was in Rome, where he was to have married a wife [he had
completely forgotten Orable for the moment],[13] when mes-
sengers arrived from France bringing him bitter news: that the
Emperor Charles was dead and his domain left to Louis. The
traitors, may God Himself bring them to harm! wanted to take

the son of the bearded Richard of Rouen and make him king before all the barons. William Strongarm wept from pity and came to take leave of the wise Pope, who entrusted to him a thousand knights-at-arms and thirty pack-horses laden with gold and silver. When it came to the departure, all the noble men wept. The count rode off, he did not delay at all; he crossed the St Bernard, which fatigued him greatly. I have nothing to relate of their journeying; until they arrived in Brie, they did not halt or delay. [1449]

35. The marquis William Shortnose rode off and I cannot give a daily account of his journeying. As far as Brie, he did not halt. There he met a pilgrim on the road, with his scrip hanging from his neck and his ash-wood staff in his hand; you never saw such a sturdy pilgrim though his beard was white as an April flower. When William saw him, he questioned him: 'Where have you come from, brother?'—'From St Martin's city of Tours.'—'Tell us then, have you any news?'—'Yes, fair sir, about little Louis. Charles the king of Saint-Denis is dead and the country has passed to Louis. The traitors, God curse them! want to take the son of Richard of Rouen with the white beard, and make him king to rule over France. But a well-born abbot, may God bless him! has hidden the young lad along with himself in a crypt at St Martin's church; they do not know the hour when they may be murdered. Ah! God help us!' said the honest pilgrim, 'where have all the noble knights gone now, and the lineage of the bold Count Aymeri? They are the ones who always supported their lord before. By that Cross where the Body of God was hung, if I were a man able to help him, I should already have done such damage to the traitors that they would have no more desire to betray their lord!' When William heard this, he gave a laugh; he called Bertrand and said: 'Did you ever meet such a well-spoken pilgrim? If he were a man who could bring his lord any help, no evil plot would ever be concocted by him.' They gave the pilgrim ten ounces of gold and sent him merrily on his way. [1484]

William rode on, continuing his journey. How fortunate is the man who has many friends! He looked along the road in

front of him and saw seven score knights riding towards him,
with shining armour and valuable horses. They were led by the
marquis Gualdin the Brown and with him was the bold Savari,
both of them nephews of the marquis William, all coming to
France to the aid of Louis. They were greatly surprised when
they all met together; they exchanged kisses as nephews and
friends. The abbot of noble birth who had Louis in his care
knew nothing of this. If he could defend and protect him a
short time longer and keep him from the clutches of the
descendants of Alori, help would arrive before three days were
over. [1500]

36. William the noble warrior rode on his way and with him
were twelve hundred knights. He had a summons proclaimed
throughout his company; everyone spurred forward his horse
or his charger and he told them straight away that they must
have no thought of sparing their mounts: if anyone lost a hack,
he would give him a charger in exchange. 'I want to arrive at
the start of this evil affair,' he said, 'I want to know and learn
in good time who is hoping to be king and govern France. Yet
by the apostle that palmers go to visit, there is one who at this
moment bears himself proudly and haughtily, but I shall give
him a crown to wear on his head that will bring his brains
pouring down to his feet.' The Romans cried: 'This man has
a bold heart. God bring to grief any man who fails him!' I have
no need to tell of their journeying; they came to Tours without
delay. William wanted to operate wisely; he left a thousand
knights in four ambushed parties and led on two hundred, all
very well equipped, wearing their white double-mesh armour
with their green helms laced on under their hoods and their
burnished steel swords girded on. Close behind them came the
squires with the stout shields and sharp spears, so that the
knights could turn to them if the need arose. From there to the
city gates they went without delay. [1528]

At once they called out to the porter: 'Open the gate, do not
keep us waiting here! We have come to the aid of Duke
Richard; this very day his son will be crowned king in the
abbey church, for so the French have decided.' When the
porter heard this, he almost went mad; he called upon God the

just Father: 'Holy Mary!' said the well-spoken porter, 'Louis, my lord, what a poor rescue this is! If He who governs all things does not look to it, you will never leave here without having your limbs cut off. Ah! God help us!' said the well-spoken porter, 'where have all the valiant knights gone now and the lineage of the warlike Aymeri who used to support their rightful lord so well?' And he said to William: 'You shall not set foot in here! There are too many vile traitors in here already, I do not want to increase their numbers. It is a great marvel that the earth still bears you. Would to the glorious King of Heaven that the earth might give way under your feet and that Louis were back in his fief! Then the world would be rid of evil men!' When William heard this, he was joyful and merry; he called Bertrand: 'Listen to me, nephew, did you ever hear a porter speak so well? If we were to reveal our hearts to him, he could stand us in good stead this day.' [1556]

37. 'My friend, good brother,' said the warlike William, 'you have been overbold in refusing to let me in, but you do not know what land I was born in or of what people and of what family. Yet, to judge by the sermon I have just heard, you would in fact open the gate to me gladly and willingly.' When the porter heard this, he rose to his feet and opened the peep-hole enough to have a look at him. 'Noble lord,' he said, 'if I might make so bold, I would ask you what country you were born in and of what people and what family.'—'Indeed,' said William, 'you will hear the truth, for never have I hidden my name from any man. I am William of Narbonne.' The porter said: 'God be praised! Lord William, I know well enough what you want here. Your line has never shown cowardice. The wicked Richard has entered this city with seven hundred armed knights; you, my lord, have very few men to stand up to this strong force.' And William said: 'We shall have enough. There are four ambushed parties left out there, a thousand knights in all, armed and ready to fight, and here I have two hundred men all well equipped, for under their clothes they are wearing their hauberks and under their hoods they have their jewelled green helms; there are plenty of squires behind

us, to whom we can turn if need be.' The porter said: 'God be
praised! If you were to ask my advice, I should say, let the
whole ambush be given up at once and send a messenger to
bring the men here secretly. The traitors are all gathered in
this city; why look for them elsewhere when you have found
them here? The truth is, this very day or before it gets light
tomorrow, you can do whatever you wish with them. But the
man who undertakes such a task must be fiercer than the wild
boar in the woods.' When William heard this, he lowered his
head, then called to Bertrand: 'Listen to me, nephew, did you
ever hear a porter speak so well?'   [1599]

38. When the porter heard this news about the bold William
whose valour was obvious, he turned to face the palace and
took a glove and put it on his right hand, then he called out in
his fine loud voice: 'I renounce you, Richard, you and your
land! I no longer wish to be in your service. Since you are trying to
commit treason, it is right and proper that you should be the
loser.' The gate was quickly opened to William; it was un-
bolted and unbarred straight away. William entered with his
fine company and the porter called out to him softly: 'Noble
knight, go and seek vengeance on the traitors who are rebelling
against you here!' When William heard this, he bowed his
head towards the ground. He quickly called a squire: 'Go and
tell Lord Walter of Tudela and tell the news to Garin of Rome
that the gates have been opened to me. Let all those who want
to gain booty come here at once, but without noise or merri-
ment.' The squire went off without delay; immediately the
ambush was raised and the companies came into the city, for
the gates were opened to them. When those of the city saw
them from the walls and windows, they thought it was the
troops they had sent for themselves. But they were to know
better about them before the day was out, to their sorrow and
grief.   [1628]

39. Count William called to the porter: 'My friend, good
brother, would you like to give me your advice? I have a great
many people here to find lodging for.'—'In God's name, my
lord, I do not know what to advise, for there is no vault or
crypt or cellar that is not full of arms and chargers and the

knights are housed in all the arcades. But you have the better part of the bargain: seize and remove all their equipment and any who will not hand it over willingly, let him risk nothing less than having his head cut off.'—'Indeed,' said William, 'you have advised me well. By St Denis, I seek no better. You shall be a watchman and gatekeeper no longer; instead you shall be my chief counsellor.' He called to Bertrand: 'Listen to me, nephew, did you ever hear a porter speak so well? Equip him now and dub him a knight!' Bertrand replied: 'Gladly, fair lord!' He looked closely at the man, at his hands and his feet, and saw he was handsome and noble-looking and slender and so he equipped him as befits a knight, with a strong hauberk and a steel helm, a fine sword and a sharp spear, and gave him a horse, a hack and a squire, a palfrey, a mule and a pack-horse. And so he gave him a fine reward for his services. [1655]

Count William called Walter of Toulouse, his sister's son and a noble knight: 'Go, son of a highborn lady, to that gate that faces towards Poitiers and take twenty knights with you. See to it that not a single man alive gets out that way, nor cleric nor priest, however much he prays you, without having all his limbs cut off.' And Walter replied: 'Gladly, fair lord!' [1665]

40. Count William Shortnose, the marquis, called Seier of Le Plessis: 'Go, noble and highly esteemed knight, to that gate that leads towards Paris and take with you up to twenty knights. See to it that not a single man born of woman gets out that way without being cut to pieces and killed.' And he replied: 'I shall do as you wish.' There was not a barrier nor a gate nor a postern where the count did not post some of his knights. [1675]

He went then without hindrance as far as the abbey church [14] and dismounted in the paved yard in front of it. He went into the church, making the sign of the cross before his face. Then the marquis William knelt down on the marble floor in front of the crucifix and prayed to God who was hung on the Cross to send him Louis, his lord. At that, suddenly a cleric called Walter [15] appeared. He recognized the marquis

William and laid a finger on his shoulder; he prodded the
count until he noticed him. The count raised his head and
turned to face him. 'What do you wish, brother?' he asked.
'See you tell me the truth.' And he replied: 'I can soon tell
you. Since you have come to rescue Louis, have all the doors of
St Martin's church closed. There are eighty clerics and canons
inside and bishops and abbots of great importance who, for
gain, have brewed up this evil plot: Louis is to be disinherited
this very day unless God and you yourself are prepared to
protect him. Take all their heads, I beg you in God's name! I
take all the sin of desecrating a church upon myself, for they
are all traitors and renegades.'   [1699]

When William heard this, he gave a laugh and said:
'Blessed be the hour that such a cleric was nurtured! Where
shall I find my lord Louis then?'—'In God's name, my lord,'
the cleric replied, 'I shall bring him to you, God willing and if
I live.' He went without delay straight to the abbey and
quickly went down into the crypt; there he found his lord
Louis. The noble cleric seized him by the hand: 'Son of a good
king,' he said, 'do not be afraid any longer, for, so help me
God, you have more friends than you thought when you got up
this morning. The marquis William has arrived with twelve
hundred knights of mark and the count has come seeking you
in the abbey-church. There is not a barrier nor a gate nor a
postern where he has not posted some of his knights.' When
Louis heard this, he rejoiced greatly. He went without delay
straight to the church. The noble abbot addressed him, saying:
'Son of a good king, do not be afraid; look, there is William
who pledged his loyalty to you: go and fall at his feet and crave
his mercy.' The young man replied: 'I shall do just as you
wish.'   [1723]

41. The noble abbot addressed him first: 'Son of a warrior,
there is no need to be afraid. Look, there is William; go and
fall at his feet.' The young man replied: 'Gladly, fair lord!'
He went and knelt down before the count; he clasped his feet
and kissed the boots that the count was wearing. The warlike
William did not recognize him, for there was little light in the
church. 'Rise up, young man,' said the much-valued count,

'God has not yet created the man that I would not gladly and willingly forgive, however much he had angered me, if he went so far as to throw himself at my feet.' Then the abbot who was the young man's spokesman said: 'In God's name, my lord, I will speak frankly: this is Louis, the son of Charles of the proud countenance. This very day he is to be killed and hacked to pieces unless God and you, yourself, are prepared to help him.' When William heard this, he rushed to embrace the lad; he took him by his two sides and raised him up at once. 'In God's name, young man,' he said, 'he who bade you throw yourself at my feet played an evil trick on me, for I above all men should bring you help.' He called out to his noble knights: 'I want you to give me your judgement. When a man has been tonsured in an abbey and ought to live to read his psalter, should he then commit treason for gain?'—'No indeed, fair lord,' said the knights. 'And if he does so, what should be his reward?'—'He should be hanged like a highway robber!' The count replied: 'You have given me good advice, by St Denis, and I do not ask for better. Yet I do not wish to degrade God's holy orders; none the less, they will pay dearly for what they have done.' [1758]

42. Count William with the stout heart heard the judgement of his barons. With all speed he went to the chancel of the church. There he found the bishops and abbots and all the clerics who were false to their lord. He snatched their croziers from their hands and handed them over to Louis, his rightful lord. The noble count embraced him round the waist and kissed him four times. Count William lost no time at all. With all speed he went to the chancel where he found bishops and abbots. Because of the sin involved, he was not prepared to have weapons used against them, but they hacked them and beat them with sticks and dragged and chased them from the church and commended them to eighty devils. Any man who is willing to commit treason against his lord fully deserves to suffer harm because of it. [1776]

43. Count William was a very valorous knight. He addressed Louis, his lord, and said: 'My lord, hear what I have to say. I think we should send a messenger to Acelin to tell him on your

behalf to come and submit to Louis his lord.' Louis said: 'My
lord, we grant this gladly.' The count called the warrior
Alelme and said: 'Go and tell the haughty Acelin to come
straight away and submit to his lord Louis, who has great
cause of complaint against him.' Alelme replied: 'Must I go
alone, then?'—'Yes, fair brother, taking a staff in your hands.'
—'And what if he asks what forces we have?'—'You will tell
him you have forty companions. And if he rejects this sum-
mons out of hand, you will tell him clearly, in the hearing of his
companions, that before sunset he will be brought to such
shame as he would not face for all the gold of Avalon.' Alelme
replied: 'I shall do as you wish. By the apostle men visit in
Nero's Meadow, we have nothing to lose by sending a message.
He mounted an Aragonese mule and went spurring through
the streets and did not halt until he came to the lodging where
he found Acelin with a large body of companions. [1802]

    He called out to him loudly, so that all could hear: 'Lord
Acelin, noble and highborn man, do you know the demand of
the noble William, of Strongarm who has the heart of a lion?
It is that you come straight away and submit to your lord,
Louis, who has great cause of complaint against you.' When
Acelin heard this, he lowered his chin. 'Friend,' he said, 'I
understand what you have said. Tell me though how many
companions your uncle has.'—'In God's name, my lord, there
are thirty knights in all.' Acelin said. 'Blessed be God! Go now
and tell bold William from me to agree to what all the others
are doing. The gift of the crown has been granted to me.
France would be ruined if it went to that servant-boy, for Louis
will never be worth a button! Count William is an extremely
fine man, yet he has no land or provision so far. I shall give him
whatever he chooses for himself. He shall have a whole
province at his disposal and ten mules laden with gold and
double-bezant pieces, then he will be a wonderfully wealthy
man!'—'Indeed,' said Alelme, 'this is all idle talk! He would
never do such a thing for all the gold of Avalon. He sends you
another message—why should I not reveal it?—a more cruel
one than I have told you. If you reject this summons out of
hand, before sunset you will be brought to such shame as you
would not face for all the wealth in the world!' Acelin cried:

'Blessed be God! Since I find neither peace nor love in him, I challenge him! That is the reply you can take back to him.' And Alelme said: 'Now we have heard your answer. In return, I say to you on behalf of us all, in the hearing of your barons, that I challenge you!' [1837]

44. Acelin was very proud and haughty. He looked closely at Alelme, at his hands and his feet, and saw that he was very handsome and straight and slender; he saw clearly that he was a squire. 'My friend, fair brother,' he said, 'you are very ill-bred to shame me in the hearing of my knights, and besides I do not give a penny for your uncle! Since I find neither peace nor friendship in him, my challenge is that I will cut off his head and this very day hack him limb from limb, for I have with me some seven hundred knights and four counts who are highly thought of; they will not fail me even if they have their limbs cut off. If you were not a messenger, I would have that head of yours cut off and your whole body mutilated and destroyed!' And Alelme said: 'God curse the man who fears you!' He left the court without asking permission to withdraw and Acelin ordered his men to prepare for battle. [1856]

The noble Alelme mounted his charger and rode with loosed reins through the streets. William the warrior was the first to meet him. He asked him: 'How did you fare?'—'In God's name, my lord, there is no friendship there and he does not recognize Louis as his lord. When I told him the number of your knights, you yourself were threatened immediately and challenged with having your head cut off. If it had not been that I was a messenger, he would have had me hacked limb from limb or burned with fire or drowned in water.' When William heard this, he went mad with rage. Then they seized and searched all the lodgings; they threw out all the equipment in a heap and any man who did not allow it willingly risked nothing less than having his head cut off. The burghers took to flight; the count had them caught and bound. The traitors who had launched the evil plot—God give them grief!—turned and fled, forcing their chargers to the limit. As far as the gates they spurred without stopping, but at each gate they found a rough porter: they had to pay such a toll that day

that they could never again answer a call to fight in a battle
for any man on earth, no matter how much he pleaded.
[1883]

Count William set spurs to his horse and rode straight to the
lodging of the free burgher Hungier. He came upon Acelin
sitting on the mounting-block; so haughty and proud he was
that he did not deign to stand up to meet him. When William
saw this, he almost went mad with rage. Because he was alone
and Acelin had many men, he sounded a high-pitched bugle
call. You should have seen the ambushed men pouring out
then! At once Bertrand and Walter appeared with a thousand
knights in their company. Then you would have seen a fierce
battle engaged, so many shafts splintered, so many shields
pierced and so many hauberks torn and unravelled! When the
enemy saw such a battle engaged and William's men support-
ing him so fiercely and that their own force was of no avail,
they threw down their naked swords at their feet and came
with clasped hands begging for mercy. The count had them
taken prisoner and bound, but Acelin loosed his reins and fled.
Count William followed close on his tail and shouted a harsh
taunt: 'Lord Acelin, turn back now, will you, and come and
be crowned in the church! We shall give you a crown to wear
on your head that will bring your brains pouring down to your
feet!'   [1910]

45. Count William with the proud bearing faced Acelin and
spoke to him harshly: 'Villainous traitor, may God Himself
confound you! Why have you acted so shamefully towards
your rightful lord? Richard your father never wore a crown!'
Bertrand came up with his long sword; when William saw him,
he called out to him proudly: 'Fair nephew,' he said, 'we
should like your advice about this traitor. How should he be
destroyed?' And Bertrand said: 'Why bother to consider the
matter, fair uncle? Let us give him such a crown to wear on his
head that his brains gush into his mouth!' He stepped forward,
holding his long sword; he was about to strike him before the
eyes of a hundred men when Count William his uncle shouted:
'Fair nephew, do not touch him! May God who created the
whole world forbid that he should ever die by the weapon of an

honest man! Instead I shall kill him in a most shameful way, so that all his heirs will suffer great reproach for it.' [1930]

46. Count William was a very fine knight; towards the haughty he was always as fierce as a man-eating leopard. He did not deign to touch this man with the weapon he bore. Seeing a sharp stake in a vine-trellis, he stepped forward and pulled it out, then struck Acelin with it on the crown of his head; his blood and brains came pouring down to his feet. He struck him down dead without more ado, then cried: 'Mountjoy! St Denis be my help! Louis is well avenged on this king!' Count William set spurs to his horse and rode to the main church; he came up to Louis his rightful lord and hastened to embrace him around the waist: 'My young lord,' he said, 'who else has given you cause for complaint? I have avenged you well on Richard's son: he will never again answer a call to go fighting in battles for any man on earth, no matter how much he pleads!'—'God' said the youth, 'receive my hearty thanks! If I were now avenged on his father, I should be merry, joyful and glad.'—'God!' said William, 'who can tell me where he is?' [1953]

They told him he was inside the abbey church; the count rode there spurring with loosed reins and eighty knights followed him. He found Richard leaning on the altar, but he did not spare him because he was in a church. He grabbed him by the hair with his left fist, pressed down his head until he was bent double, then raised his right and brought it down on his neck and toppled him to the ground stunned at his feet. Anyone could have hacked all his limbs off and he would not have been able to move hand or foot. When William saw this, he began to shout: 'Out on you, coward! God give you grief!' He called for shears and cut off his hair and left him lying flat out on the marble floor. Then he called out in the hearing of all the knights: 'This is justice fitting for a traitor who tries to betray and wrong his lord!' But the counts and the barons pleaded with him until they finally restored peace between Richard and William. Richard first declared himself acquitted of the death of his son, then they swore peace to each other before he left the church, kissing each other in the sight of many knights. But this reconciliation was not worth a penny, for afterwards they tried to murder William in a wood and mutilate him with a steel knife, but God would not endure or permit it.   [1980]

Count William did not wish to delay any longer; he called out to the good Abbot Walter: 'I am going off now to the realm of Poitiers; there are a great many traitors hiding there, but, God willing, I shall rout them out. I should like to leave my rightful lord in your charge. Guard him well! If he wants to go out to seek distraction, let him take at least a hundred knights with him, for, by the apostle that palmers go to visit, if I should hear when I get back that Louis has come to any harm, all your holy orders would not keep me from having you hacked limb from limb!' The abbot said: 'You are talking idle words. He will be more safely guarded than the relics of this church.'   [1995]

Count William was a very fine knight. Throughout the whole land he sent his writ and summoned all the brave knights; before a fortnight was up he had gathered together more than thirty thousand, then they went off all together to Poitiers. After that for three whole years there was not a single day, however high and holy, that William did not have his burnished helm laced on and his sword girt at his side, riding fully armed on his charger. There was not a feastday when men should go to worship, not even Christmas Day which should be set above all others, that he was not dressed in his hauberk and armed. The knight suffered a great penance to support and aid his lord.   [2010]

47. For three whole years William the warrior was in Poitou, conquering that province. There was not a single day, however great an occasion, not even Easter Day or Christmas or the feast of All Saints that should be kept most solemnly, that he had not his burnished helm in place and his sword girt at his side, riding fully armed on his horse. The young knight suffered a great penance to protect and defend his lord.   [2019]

48. Count William with the proud bearing turned from there to Bordeaux on the Gironde. There he defeated the mighty King Amarmonde, who then received his crown from Louis

and held all his lands, which were great and wide, as his vassal.
[2024]

49. Count William with the stout heart turned from there
towards Peralada. There he defeated Dagobert of Carthage,
who thereafter held his lands, which were great and wide, as a
vassal of Louis the wise.   [2029]

50. Count William with the judicious expression went on his
way towards Andorra and then one morning attacked Saint-
Gilles. He took the township without difficulty and acted in a
way pleasing to Jesus when he spared the church there from
being laid waste. He captured Julian who ruled that land, then
received in exchange all the hostages he asked for and, on this
surety, accepted his oath of peace. After that William called
his men together and spoke in a way that was pleasing to many
of them: 'Take your equipment, freeborn and honoured
companions, and let each of you go back to his own district and
the bride he wants to marry.'   [2043]

51. Count William Shortnose the warrior turned his mind to
riding back to sweet France, but throughout Poitou he left
knights in the fortresses and great castles. He took with him
only two hundred well armed knights and, skirting the whole
of Brittany, travelled without a break to Mont-Saint-Michel.
He stayed there two days, then left on the third and set out on
his return journey through the Cotentin. I cannot give a day-
by-day account of his travelling; he came without delay to
Rouen and took lodging in the main part of the town. But it
was a most ill-advised act on his part to dare to ride through
the lands of old Duke Richard, whose son he had killed with
the great beam. The noble count was relying on the fact that
they had been reconciled and sworn peace, but that recon-
ciliation was not worth a penny, for afterwards they tried to
murder and mutilate him.   [2063]

'Indeed,' said Richard, 'it is enough to make me go mad
with rage to see that man riding through my lands who
deprived me of the best heir that ever lived to govern a
domain. But, by the apostle that palmers go to visit, before he
leaves my land he shall be sorely afflicted!'—'In God's name,

lord,' said his knights, 'you shall not touch him in this town, for the burghers would try to help him. It is not a good thing to stir up treachery.' And Richard said: 'I am all the more vexed for that. Instead I shall send to him in friendship and say I want to ride with him to sweet France. There shall be sixteen of us, all well armed. If we can get him separated from his men, each of us will produce a good steel knife and then he will be murdered and mutilated.' Fifteen knights swore themselves to this; it would have been better for them if they had kept out of it, for later they were all brought to disgrace and shame. God! alas that the proud-faced count knew nothing of this! [2084]

He mounted his horse in the morning, meaning to ride as far as Lyons, a huge and mighty forest. They dismounted in a clearing and the peasants brought them food. When the noble knights had dined, some of them fell asleep, for they were worn out with fatigue. When William saw this, he felt very sorry for them. He called for his arms to get ready to ride out himself and they were brought at once; he put on his hauberk, laced on his steel helm and girded on his sword with its chased gold pommel. They brought him his charger Alion and the count mounted by the left stirrup; he hung his quartered shield at his neck, in his fist he held a stout sharp spear with his banner attached to it by fifteen nails. Taking only two knights with him, he rode out to seek sport along the riverbank. At this, old Duke Richard appeared; he had had his spies watching all day long and now he came up with fifteen brave knights. When William saw this, he was greatly dismayed. [2106]

52. Count William came riding round the side of a hill and Duke Richard the Red appeared with fifteen companions. When William saw this, he was seized with great fear. He called his two companions, speaking to them very softly: 'Barons,' he said, 'tell me what we should do. Here is Duke Richard the Red coming at us; he hates me with very good cause: I killed his son, as everyone knows. And yet we were reconciled over it and swore peace to each other in the abbey of Tours.' And they replied: 'Why fear him then? Ride and spur your horse up to the bridge and greet him in honour and

friendship. If in any way he rejects what you have to say, rely on your shield with its lion and we will not fail you for all the gold in the world.' William replied: 'My hearty thanks, barons.' [2125]

53. Count William rode up in front to the bridge, faced the duke and addressed him: 'Duke,' said the count, 'God preserve you from harm! Is there any reason for me to be on my guard against you? We have been reconciled and have made peace with one another; we both swore an oath in the abbey church at Tours and kissed each other in the sight of many knights.'—'Indeed,' said Richard, 'you are very good at preaching! You deprived me of the best heir that ever lived to govern a domain. But, by the apostle that palmers go to visit, before you leave my land, you shall be sorely afflicted. Neither God nor man can protect you now or keep me from having your head cut off and all your limbs torn from your body!'—'Scoundrel!' said William, 'God give you grief! I count you no better than a mad dog!' [2142]

He pricked Alion with his spurs of pure gold and struck Richard on his quartered shield; he split and pierced it under the boss, ripped and unravelled his white hauberk and drove his steel into his left flank so that blood streamed down on both sides of his body. The fine horse shook off its heavy burden; the duke's stirrups turned up towards the sky and the point of his helm was driven into the ground with such force that two of the laces snapped. William reined up over him and drew his steel blade; I fully believe he would have taken his head straight away, but suddenly the fifteen appeared, God give them grief, and rushed upon the warlike William. If you had seen the count then, defending himself against all of them and dealing mighty blows with his steel blade, you would have felt very sorry for the noble knight. His two companions came to his aid and each struck down his opponent at once. The just Father stood by them all so well that they killed and hewed down ten of the attackers; the other five took to flight, wounded and disabled. Count William followed close on their tails and shouted a harsh taunt. [2166]

54. The five rode off in flight over a hill; Count William

chased after them and pressed them hard. In a loud voice he
shouted a fine gibe: 'Noble barons, by God the heavenly King,
how will you ever bear such a great disgrace? Your rightful
lord is going to be led off bound to his horse. God! what a feat
that would be if you could rescue him!' And they replied:
'For God's sake, have mercy on us, William! Noble knight,
you should be a king or the emir of a great and powerful land.
God help us, you can easily capture us, for our bowels are
hanging out over our saddles. Even the fittest of us could not
face being led off on a horse!' When William heard this, he
pulled in his rein.   [2180]

55. When William realized they had begged for mercy he
would not have touched them for all the gold of Montpellier.
At once he turned back his horse. They removed the armour
of the other ten and took Duke Richard and bound him.
Trussed like a chest on a pack-horse, they led him off on a
swift-footed charger. Without delay they returned to the army.
When they got back, the men had woken up. 'Uncle William,'
said the warlike Bertrand, 'I see the steel of your sword all
bloody and your shield is not entirely whole. You have
been stirring up some trouble!' William replied: 'Spare me,
for God's sake, fair nephew! When I set out for a ride, I saw
you were all weary and worn out so I left you to sleep and rest
and took only two knights with me. I met old Duke Richard
who had had his spies watching me all day long. There were
fifteen brave knights with him. He held up the death of his son
against me and wanted to hack me limb from limb. But the
just Father stood by us so well that we killed and hewed down
ten of them and five took to flight, wounded and disabled. You
can see the arms and chargers of our victims here and we have
brought back Duke Richard in bonds.' And Bertrand said:
'God be thanked!'   [2209]

56. 'Uncle William,' said the valiant Bertrand, 'you look as if
you could not last much longer.'—'Nephew,' said William,
'spare me, I beg you, for I am ready to spend my whole youth
in great hardship until this king is in full possession of his great
inheritance.' Then they armed themselves and continued on
their way and travelled on by forced marches until they

reached the city of Orleans. There William found King Louis
and handed over Richard to him as a prisoner. The king had
him thrown into his dungeon and there he remained, as I have
heard tell, until at last he died of grief and languishing.
[2222]

*   *   *

Then William thought he could have a rest and spend his
time hunting in the woods and along the rivers. But that was
not to be for as long as he lived. Suddenly two messengers
arrived, spurring post haste. They had come from Rome and
completely wearied their horses, yes, worn them out, broken
them with fatigue and ruined them. They enquired after the
king and searched for him until they found Louis and William
together. They threw themselves at the count's feet, begging
his favour: 'Have pity, noble count, for the sake of the God of
Majesty! You have had little thought for the maiden to whom
you pledged yourself. The valiant Guaifier of Spoleto is dead
and many men are seeking to marry her, counts, lords and
peers; yet she will give her love to no one but you. But we are
most of all troubled by another grave matter: Galafre the
noble emir you had baptized has also died and so has the Pope;
Guy of Germany has assembled his armies and captured the
main strongholds of Rome. Noble lord, the whole country will
be brought to sorrow if you do not come to our rescue!'
[2245]

When he heard this, William bowed his head and Louis
began to weep. When William saw this, he felt himself going
mad. 'Ah! wretched king, cowardly and besotted! I under-
took to protect you and defend you against any man in
Christendom, but everyone now feels such hatred for you that
I am ready to spend my whole youth in your service, until
things are all settled according to your will. Summon your
men and your barons and let all the impoverished young
knights come, those with lame horses and unshod chargers,
with broken and tattered armour! Let all those who serve in
poor baronies come and join me! I shall give them in plenty
gold and silver and minted money, Spanish chargers and great
lively mules that I brought from the city of Rome. Besides I

have captured so much more in Spain [16] that I cannot dispose
of a tenth of it. No freeborn man will ever call me miserly
about this, for I shall give it all away and much more besides.'
And the king said: 'God reward you for it!'   [2268]

They sealed their charters and their writs and sent out their
men-at-arms and servants far and wide. Before a fortnight was
up, so many men had come and assembled that fully fifty
thousand could be reckoned up, whether men-at-arms or
armed knights. They did not let any men on foot go with them,
to make sure of a speedy rescue. Of their journeying I have
nothing to relate. They crossed the St Bernard, which caused
them great fatigue, and travelled without stopping as far as
Rome. But they could not get in through the gate, for the
German opposed them strongly. King Louis had his pavilion
set up and all his tents and awnings pitched; he had fires lit
and kitchen hearths as well. Count William led out the foragers
into the surrounding district to spoil the countryside. They
plundered the whole region, so that the men of the army were
well-off and well provided for.   [2288]

57. Count William went out again, leading the foraging party.
Guy of Germany rose to his feet and addressed a Roman peer:
'Ah, noble lord, hold your peace and listen to me. Take up
your arms now, along with a band of a thousand knights,
before the French finish pitching their pavilions, and shout out
a loud warcry as you attack them. If you have any trouble, I
shall come to your aid.' And the lord replied: 'It shall be done
as you say.' Speedily they armed themselves, putting on their
hauberks and lacing up their helms, girding on their swords
and mounting their chargers; at their necks they hung their
quartered shields and in their fists they grasped their stout
sharp spears. Then they galloped out through the gateway.
[2303]

A fog was beginning to thicken so that it was impossible to
see to ride. The French had no means of setting up a proper
watch before the Romans came hurtling in among the tents.
They led off horses and killed squires, they carried off the food
from the kitchen and killed the chief steward. Louis himself
rushed away, fleeing on foot, going from tent to tent trying to

find a place to hide, calling out at the top of his voice: 'Bertrand! William! where are you? Sons of barons, I beg you come to my rescue! So help me God, now I need your help badly!' [2315]

William the valiant was out again leading the foraging party. The first to speak was Count Bertrand his nephew. 'Uncle William,' he said, 'you must take action at once: I can hear some very fierce shouting in the army. So help me God, they need our help badly!' And the count said: 'We must ride hard in the direction of Rome with our strong helms laced on. If we can keep the enemy cut off outside and trap them, and the men of our army have time to get their hauberks on, we can all gain a very great booty, such as has not been taken since the death of Guaifier.' They set their minds to riding hard towards Rome and now the fog was becoming very thick. The Romans had no means of setting up a proper watch before William began shouting his cry. 'Mountjoy!' he shouted, 'strike hard, knights!' Then you would have seen a fierce battle joined: so many shafts splintered, so many shields pierced, so many hauberks ripped and unravelled! You would have seen one dying man tumbling and tripping over another. The men of the army donned their hauberks and so the attackers were cut off before and behind. The French did not mean to spare a single man of the thousand Romans; they wanted them all killed and hewn down, or else taken prisoner and bound. [2340]

The lord who was in charge of the attackers fled. The count pursued him at full gallop along a hillside and shouted out: 'Turn back, knight, or you shall die like a worthless scoundrel!' He drove his steel along the fellow's side and toppled him over on the neck of his charger, then drew his sword and was about to take his head when he called out for pity and mercy. 'Baron, do not kill me, if you are William! Take me alive! You have much to gain from it: I shall give you a hogshead of silver pieces!' Count William came up to him and he handed over his burnished steel sword and was sent as a prisoner to Louis. The count returned to his foraging party. Guy of Germany rose to his feet and said to his men: 'Hold your peace and listen to me. My men are dead, killed and hewn down. If

I cannot arrange a single combat for myself, a hand-to-hand
fight against a single knight, our entire force will be of no value
to us against them.'   [2361]

58. Guy of Germany called a messenger and set him on an
Arab charger. About his neck he hung a great marten-skin
cloak and in his hands he hurriedly placed a wand. Guy of
Germany told him the message he was to deliver: 'Go straight
out to those silken tents and say on my behalf to Louis the son
of Charles that he is very much in the wrong in coming to lay
waste my province. He has no right to Rome or to any of this
inheritance and, if in his arrogance he wants to have it, he will
have to fight a duel against me, either he himself or some
knight who is willing to take his place. If I am defeated in this
combat, he will have full claim to Rome and the whole
inheritance; no man will wrong him over it afterwards. But if
I overcome him with my sharp sword, let him beware if he
takes anything here worth a single halfpenny; let him go off
back to France, to Paris or to Chartres, and leave Rome to me,
since it is my inheritance.' And the man replied: 'It is right
that I should do as you say.'   [2381]

At that he rode off through the wide gate and stopped for
nothing until he reached the tents. He dismounted beside the
silken pavilion and went inside this large tent where he found
Louis, the son of Charles. He called out to him in the hearing
of all the barons: 'Rightful emperor, listen to my words. I do
not greet you. It would not be right for me to do so. Guy of
Germany has sent me with a message and I will not conceal the
summons he sends you through me. You have no right to Rome
nor to any of this inheritance and, if in your arrogance you
want to have it, you will have to fight a duel against him,
either you yourself or some knight who is willing to take your
place. If my master is defeated in the combat, then you will
have full claim to Rome and the whole inheritance; no man
will wrong you over it afterwards. But if he overcomes you with
his sharp sword, beware if you take anything here worth a
single halfpenny; rather go off back to France, to Paris or to
Chartres, and leave Rome to him, since it is his inheritance.'
[2402]

When the king heard this, he hung his head. Then he raised it and called to his barons: 'Noble lords,' he said, 'listen to my words. Guy of Germany has sent me an arrogant message: he demands a single combat between himself and me, and I am young and of tender years, so that I cannot uphold my warlike station. Is there a Frenchman who is willing to fight him in place of me?' When they heard this, the barons hung their heads. The king saw their reaction and almost went mad with rage, then he wept tenderly under his marten-skins. [2413]

At that moment William Strongarm arrived, leading back the foraging party to the camp; still armed, he came into the silken tent and found the king sighing and in tears. When he saw this, he almost went mad with rage. He shouted out: 'Ah, wretched king, may God Himself bring you to harm! Why are you weeping? Who has done you wrong?' And Louis replied without delay: 'In God's name, my lord, why should I hide it from you? Guy of Germany has sent me an arrogant message: he seeks a single combat between himself and me. There is not a Frenchman who is willing to fight him in place of me, and I am young and of tender years, so that I cannot very well face up to such a warlike encounter.'—'King,' said William, 'may God Himself bring you to harm! For love of you I have already faced twenty-eight encounters like that. Did you think I would fail you this time? No indeed, by God! I will fight this battle. Not one of your Frenchmen is worth a halfpenny!' He turned to the messenger and addressed him boldly. [2434]

59. 'My friend, fair brother,' said the noble William, 'go and tell Guy the German from me that a knight who is taking the place of his lord has accepted the combat and is longing to meet him. I claim such hostages as I desire and he may take as many as he wishes, then the victor will keep what he has settled for.' The paladin Bertrand leapt to his feet: 'Uncle,' he said, 'this is very hard on us! Everything comes to you, in combats and battles, and your valour reduces ours to nothing. My lord, I request this combat for myself. Grant it to me, by your leave!' The count replied: 'You are talking madly! When Louis was all lamenting a moment ago, there was not a single man bold or doughty enough to hold out his glove in front of

him. Did you think then that I was going to back out? I would
not do so for the fief of Abilant! Messenger, brother, tell Guy
the German to arm himself and then go out to the field. Count
William will be there to meet him!'   [2456]

The messenger went off, pricking with his spurs, and rode
back to Rome without stopping. Guy the German came to
meet him. 'My friend, fair brother,' he said, 'how did you find
things among the Franks?'—'In God's name, my lord, I shall
hide nothing. A knight who is taking the place of his lord has
accepted the combat and desires nothing more than to fight.
He claims hostages and is anxious to have them and you are to
take as many as you wish, then the victor will keep all that he
has agreed to. William is his name, as far as I know. A young
knight, Bertrand, who is his nephew (that I know for sure),
sprang to his feet and was very eager to fight the duel.'—'My
friend, good brother,' said Guy the German, 'when I have
finished the combat against William, if this nephew of his,
Bertrand, is still looking for a fight, he will not need to look any
farther. Now bring me my most precious equipment.' And the
messenger replied: 'As you command.'   [2476]

They brought it to him with no more delay. They put on his
hauberk of Algerian mail with its mesh redder than a blazing
fire. They laced on his gleaming green helm with a carbuncle
in front on the nose-piece. Then he girded on his sword at his
left side. They brought up his fine speedy charger; another
sword was hanging from the saddle-bow. He leapt at once on
to the charger without touching stirrup or saddle. At his neck
he hung a strong heavy shield; in his fists he held a stout sharp
spera; he attached his banner to it with five gold nails. Then
he went spurring out through the gate and rode at full speed to
Nero's Meadow. Count William saw him arriving in the
distance and called out to Guielin and Bertrand: 'I see my
enemy has come to the field. If I wait any longer, I would
consider myself a recreant. Bring me my most precious equip-
ment!' And they replied: 'As you command.' They brought
him his arms without more delay. Louis the valiant was present
at his arming. He donned his hauberk, laced on his gleaming
helm and girded on at his left side the sword Joyous that
Charles the mighty fighter gave him. They led up the swift

Alion and he mounted with easy agility. At his neck he hung a strong heavy shield; in his fists he held a fine sharp spear; he attached his banner to it by five gold nails. He went spurring out between the booths and rode without a stop to the mound. [2509]

60. The marquis William rode up to the top of the mound and Guy of Germany addressed him: 'Who are you then—see you tell me no lies!—you who have found such boldness in your heart that you dare to come and face me in the field of combat?'— 'Indeed,' said William, 'I shall soon tell you that. My name is William, son of Count Aymeri of Narbonne, the brave and the bold. I am going to fight you here, you who look so challenging, with my burnished steel blade and I shall tell you now on what grounds: By right, Rome belongs to the King of Saint-Denis and I myself fought in combat once already over this, on top of this very mound, against the Arab Corsolt, the strongest man who was ever born of woman. It was then that he cut the nose off my face.' [2526]

When Guy heard this, he almost went stark mad; he would rather not have been there than have held the fief of Paris. Looking straight at William, he addressed him: 'Are you really then that marquis William of Narbonne, the son of Count Aymeri? Let us make peace and be good friends and you and I shall hold Rome together.'—'Scoundrel!' said William, 'God curse you! I did not come here to preach and have no wish at all to betray my rightful lord. I would not do that, even if I were to lose all my limbs!' When Guy heard this, he almost went stark mad. He swore by the apostle who is revered in Rome: 'I consider myself vile for ever asking you for anything! Now I challenge you, by God in Paradise!' William replied: 'And I challenge you in the same terms!' [2541]

They rode apart more than a bowshot, then looked straight at each other, turning face to face. They clasped their stout shields in front of their chests and got themselves all ready to exchange rude blows. They pricked their chargers with their burnished spurs and at once came charging at each other with lowered lances. They exchanged great blows on their vaulted shields; below the bosses they split and wrecked them. But

neither could fault the other's white hauberk; their shafts were
shattered since they could not bear the strain and the splinters
from them flew right up into the air. Their bodies and chests
collided; their stout vaulted shields, their hauberks and their
valuable horses were all locked together. Their helms grated
together in front of their faces; blood and sweat streamed
down from them until all four were forced to fall flat. The two
chargers entangled on the ground, but the two warriors leapt
to their feet with drawn swords and shields at the ready. Now
they were to show how far they were from being friends!
[2562]

61. Count William had leapt to his feet again; he called upon
God, the righteous Father: 'Holy Mary, Virgin Maiden, help
me! Never before did I lose my stirrups for any man!' Guy of
Germany replied proudly: 'By God, William, that will not
help you a jot! I am fighting for Rome, for the walls and the
fief. Louis shall never inherit it!'—'Scoundrel!' said William,
'God give you grief, for by the apostle the palmers go to seek,
before evening or sunset I mean to treat your body in such a
way that nobody will think it worth a bezant!' He gripped
Joyous with its blade of steel, lunged fiercely at Guy standing
there before him and gave him such a blow on his inlaid helm
that he scattered all the flowers and the jewels. Had it not been
for the hood of the double-mesh white hauberk, he would not
have needed to strike another blow after that one. The blade
slid down to his enemy's hip and tore off more than a foot of
flesh so that the bone was laid bare at his waist. 'Indeed,' cried
William, 'I have drawn blood on this side! Now you know how
my blade can cut!' Guy the German replied proudly: 'Ah,
wicked William, God give you grief! Do you think you can
frighten me off for so little? A man can be too much weighed
down with paltry flesh! But, by the Cross that palmers go to
visit, before evening or sunset I mean to avenge my flesh on
yours!'   [2593]

He gripped his sword with its blade of steel, lunged fiercely
at William standing there before him and gave him such a
blow on his inlaid helm that he scattered all the flowers and
the jewels. Had it not been for the hood of the double-mesh

white hauberk, Count Aymeri would have been left without an
heir. But God would not suffer or allow that. Guy gained little
from striking that blow, for his blade shattered where it joined
the hilt; he drew his other sword without a moment's delay.
When William saw this, he could not help laughing. He
gripped Joyous with its rich blade of steel, lunged fiercely at
Guy standing there before him and gave him such a blow on
his inlaid helm that the blade swept right down to his shoulder
and into his chest, splitting it and cleaving it open. With a
twist, he pulled his sword out again and flung him down dead.
They were near the Tiber; he threw the body into the water
and the weight of iron on it dragged it right down to the
bottom, so that no one has ever been able to pull it up again.
When this was done, William shouted his battle-cry: 'Mount-
joy!' he cried, 'God and St Denis be my help! Now King
Louis is avenged on this man.' He mounted his charger Alion,
leading off Clinevent, for he did not want to leave him behind,
and rode back to the army without delay.   [2619]

Count Bertrand his nephew came out to meet him and with
him Louis, all merry, joyful and gay. What tears were shed by
Guielin and Walter! They had never been so afraid before in
their lives, except on the day that William fought against
Corsolt. 'Uncle William,' they said, 'are you sound and well?'
—'Yes indeed,' he replied, 'thanks be to God in Heaven! Fair
nephew Bertrand, why should I hide it from you? I want to
give you this fine swift charger because you claimed the right
to fight this combat yesterday.' Bertrand replied: 'Accept my
most hearty thanks!' The men of Rome were now all in dismay
and said to each other: 'Things have turned out very badly
for us. Our lord has been killed and hacked to pieces. Now we
must all humble ourselves. Let us go at once and beg for mercy.'
And the others agreed: 'Yes, let that be done!' With great
golden crosses of very high value, with phylacteries and incense
and psalters, they came out in procession, bearing the holy
relics of their church. They opened up the gates without delay
and gave a fine welcome to their rightful lord.   [2641]

62. The noble William was in the city of Rome. He took his
lord at once and with all speed and set him straight away on

the throne and crowned him there with the lordship of all the Franks. All his vassals came then to swear allegiance to him. Some who swore their oath that day kept it well, but there were others who did not keep it at all.   [2648]

63. The valiant William was in the city of Rome; he had crowned his lord Louis ánd secured him in his rule over the whole empire. Then he made his preparations and turned his mind to the journey. They travelled and made their way back until they arrived in the kingdom of France. The king went off to the city of Paris, Count William went on to Montreuil. Then William thought he could have a rest and find sport hunting in the woods and along the rivers. But that was not to be for as long as he lived, for the Frenchmen took to rebelling again, making war against each other and acting like madmen, burning down towns and laying waste the countryside. They would not restrain themselves at all on Louis's account. [2664]

A messenger went to tell William of all this. When the count heard it, he almost went out of his senses. He called out to Bertrand: 'Noble nephew, listen to me. For the love of God, what advice do you give me? My lord the king is completely disinherited.' Bertrand replied: 'Leave him then as he is! Let us give up France and send it to the devil, along with this king who is so besotted! He will never be able to hold on to a foot of his inheritance.' William replied: 'Leave all that as it is! I am ready to spend my whole youth in his service.'   [2674]

He had all his men and his friends summoned and they rode and travelled by forced marches until they reached the city of Paris. There William found Louis. From then on they began to wage great battles. When William Shortnose the marquis saw that Louis could not remain in that region because he had too many mortal enemies there, he took the young man who was in his care and bore him off to the city of Laon. He left him closely guarded by the men of the city and took to burning and pillaging the enemies outside. So he began chopping down their stout barriers and piercing and breaking down their high walls. Within a year he had dealt out such punishment to the rebels that fifteen counts were forced to present themselves at

court and do homage for their inheritance to Louis who held
command over France. He gave his sister in marriage to Louis
and so the king was established in his high station. But when
he was fully in power, he showed no gratitude to William.
[2695]

D. G. HOGGAN
Aberystwyth

NOTES

This is a translation of the second, revised edition of *Le Couronnement de
Louis* published by Ernest Langlois in the *Classiques français du moyen
âge* series, Paris (Champion), 1925, which replaced his earlier edition
in the *Société des Anciens Textes Français* collection, Paris, 1888.

The poem is preserved in eight manuscripts (with fragments of
another) of the 13th and 14th centuries, all of these being 'cyclic'
manuscripts which also include *The Waggon-train* and *The Capture of
Orange*. Langlois's classification of the manuscripts has been found to
apply equally to these subsequent poems by their editors and also by
Madeleine Tyssens (see Bibliography).

Both of the Langlois editions of *Le Couronnement de Louis* are critical
editions in the sense that they attempt to reconstitute the text of the
original poem by collating the readings of all the existing manuscripts.
From the point of view of the translator, this can only be considered
an advantage, especially as very few of Langlois's readings have ever
been seriously challenged. Similarly, his dating of the original poem,
c. 1130, is still generally accepted.

The text has been translated into modern French prose by André
Lanly, under the title *Le Couronnement de Louis, Chanson de geste du
XIIe siècle*, Paris (Champion), 1969.

[1] Old French *mostier* usually means a church, normally a monastic one
(cf. English *Minster*), but it can also be applied to the abbey or
monastery as whole.
[2] This summary treatment of traitors becomes one of William's main
hallmarks. It is repeated in *laisse* 46; in *The Waggon-train*, 26 and 53;
and applied to Guielin in *The Capture of Orange*, 55.

[3] This line, which makes nonsense of the internal chronology of the poem, is almost certainly a late interpolation.

[4] The verb in these frequently recurring oath-formulas (*querre* or *requerre*) is commonly understood in the sense of 'invoke' (cf. English 'request'). However, the verb 'visit' perhaps renders the sense more accurately. Chaucer's line, 'The holy blissful martyr for to seek', suggests another verb that, given the uncertainty as to the precise meaning of *(re)querre*, could be used in this type of context. See the 'Index of Proper Names' under *Ark, Galicia, Nero's Meadow, palmers* and *Rome*.

[5] These lines contain an extremely garbled version, probably ironical in intent, of a plenary indulgence, the first of which was offered by Urban II in 1095 for all those taking part in the First Crusade.

[6] The twelve names given here are intended to correspond to the group of the Twelve Peers of Charlemagne's army at Roncevaux, but in fact only the first six and the last two properly belong to the list as indicated in the *Song of Roland* (lines 2403 f.).

[7] This prayer, like the other in *laisse* 26 below, is a particularly elaborate example of a type frequently found in French epic: see Sister M. P. Koch, *An Analysis of the Long Prayers in Old French Literature* (Washington, 1940) and E.-R. Labande, 'Le *credo* épique . . .', in *Recueil de travaux offerts à M. Clovis Brunel* (Paris, 1955), t. II.

[8] These two lines are garbled in different ways in all the manuscripts and Langlois's text does not give a very clear sense. The meaning has been reconstructed from Genesis 4:12.

[9] In accordance with common medieval practice, the account of the anointing of Christ's feet in the home of Simon the Leper (Matthew 26:6 f.; Mark 14:3 f.) is here conflated with John 12:1 f., where Mary Magdalene performs this office, and Luke 7:36 f., where a 'woman who was a sinner' washes Christ's feet with her tears.

[10] This is the 'canonical' list of the names of William's six brothers with their traditional titles or epithets.

[11] No doubt an explanation current among the Crusaders for the Mohammedan's well-known abstention from alcoholic drink and the flesh of swine.

[12] Langlois's note to line 1422 explains that William would have committed treason if he had accepted that Galafre remain in charge of Rome *on his behalf*, since the overlordship of Rome was the emperor's prerogative.

[13] This line is generally recognized as a late interpolation, since the tradition that William had contacts with Orable before the action of this poem contradicts the situation at the beginning of *The Capture of Orange*.

14 There is some confusion in the original because the term *le mostier* is applied to two different places and it has often been thought that two distinct *churches* were involved. It seems better to assume that only the Abbey of St Martin is intended, sometimes the church itself and sometimes the monastic buildings more generally.

15 The 'cleric Walter' introduced here is clearly identical with the Abbot of St Martin's, named Walter in *laisse* 46.

16 'Spain' here, as in *The Waggon-train* (*laisses* 18, 19, 24, 25, 26, 30, 44, 48), *The Capture of Orange* (*laisses* 1, 7, 19, 57, 59, 61), and *The Song of William* (*laisses* 153, 157, 162, 181, 182), includes those parts of the South of France that had been invaded by the Moors who occupied much of Spain.

The Waggon-Train

1. Hearken, my lords! May God, the Glorious, the King of Majesty, grant you greater valour! Will you hear a fine tale of the best man who ever believed in God? It is about William, the marquis of the short nose, and how he captured Nîmes by leading in the waggon-train. Then he won the city of Orange and had Guibourg baptized, whom he took away from Tibalt, king of the Slavs, and married her, taking her as his wife and his equal. He killed Corsolt [1] in the meadows below Rome. He greatly exalted holy Christianity and such were his deeds on earth that now he wears a heavenly crown. [13]

It was in May, in early summer when the woods are in leaf, the meadows grow green again, and the birds sing sweet, melodious songs. Count William was returning from hunting in a forest where he had been for a long while. He had bagged two stags in ideal condition and had loaded them on three Spanish mules. The count had four arrows at his side and was bringing back from the hunt his bow of laburnum wood. With him were forty youths, sons of counts and of enfeoffed princes, who had recently been dubbed knights. They held falcons for their entertainment and had packs of hounds with them. They entered Paris by the Petit Pont. [28]

A noble and a valiant man was Count William. He had his venison taken to his lodging. On the way, he met Bertrand and asked him: 'Where are you coming from, nephew?' Bertrand replied: 'You shall hear the truth. I come from the palace where I have been for some time. I heard a great deal there. Our emperor has been distributing fiefs to his barons: to one he gives land, to another a castle, to another cities, to another a town, as he thinks appropriate: you and I, uncle, are overlooked. It does not matter about me—I am a mere youth—but it does matter about you who are so valiant and have undergone great toil and travail, going without sleep by night and without food by day.' William heard him and laughed. 'Nephew,' he said, 'no more of this. Go quickly to your lodging and equip yourself in fine style. Meanwhile I shall go and talk to Louis.'—'As you command, sir,' said Bertrand, and returned quickly to his lodging.   [50]

A noble and a valiant man was Count William. He had no mind to stop until he reached the palace. He dismounted beneath the spreading olive-tree then went up the marble steps. He strode so energetically across the floor of the hall that he burst the uppers of his Cordovan leather boots; there was not a baron present but was scared. Seeing him, the king rose to greet him, saying: 'William, do be seated.'—'No, sire,' said valiant William, 'but I would like to speak to you a little.'—'As you command,' said Louis, 'you will, I think, have a fair hearing.'—'Louis, my brother,' said valiant William, 'I have served you, not by massaging you at night or by robbing widows and children of their inheritance, but by valiantly taking up arms. Many a hard pitched battle have I fought for you, in which I have killed many a noble youth and incurred the guilt of that sin. Whoever they were, God made them. God preserve their souls and forgive me!'—'My lord William,' said valiant Louis, 'I pray you, bear with me a while. Winter will pass, summer will come again. One of these days, one of your peers will die. I will give you all his lands, and his wife too if you wish to take her.' Hearing this, William was beside himself with anger: 'O God who suffered on the Cross!' said the Count, 'how long a wait has the poor youth who has nothing to take for himself and nothing to give another. I have to feed my horse, but do not know where to find the wherewithal. God! what a long valley must he pass through and what a great mountain must he climb whose fortune waits on the death of another!   [86]

2. 'God!' said William, 'what a long wait there is for a young man of my age! He has nothing to give and nothing to take for his needs. I have to provide fodder for my horse, but do not yet know where to find corn to do so. Do you think, O King, that I am not grief-stricken?   [93]

3. 'My lord Louis,' said proud William, 'were it not that my peers would have held me faithless, I would have left you fully a year ago, when the letters sent me by the mighty King Guaifier reached me from Spoleto, offering to give me a share of his land, one half of it and his daughter too. I could have waged war on the king of France.' The king heard him and thought he would go out of his mind. He said things he ought to have left unsaid. And so the discord began to grow worse and the ill-feeling between them to intensify. [105]

4. 'My lord William,' said King Louis, 'there is no man in all this country, neither Guaifier nor any other, nor the king of Spoleto himself, who would dare accept the services of a single one of my men without being killed or captured within a year, or driven into exile.'—'God!' said the Count, 'What a plight is mine, to be wholly dependent on you for my sustenance. Shame on me if I ever serve you again! [114]

5. 'My noble knights,' said valiant William, 'go quickly to your lodgings, equip yourselves in fine style and have the baggage loaded on to the pack-horses. I am so angry I must leave the court. Since it was for sustenance we stayed with the king, he can say that he has done well.' And his men replied: 'As you command.' William stood on a raised hearth and leaned for a while on his bow of laburnum wood, that he had brought back from the hunt, with such force that it snapped in two and the pieces flew up to the beams and then fell right in front of the king. He began to address the king in strong terms, for he had served him for a long time: 'Am I to be reproached for the great deeds I have accomplished in your service, the great combats and the pitched battles? My lord Louis,' said valiant William, 'do you remember the great battle I fought for you in the meadows below Rome? There I fought the Emir Corsolt, the strongest man in Christendom or in the pagan lands. With his naked sword he dealt me such a blow on my gold-and-jewel-studded helmet that he brought the crystal [2] crashing down. He sliced through the nose-piece of my helmet just where it covered my nose and slid the blade right down to my nostrils. I had to hold my nose together with both hands and when it had been patched up there was a great bump in it.

Curse the doctor who was supposed to mend it for me! That is why they call me "William Shortnose". I feel great shame when I come amongst my peers and before the king amongst the assembled nobles. No-one was ever given so much as a lance by him, or a pike, or a shield or an iron-shod palfrey or a steel blade with its pommel. [152]

6. 'King Louis,' said prudent William, 'rightful Emperor, you were indeed the son of Charlemagne, the best king ever to bear arms, the most terrible, the most just. Remember, O King, a fierce battle I fought for you at the ford of Peralada. I captured Dagobert who will remain at your court: there he is, dressed in his fine sable. If he denies it, I can be called to account. Then I fought another battle for you: when Charlemagne wanted to make you king and the crown was set on the altar, for a long time you did not move from your place. The French saw that you were of little worth and wanted to make you a cleric, or an abbot, or a priest, or they would have made you a canon somewhere. In the church of St Mary Magdalene, when Arneïs, because of his powerful family, wanted to take the crown for himself, I saw what was afoot and did not like it. I dealt him a mighty blow on the neck and laid him flat on his back on the marble floor. I was hated by his powerful family for it. I crossed the whole breadth of the court, in full sight of everyone, including the Pope and all the patriarchs; I took hold of the crown, and you left with it on your head. You did not remember this service I did you when you overlooked me in distributing your lands. [181]

7. 'My lord Louis,' said noble William, 'do you not remember the arrogant knave who came and defied you here in your own court? "You have no right to rule France," he said in the hearing of all. In the whole of your empire you had not a single baron, rightful Emperor, to answer him yea or nay, but I was mindful of my natural lord. I stepped forward and, like a madman, tied him to a stake like the traitor he was. I had my reward later, when I was returning from Mont-Saint-Michel and met the aged Richard the Red, the father of the arrogant Norman. He had twenty men, I had only two. I drew my sword and put up a gallant fight. With my naked blade I

killed seven of them, and struck down their leader before their eyes. I handed him over to you at your court in Paris and later he died in your great tower. All this barely occurs to you when you overlook me when making gifts of land. Remember, O King, Guy the German: when you were going to St Peter's he claimed from you the French and the Burgundians, the crown and the city of Laon. I engaged him in combat, as many barons saw, thrust my gonfalon through his body, and flung him into the Tiber; the fish ate him. I would have considered myself a fool for that, when I came to my host, Guy, who made me put to sea on a galley.[3] Remember, O King, Otto's vast army: with you were the French and the Burgundians, the Lorrains, the Flemings and the Frisians. Over the great St Bernard and past Monbaldone you went right on to Rome, to the place called Nero's Meadow, and I myself pitched your tent and served you superb venison. [219]

8. 'When you had eaten, I came to you to ask leave to go. You granted it freely and willingly, thinking that I would go and lie down in my tent to rest my limbs. I ordered two thousand knights into the saddle and came to keep watch over you in a patch of pines and laurels behind your tent, bidding my men take cover there. You would not deign to keep a lookout for the Romans. There were more than fifteen thousand of them. They arrived in front of your tent ready to hurl lances, cut your guy-ropes and overturn your tents, pull away the table-cloths and scatter your food. I saw your steward and your door-keeper captured. You were fleeing on foot from one tent to another in the crush like a wretched hound. You called out at the top of your voice: "Bertrand! William! Come to my aid!" I took great pity on you then, my lord king. I took on seven thousand strong men in battle, and captured more than three hundred knights for you there with their fiery war-horses. I saw their leader leaning against a wall and recognized him by his fine helmet strengthened with bands and by the carbuncle which shone on its nose-piece. I struck him so hard with my sharp lance that I knocked him down on the neck of his horse. He cried for mercy: "Good sir, do not kill me if you really are William!" and so I took pity on him. I brought him

to you without delay. As a result, you still have an important
fief in Rome. Now you are a mighty man and I am held in
low esteem. All the time I have served you I have defended
you. I have not earned a penny by it and the Picards call me
"Sir-Hang-around-Court".   [255]

9. 'My lord Louis,' William continued, 'I have served you till
my hair has turned white, but I am not a penny better off, not
so as to be any better dressed for it in your court. I have no
home to call my own. My lord Louis, what are you thinking
of? It used to be said that I was your bosom friend, and I used
to ride the fine horses with flowing manes and I served you in
all kinds of terrain.[4] No-one ever gained anything by serving
you, not even to the extent of having an extra stud in his shield
unless he received a mighty blow from another lance.[5] I killed
more than twenty thousand unbelieving Turks; but, by Him
who dwells on high in Heaven, I shall turn against my liege.
You can destroy our friendship.   [271]

10. 'O God, born of a noble Virgin,' said William, 'for what
have I killed so many fine young men? For what have I made
so many mothers grieve, so that the sin of it weighs on my
heart? So long have I served this wicked king of France and
am not a whit better off.'   [277]

11. 'My lord William,' said valiant Louis, 'by the apostle
whom they seek in Nero's Meadow,[6] I have sixty other of your
peers to whom I have neither promised nor given anything.'
And William said: 'My lord king, that is a lie. I have no peer
in Christendom except yourself and you are a crowned king—
and I do not claim to be above you. Take now those men you
have mentioned, bring them out one by one into the meadow,
on horseback, equipped and armed; if I do not kill them all
and more—you too if you wish to join in—then let me not have
any part of your inheritance.' The king heard him and bowed
in his direction. As he raised his head, he addressed him
thus: [293]

12. 'My lord William,' said noble Louis, 'now I see clearly
that you are filled with anger.'—'Truly,' said William, 'so
were my parents. Thus it happens when one serves wicked

men: one does all one can, and gains nothing; on the contrary, things grow steadily worse.' [299]

13. 'My lord William,' said worthy Louis, 'now I can see that you are a very angry man.—'Truly,' said William, 'so were my ancestors. That is the lot of a man who serves a wicked lord: however much he does to enhance his lord's reputation, he himself is little better off.'—'My lord William,' Louis answered, 'you have defended my interests and served me devotedly, more than anyone else in my court. Come forward, and I will give you a fine gift. Take the estate of the worthy Count Foucon: you will have three thousand companions to serve you.'—'Indeed I will not, sire,' William answered. 'The noble Count has left two children who will be well able to administer his lands. Give me a different estate, for I am not prepared to take that one.' [314]

14. 'My lord William,' said King Louis, 'since you will not accept this estate or deprive the children of it, take the lands of Aubrey the Burgundian and his step-mother Hermensaut of Tori, the finest woman who ever quaffed a draught of wine: you will have three thousand iron-clad men to serve you.'— 'Indeed I will not, sire,' William replied. 'The noble count has left a son called Robert, but he is tiny and cannot yet dress himself or pull on his breeches. If God grants that he grow big and strong, he will be well able to administer all his lands.' [327]

15. 'My lord William,' said proud Louis, 'if you do not wish to deprive this child of his inheritance, then take the lands of Marquis Béranger. The marquis is dead, so marry his widow: you will have two thousand knights to serve you, equipped with shining weapons and swift horses—and they will not cost you a penny of your own money.' William heard him and was beside himself with anger. He began to shout, in a loud, clear voice: 'Listen to me, noble knights, hear how Louis, my rightful lord, defends the interests of those who freely serve him. I will tell you about Marquis Béranger, who was born in the Val de Riviers. He killed a count and could not afford to pay the blood-money. He fled to the imperial residence at Laon and there fell at the feet of the emperor who received him

readily and gave him lands and a wife of noble birth. Béranger thereafter served him blamelessly for a long time. Some time later, the king happened to be fighting the Saracens, the Turks and the Slavs. There was an astonishingly fierce battle and the king was struck down from his horse and would never, ever, have been able to remount, but then Marquis Béranger arrived on the scene and, seeing his lord hard pressed, came galloping up. In his hand he held his sword of furbished steel and cut down those around him like a boar in the middle of a pack of hounds. Then he dismounted from his swift steed to come to his lord's rescue. The king remounted with the marquis holding the stirrup for him, and fled like a hound with its tail between its legs. Marquis Béranger stayed behind and we saw him killed and cut to pieces and could do nothing to help him. He has left a noble heir, called young Béranger. Anyone who wishes to harm the child's interests is an arrant fool and, so help me God, a traitor and a renegade. The emperor wishes to bestow his fief on me: I will have none of it and I wish you all to hear me say so. And there is one thing I must make clear to you: by the apostle whom they seek in Rome, there is no knight in the whole of France so bold that, if he takes young Béranger's land, he will not have his head struck off at once by this sword of mine!'—'We thank you, sir,' said the knights of young Béranger's household, bowing to him and embracing his feet and legs.   [379]

'My lord William,' said Louis, 'listen. Since you find this honour unacceptable, so help me God, I will now give you such a fief that, if you are reasonable, you shall obtain a position of eminence. I will give you one quarter of France, a quarter of the abbeys and a quarter of the markets, a quarter of the towns and a quarter of the archbishoprics, a quarter of the footsoldiers and a quarter of the knights, a quarter of the vavasours and a quarter of the footmen, a quarter of the girls and a quarter of the women, a quarter of the priests and a quarter of the churches; I give you a quarter of the horses in my stables; I give you a quarter of the ready money in my treasury; I willingly bestow on you a quarter of the empire that is mine to govern. Accept it, noble knight.'—'That I will not, sire,' William replied. 'I would not do so for all the gold in the world, for these worthy knights would say at once: "Look how William, the proud-faced marquis, has deceived his rightful lord! Louis gave him half of his kingdom, and receives not a pennyworth in return. William has been cutting into his resources!'" [403]

16. 'My lord William,' said valiant Louis, 'by the apostle whom they seek in Nero's Meadow, if you are not willing to accept this honour, I do not know what in this land I can give you, nor can I think of any other honour to offer you.'—'Sire,' said William, 'then leave things be. I do not wish to discuss the matter any further at present. When it suits you, you will give me castles and borderlands, strongholds and fortresses in abundance.' So saying, the count turned away and strode angrily down the steps. On the way, he met Bertrand who asked him: 'Where are you coming from, uncle?' And William said: 'You shall hear the truth: from the palace, where I have been for a long while. I have had a quarrel with Louis and spoken angrily to him. I have done a great deal in his service, and he has given me nothing.'—'God's curse!' said Bertrand, 'you must not provoke your rightful lord but, on the contrary, serve him and honour him, and protect and defend him against all comers.'—'Away with you!' said William. 'He has so treated me that I have spent my life serving him and am not an ounce better off.' [427]

17. William said: 'Sir Bertrand, my nephew, I have devoted my life to serving the king, and by the strength of my own hand upheld and exalted him. Now he has granted me a quarter of France. Exactly as if it were a reproach, he wishes to pay me for my services. But by the apostle whom they seek in Rome, I feel like knocking the crown off his head: I placed it there and am prepared to take it off again.' Bertrand said: 'Sir, what you say is unworthy. You must not threaten your rightful lord, but uphold and exalt him, and help him against all who come against him.' And the count said: 'What you say is true, nephew. One must always cherish loyalty: that is the command of God who shall judge all things.' [443]

18. 'Uncle William,' said Bertrand wisely, 'let us go now, you

and I, and talk to Louis in that vast palace to ask for a gift that
has sprung to my mind.'—'And what would that be?' asked
valiant William. 'You shall hear the truth,' said Bertrand.
'Ask him for the kingdom of Spain,[7] including Tortolouse and
Portpaillart on the coast, and also the fine city of Nîmes, and
finally Orange, which is such an admirable place. If he grants
it to you, no thanks are called for, for no-one ever bore a shield
for him in those parts, nor was any knight ever hired to serve
him there. He can easily give you that domain and his king-
dom will hardly be harmed thereby.' When William heard
this, he laughed aloud and said : 'Nephew, blessed is the hour
you were born ! I too had thought of that but wished to discuss
it with you first.'   [462]

    Taking one another by the hand, they went up to the palace
and did not stop until they reached the hall. The king, seeing
them, stood up to receive them and then said; 'William, be
seated.'—'No, sire,' said the well-born count, 'but I would like
to speak to you briefly to ask for a gift that has sprung to my
mind.'—'God be praised !' said the king, 'if you want a castle
or a town, a tower or a city, a stronghold or a fortress, it shall
at once be granted to you. Half my kingdom, if you wish to
take it, I give you, sir, freely and willingly; for I have always
found you a man of great loyalty and it is because of you that
I am called King of France.' Hearing him, William laughed
aloud and addressed the king there as he stood before him :
'That is not the gift that we shall ask for. Rather I ask for the
kingdom of Spain, and Tortolouse and Portpaillart on the
coast, and the city of Nîmes, and Orange which is such an
admirable place. If you give it me, no thanks are called for, for
no-one ever bore a shield for you in those parts nor did you
ever have a knight in your pay there, and your estate will not
be impoverished thereby.' The king, hearing him, laughed
aloud.   [489]

19. 'Louis, sire,' said mighty William, 'give me in God's name
all the passes into Spain; the land shall be mine, the treasure
shall be yours; a thousand knights will campaign there with
you.   [493]

20. 'Grant me, sire, Nauseüre the Great, and with it, Nîmes and

its strong fortress: I will drive out thence the foul pagan Otrant who for nothing has slain so many Frenchmen, and has put them to flight from so many lands. If God be my helper, and if it is according to His will, I will ask you, sire, for no other land. [500]

21. 'Give me, sire, Valsoré and Valsure, give me Nîmes and its pointed towers, and also Orange, that formidable city, and the land round Nîmes with all its pastures, where the Rhône flows through the ravines.' Louis said: 'God be my helper! Shall all this be held by one man alone?' And William said: 'I have no care to stay. I shall ride through the evening and by moonlight, clothed in my padded hauberk, and will drive out the vile race of Saracens thence.' [510]

22. 'My lord William,' said the king, 'hear me. By the apostle whom they seek in Nero's Meadow, that land is not mine, I cannot give it to you. On the contrary, it is occupied by the Saracens and Slavs, by Clarel of Orange and his brother Aceré, and Golias and King Desramed, and Arragon and Morant and Barré and Quinzepaumes and his brother Gondré, Otrant of Nîmes and King Murgalé. King Tibalt is to be crowned there. He has taken as his wife Orable, the emir's sister, the most beautiful woman you could hope to find in Christendom or in the pagan lands. I fear therefore that if you thrust yourself in their midst, you will not be able to liberate that country. But, if you will, stay in this country. Let us divide our towns out equally: you shall have Chartres and leave me Orleans, and you shall have the crown too for I no longer wish to wear it.'—'Indeed I will not, sire,' said valiant William, 'or else these high-born barons would say: "See how William, the marquis of the short nose, has now served the interests of his rightful lord: Louis has given him half of his kingdom, but he has not paid a penny in return. He has been cutting into Louis's resources."' [537]

23. 'My lord William,' said the king, 'noble warrior, what do you care if people blame you unjustly? I do not want you to leave me here in this country. You shall have Chartres and let me have Orleans and the crown, for I ask for no more.'—'No,

sire,' replied William, 'I would not do so for all the gold in the world. I do not wish to diminish your estate in any way, but rather to enhance it by iron and the sword. You are my lord, I do not wish to do you wrong.—It was at Michaelmas. I was at Saint-Gilles-de-Provence, at the house of a worthy man. The noble knight lodged me, gave me food and drink, and hay and oats for my fiery steed. When we had eaten, the courtly knight went to enjoy himself in the fields with his followers. [*Line or lines missing*] . . . when his wife seized my reins. I dismounted and she held on to the stirrup, then led me down into a cellar, and from the cellar into an upper room. Before I realized what was happening, she fell at my feet. I thought, sire, that she was making amorous advances, asking for what a woman asks from a man. If I had known this for certain, I would not have gone near her for a thousand pounds. "My lady, my good woman, what are you after?" I asked. "Have mercy, William, noble knight! For the love of our crucified Lord, take pity on this land!" She made me look out of the window. I saw the whole country full of demons who were burning cities, desecrating churches, destroying chapels, overturning belfries, and twisting the breasts of noble women so that I felt deep pity for them in my heart and wept tenderly. And there and then I swore to the Glorious One in Heaven and to St Giles, to whom I had just been praying, that I would go and help the people in that land with as many men as I could have under my command.' [579]

24. 'My lord William,' said noble Louis, 'that this country does not appeal to you, so help me God, saddens and distresses me. Noble knights, come forward. I will do, truly, what you wish. Have Spain as your fief, take this glove in token. I give it to you on this understanding that, if toil and hardship mount up for you, I shall have no responsibility for you either here or elsewhere.' William said: 'I ask for nothing more, except your help once in seven years.' Louis said: 'I agree readily. Now indeed I shall do according to your behest.'—'Many thanks, sire,' said the count, 'now wait.' Count William then looked around him and saw standing there his nephews, Guielin and Bertrand, the sons of Bernard of Brubant. He called them

loudly as they stood listening: 'Come forward, Guielin and Bertrand. You are my friends and my close kinsmen. Present yourselves to the king and, along with me, accept the glove in token of the fief that I am now asking for. You shall share with me the rewards and the hardships.' Hearing this, Guielin feigned a smile and said under his breath so that no-one heard him: 'I shall bring great sorrow upon my uncle.'—'Indeed you will not, sir,' said Count Bertrand, 'for brave William is a proud-hearted man.'—'What do I care?' said proud Guielin. 'I am too young, only twenty years old. I cannot yet endure such great hardship.' His father, Bernard of Brubant, heard him and nearly went mad with rage. He raised his hand and struck him. 'Ah! you treacherous fool! You have filled me with sorrow! I will bring you into the king's presence. By the apostle of the penitents, if you do not accept the glove along with William I shall deal you such a blow with this sword that no doctor now or hereafter will ever heal you in the whole of your life. Go and look for a fief, as you totally lack one, just as I did whilst I was still a young man. For by the apostle of the penitents, you shall not have as much as a handsbreadth of mine: I would rather give it away just as I please.' Guielin and Bertrand stepped forward and, standing on a table, declared in a loud, clear voice: 'Master Bernard of Brubant has had the better of us. But, by the apostle of the penitents, the Saracens and the Persians will pay dearly for this. They can consider that they have entered on an unlucky year. They will die in their hundreds and their thousands.' [634]

25. William climbed on to a table and began to cry out in a loud, clear voice: 'Listen to me, barons of France. So help me God, this I can claim that I have more land than thirty of my peers, although I have not yet liberated an acre of it. This I say to the needy young men with their lame cart-horses and their tattered garments: though they have served and gained nothing thereby, if they will put themselves to the test with me in battle, I will give them money and estates, castles and borderlands, strongholds and fortresses, if they help me to conquer the land and exalt the true faith. This will I say to the needy young men, to the squires with their tattered garments:

if they come with me to conquer Spain, and help me to liberate
the country and exalt the true faith, I will give them in
abundance money and shining silver, castles and borderlands,
strongholds and fortresses, and Spanish horses, and they shall
be dubbed knights.'   [656]

26. When they heard him, the men were jubilant and began to
call out: 'Lord William, in God's name, waste no time. Those
of us who have no horse will go with you on foot.' What a sight
were the poverty-stricken squires and knights! They went to
William, the proud-faced marquis. Soon there were thirty
thousand of them, armed as best they could, all of whom had
sworn and affirmed that they would not fail him, were their
limbs to be cut off. Seeing this, the count was jubilant and
thanked them in the name of the King of Glory. Count
William acted most admirably. He went to take leave of Louis,
which the king granted readily: 'Go, good sir, in the name of
the King of Glory! May Jesus who dwells in glory grant you
success and safe return!' William, the proud-faced marquis,
then left and with him many a noble knight.   [677]
   Then across the hall the aged Aymon made his appearance.
God confound him! When he saw the king, he addressed him
thus: 'Noble Emperor, how you have been tricked!'—'In
what way, good sir?' Louis replied. 'Sire,' he said, 'I will tell
you: William, the warrior, is leaving this very moment, and in
his company many a noble knight. In this way he has deprived
you of the flower of France. If war breaks out, you will be
defenceless. And I have no doubt he will come back on foot,
and all the rest will be reduced to beggary.'—'That is an
unworthy way to speak,' Louis replied. 'William the warrior
is a very worthy man, there is no better knight in any land.
He has served me well with iron and the sword. May Jesus who
dwells in glory grant that he return safely, having liberated the
whole of Spain!' There was present there a noble knight
known as Walter of Toulouse. When he heard William being
abused, he was greatly distressed and angered. He strode
quickly down the floor of the hall, came to William, seized the
stirrup and reins of his swift horse, and said: 'Sir, you are a
very fine knight but in the palace you are of no account.'—

'Who says that?' asked proud William. 'Sir,' he replied, 'I must not conceal it from you: I give you my word that that is what the aged Aymon says. He intends to turn the king against you.' William said: 'He shall pay dearly for this. If God grant that I may return, I will have his every limb cut off, or have him hung on the gallows or put to death by drowning.' And Walter said: 'I am not interested in threats. Any worthless man can threaten. But one thing I would ask of you: reward him according to his services. It is here that you must begin to wage your war: this is the first man to have opposed your expedition.'—'By my head,' said William 'what you say is true.' [719]

The count dismounted whilst Walter held his stirrup and, side by side, they walked up the floor of the hall. When he saw William, the king stood up to receive him. He placed both arms round William's neck, embraced him three times in most friendly fashion, and spoke to him very courteously: 'My lord William, is there any gift of gold or silver I can grant you that you would like? You shall have what you want without restraint.'—'Many thanks, sire,' William replied, 'I have everything I need. But one thing I would beg of you, namely not to take scoundrels as your advisers.' Then William looked behind him and noticed the aged Aymon in the midst of the hall. Seeing him, he began to hurl abuse at him: 'Ah! you rogue, you scoundrel, God damn you! Why do you go to such pains to criticize an honourable man when I never wronged you in all my life? Why do you strive to do me such harm? By St Denis, before you leave I intend to make you pay dearly for it!' He stepped forward, and when he had rolled up his sleeves, he clouted him on the head with his left fist, raised his right fist and struck him on the nape, breaking his neckbone, and flung him down dead at his feet. Count William seized him by the head and Walter of Toulouse took him by the feet and they threw him out of the window into the orchard on to an apple tree, breaking his body in two.[8] 'Away with you,' they said, 'you treacherous scoundrel. You shall not profit by so much as a penny from your slanderings!'—'My lord Louis,' said proud William, 'never trust a scoundrel or a slanderer, for your father never had any regard for them. I

shall go off on my wanderings in Spain. The land shall be
yours, sire, if I conquer it.'—'Go, good sir, in the name of the
Heavenly King. Jesus grant you success and that I may see you
again, safe and sound and whole.' William, the proud-faced
marquis, went away with many princes in his company, and
Guielin and Sir Bertrand, his nephews, taking with them three
hundred beasts of burden. I can tell you what the first carried:
golden chalices, missals, psalters, silken copes, crosses and
censers. When they came to the devastated realm, they would
all first serve the Lord.   [769]

27. I can tell you what the second carried: vessels of pure gold,
missals and breviaries, and crucifixes and rich altar-cloths.
When they came to the desolate realm, they would use them
in the service of the Heavenly Jesus.   [774]

28. I can tell you what the third carried: pots and pans,
cauldrons and tripods, and sharp hooks, tongs and fire-dogs,
so that, when they came to the devastated realm, they might
be able to prepare their food properly, serving William the
warrior and after him all his knights.   [781]

29. William went away with his fine company of men, com-
mending to God, France and Aix-la-Chapelle, Paris and
Chartres, and all the rest of the country. They passed through
Burgundy and Berry and Auvergne. One evening, they came
to the ford for the mountain passes, and set up their tents and
their quarters.   [787]

30. They lit the fires in the cook-houses and the cooks hastened
to prepare the food. Count William was in his tent and began
to sigh deeply and to ponder things in his heart. Seeing him,
Bertrand began to look at him: 'Uncle,' he said, 'Why are you
so sorrowful? Are you a woman weeping over her widow-
hood?'—'Indeed, no, nephew, but because I have something
else on my mind. What will the noble knights say now? "Look
how William, the proud-faced marquis, has dealt with his
rightful lord. The king wanted to give him half his kingdom
and he was mad enough not to accept it gratefully but to take
Spain to which he had no rightful claim." I shall never again
see four men gathered together without thinking they must be

talking about me.'—'Enough of this, uncle. There is no call for
you to be angry on that account: the outcome is entirely in the
hand of God. Ask for water and let us have supper.'—'That is
easily granted,' said the count. They sent for water by bidding
the trumpeters sound, and sat down together to supper. They
were well-provided with boar-meat, cranes, wild geese and
peacocks spiced with pepper, and when they had eaten
copiously the squires came to remove the table-cloths. The
knights returned to their lodgings until dawn next morning
when they mounted their fiery steeds. They went and asked
William the marquis: 'Sir, what decision have you come to?
Say which way you wish to go now.'—'Noble knights, you are
all alarmed. We have not long since left home. We shall go
straight to Brioude where the saint's body is revered, and to
Notre-Dame-du-Puy: there we must make an offering and Our
Lady will intercede for Christendom.' And they answered: 'As
you command.' Then they rode on in serried ranks and crossed
the hills and the mountains.   [830]

31. They crossed through Berry and Auvergne as William had
instructed them, leaving behind Clermont-Ferrand on the
right. They avoided the city and the rich dwelling-places, for
they had no wish to harm the townsfolk.   [835]

32. They slept there that night and in the morning packed up
their tents, and loaded them on the pack-animals. They carried
on along the Regordane Way and did not stop until they
reached Le Puy.   [840]

33. Count William went to pray in the church. He placed on
the altar three silver marks,[9] four pieces of silk and three
mats with circular patterns. Great was the offering the
princes made: its like has never been seen before or since.
William Shortnose came out of the church and, seeing his men,
addressed them: 'Barons,' he said, 'hear what I have to say.
Here we are in the pagan marches. From now on, go where
you may, you will not find a single man of woman born who is
not a Saracen or a Slav. Take up your arms, mount your
horses, and go out to forage, my renowned and noble knights.
Whatever good thing God henceforward brings your way, take

it. Let the whole country be laid open to you.' And his men
replied: 'As you command.' They donned their hauberks,
laced up their jewel-studded helmets, girded their swords with
the pommels adorned with enamel and gold, and climbed into
the saddles of their fiery horses. At their necks they hung their
strong shields with the centre boss, and held in their hands
their enamelled lances. They left the town in serried ranks
with the oriflam carried before them, and made directly for
Nîmes. There were so many helmets gleaming there! In the
van were the renowned Bertrand, Walter of Termes, L'Escot
Gilemer, and Guielin the doughty and the shrewd. Valiant
William brought up the rear with ten thousand well-armed
Frenchmen tried in battle.   [873]

They had not gone four leagues when along the road they
came across a peasant who was returning from Saint-Gilles,
with four oxen he had acquired and three children he had
fathered. The peasant had been shrewd enough to realize that
salt was dear in the country where he was born, so he had
loaded a barrel on to his cart and filled it to the brim with salt.
His three children were laughing and playing and had plenty
of bread to eat. They were playing marbles on the salt and the
French laughed at the sight—what else could they have done?
Count Bertrand addressed him: 'Tell us, peasant, in the name
of your religion, where do you hail from?' And he replied:
'You shall hear the truth. By Mahomet, sir, I am from Laval
on the Cler. I am now on my way from Saint-Gilles where I
have been buying supplies and I am going back home to get
my wheat in—if Mahomet has protected my crop, I should do
well out of it, I sowed plenty.' The French said: 'You talk like
a fool! If you believe that Mahomet is God, that *he* can bring
you wealth and plenty, cold in winter and heat in summer, you
deserve to have all your limbs chopped off!' And William
said: 'Barons, enough of that! I want to talk to him about
something else.'   [901]

34. Count William began to address him: 'Tell me, peasant,
in the name of the faith you practise, have you been to Nîmes,
the strongly fortified city?'—'Yes, indeed, sir, they wanted me
to pay a toll. I am too poor, I couldn't give it them. But they

let me through when they saw my children.'—'Tell me, peasant, what the town is like.'—'I can tell you that all right. We got two big loaves for a penny, that's twice as much for a pennyworth as in other towns. So it's a good place to live, if things haven't got worse since.'—'That's not what I am asking about, you fool,' said William. 'I am asking about the pagan troops in the town, about King Otrant and his followers.'— 'I don't know anything about that,' said the peasant, 'and you won't hear any lies from me about it.'   [917]

Amongst those present was Garnier, a noble knight; he was a vavasour, a cunning fellow and a master of deception. 'Sir,' he said, 'God be with me, if one had a thousand barrels like that one on the cart and filled them with knights and took them all the way to Nîmes, that would be a way of capturing the town.'—'By my head, you are right!' said William, 'I will do it if my men agree.'   [929]

35. Acting on Garnier's suggestion, they induced the peasant to stay with them and brought him plenty to eat, bread, wine, spiced drinks and sweetened wine, and he ate for he had been longing for food. When he had eaten his fill, Count William sent for his barons who came without delay and, as soon as he saw them assembled, he addressed them: 'Barons,' he said, 'hear what I have to say. If one now had a thousand banded barrels like the one you can see on that cart, full of armed knights, and took them along the stony road right up to the fair city of Nîmes, one could get into the city like that without a fight.'—'What you say is true, noble lord William,' his men replied, 'so put the plan into effect. There is certainly enough transport hereabouts, there are plenty of wagons and carts. Send your men back along the Regordane Way that we came by and have them seize the oxen by force.'—'It shall be seen to,' said William.   [954]

36. Following the advice of his worthy knight, Count William sent his men back fourteen leagues along the Regordane Way. They seized the carts, the oxen and the barrels, and the worthy peasants who made and assembled the barrels fixed them on the carts and doubled up the teams of oxen. Bertrand did not care if his peasants grumbled: anyone who spoke up paid for it

dearly, having his eyes put out and being hanged by the neck. [963]

37. Anyone who saw the hardy peasants bustling about, wielding adzes and axes, binding up and repairing all the barrels, fitting the carts and waggons with pegs and bars and the knights getting into the barrels, would have found it a memorable occasion. Each one was given a big mallet so that, when they came to the city of Nîmes and heard the bugle sound, the Frenchmen would be able to fend for themselves. [973]

38. In the other barrels were put the lances, and two distinguishing signs were placed on each barrel so that when they reached the land of the fearsome race, the soldiers of France should make no mistake.   [977]

39. In other barrels were put the shields, and two marks were made on the top of each barrel so that when they were amongst the Saracens the French should not be taken by surprise. [981]

40. The count hastened to get the waggon-train ready. Anyone who saw the peasants of that realm binding up and repairing barrels and fitting them with bottoms, and the great waggons being turned round, and the knights getting into the barrels, would have found it a memorable occasion.   [987]

Now we must tell of Sir Bertrand and how he was attired: he had on a surcoat of dark homespun and amazing footwear, great oxhide shoes with split uppers. 'God in heaven!' said Bertrand, 'my feet will soon be crushed in these.' Hearing him, Count William laughed and said: 'Listen to me, nephew, drive these oxen down that way.'—'It is pointless asking me to do that,' said Bertrand, 'I do not know how to get oxen moving either by goading them or by shoving them.' William laughed when he heard him, but a bad mishap befell Bertrand because he was not trained for the work. Before he knew what was happening, he had gone into the mud with the waggon up to its axles. Seeing what had happened, Bertrand nearly went berserk. Anyone who saw him making his way into the mud and heaving the wheel up with his shoulders would have marvelled at the sight. His mouth and nose were bruised and when William saw him he began to tease him: 'My dear nephew, listen to me. You have been dabbling in a task that is clearly beyond your experience.' Hearing him, Bertrand nearly went berserk. In the barrel that he was supposed to be leading along were Gilbert of Falaise, Walter of Termes and L'Escot Gilemer: 'Sir Bertrand, take care with your driving. We shall be overturned at any minute.'—'You will get there in time,' said Bertrand.   [1021]

We must now tell of the men with the carts who were to lead the waggon-train along. They wore straps and bags and baldrics, and large wallets for changing money, and rode mules and broken-down pack-horses. If you had seen them wending their way up towards you, you would have been put in mind of a wretched mob. Wherever they went in that country, if it was daylight and they could be seen, they would pass for merchants. They crossed the Gardon by the causeway at the ford and camped in a meadow on the other side.

Now we must tell of William and the way he was attired. [1035]

41. Count William put on a tunic of local homespun, great purple breeches and oxhide boots that fitted closely over his leggings; he girded himself with the baldric of a townsman of those parts, and hung at his side a knife and a fine sheath. He mounted a very feeble mare, with a pair of old stirrups hanging from the saddle, his spurs were not new—they could well have been thirty years old—and he wore a woollen cap on his head. [1045]

42. Beside the Gardon, down along the bank, they left two thousand men-at-arms of the household of William Strongarm. They made all the peasants go back so that the news should not leak out through any of them about the kind of goods they would be producing from the barrels. Over two thousand of them sharpened their goads, and cut and thrust, and started on their way. They did not stop until they came to Vesene, and then to Lavardi where the stone that the towers of Nîmes were built of was quarried. The townspeople were going about their business; they looked and said to one another: 'Here come a

lot of merchants.'—'Indeed,' said another, 'I have never seen
the like.' They crowded around them until they reached the
leader and asked him: 'What sort of goods are you carrying?'
—'We have silks and ciclatouns, purple garments, scarlet
cloth, green and brown fabrics of great value, sharp lances,
hauberks, green-painted helmets, weighty shields and keen-
edged swords.'—'There is great wealth here,' said the pagans;
'go on to the main customs point.'   [1069]

43. The French rode on their way, crossing valleys and
mountains and hills, until they came to the city of Nîmes. They
led their waggon-train through the gateway, one at a time as
the way was so narrow. The cry went up all over town: 'There
are rich merchants from another country bringing goods such
as have never been brought before, but they have packed them
all into barrels.' King Otrant, hearing about it, went down the
steps with Harpin; they were brothers, who must have loved
one another dearly, and lords of that fine city. They took two
hundred pagans with them and did not pause until they
reached the market-place.   [1084]

44. Hear me, my lords, may God the Glorious One, the Son of
Mary, bless you. This tale I propose to tell you is not a tale of
pride or folly, nor is it based on lies. It is a tale of noble men
who conquered Spain and in the name of Jesus exalted His
religion. This city of Nîmes that I sing of is on the road to
Saint-Gilles. To one side of the town [*line missing*], but there
was nothing at that time; rather there was the religion of the
pagan race, where they prayed to Mahomet and to idols, and
to Tervagant to invoke his aid. They held their law-courts and
their council meetings there, assembling from all over the
town.   [1100]

45. William Strongarm went straight to a market-place where
there was a mounting-block hewn out of green marble and
there he dismounted, took out his wallet and, untying the
strings, pulled out a fistful of coins. He asked for the man
who took the tolls as he was most anxious not to harm their
interests. 'You need not worry,' said the pagans, 'if anyone,
however powerful his family, were to address you haughtily

or insolently, he would be hanged by the neck from a tree.'
[1111]

46. Whilst they were thus engaged in conversation and dis-
cussion with Count William, along came Harpin and Otrant
asking for the worthy merchant. 'There he is,' said the pagans
who were there staring at him, 'that fine-looking man with the
hat and the great beard who orders the others about as he
pleases.' King Otrant called him to come forward: 'Where are
you from, my merchant friend?'—'Sire, we are from the great
country of England, from Canterbury which is a splendid city.'
—'And have you a wife, my merchant friend?—'I have, a very
gracious one, and eighteen children, all of them little, apart
from two who are grown up, one called Bègue and the other
Sorant: there they are if you do not believe me.' And he
pointed out his two nephews, Guielin and Bertrand, the sons of
Bernard of Brubant. The pagans stared at them and said: 'You
have wonderfully handsome children, if only they knew how to
dress properly.' Immediately after this, King Otrant asked him:
'What is your name, my merchant friend?'—'Indeed,
my noble lord, it is Tiacre.'—'That is an outlandish name.
What sort of goods do you bring, brother Tiacre?'—'Many
kinds of fine silk and other cloth, my lord, fine green cloth and
blue cloth, white hauberks and strong, gleaming helmets, sharp
lances and fine, weighty shields, and shining swords with
gleaming golden pommels.' And the king said: 'Show us some
of your wares, my friend: you will not lose by it.' [10]—'Please be
patient, my lord,' said William, 'the best of our wares are yet
to come.'—'And what then is here in front?'—'Ink and
sulphur, incense and quicksilver, alum and cochineal and
pepper and saffron, hides, and basan and Cordovan leather
and marten pelts of the right age.' Hearing him, Otrant
laughed with glee and the Saracens were delighted. [1153]

47. King Otrant addressed him again: 'Brother Tiacre, by the
faith you hold, be so good as to give us a true account. You
have, I think, great wealth and are bringing it here in a
waggon-train; be so kind as to give us some of it, to me and
these others who are all of us young men. It will be to your
advantage, if you are continuing your journey.' William said:

'My noble lord, please be patient. I shall not leave the city today: it is a good town to be in and I want to stay. But before midday tomorrow, before the bell rings for vespers, before the sun goes down, I shall let you have so much of my wealth that the strongest of your men will have all he can carry.'—'You are a most noble man, merchant,' said the pagans; 'you are very generous, but only in words: we shall find out well enough whether you are an honourable man.'—'Indeed I am,' he said, 'more so than you may think; I have never been deceitful or niggardly. All I have I freely give to those who are my bosom friends.' The count called one of his men: 'Hey, there! is the whole of my waggon-train in yet?'—'Yes indeed, sir, thanks be to God!' He began to guide them through the streets and they unloaded in the wide open spaces of the town, for he did not wish to be hampered in any way from making his escape should need arise. They so blocked the door of the palace that it would be difficult for the Saracens to enter.   [1184]

48. King Otrant began to say: 'Brother Tiacre, by the faith you live by, where did you come by such great riches, and in what country and in what fiefdom is your home?' And William said: 'That I can easily tell you: I came by some of it in France. And now indeed I am off to Lombardy and Calabria, to Apulia and Sicily, to Germany and as far as the Romagna, to Tuscany and thence to Hungary. Then I am coming back to go to Galicia, via Spain, a prosperous area, and to Poitou and as far as Normandy. My way of life takes me to England and Scotland. I shall keep on as far as Wales. I shall lead my followers right to the Crac des Chevaliers, to a fair of great antiquity. I change my money in the kingdom of Venice.'—'You have sought out many countries,' said the pagans, 'it is no wonder you are rich.'   [1204]

49. Hear, my lords, in the name of the God of Majesty, how William was found out that day. King Otrant began to look at him when he heard him talk like that, and saw the bump on his nose. Then he was reminded of William Shortnose, the son of Aymeri of Narbonne. When he saw this, he nearly went ber-serk. His blood curdled in his veins, his heart missed a beat, and he nearly fainted. But he spoke to him courteously and

addressed him as follows: 'Brother Tiacre, by the faith you
follow, that great lump you have on your nose, who did it to
you? Take care not to hide anything from me. I am reminded
of William Shortnose, the son of Aymeri, who is held in such
awe and who slew my mighty kinsmen. By God who is my pro-
tector, and Tervagant and his holy virtues, if I had William
hemmed in here like you whom I now see before me, by
Mahomet, he would be made to suffer for it, he would be
strung up on the gallows and made to hang in the wind, or
burnt in the flames or put to a shameful death.' When William
heard him, he laughed: 'Sire,' he said, 'pay attention to me.
As for what you are asking about, I will answer freely and
willingly. When I was a young man, a mere lad and a novice,
I became a marvellous thief and trickster: I never came across
anyone as good at it as I was. I used to slit open purses and
well-secured wallets. The young men and merchants I had
robbed caught me at it and slashed my nose with their knives,
and then let me go. I began to earn my living in the way you
see. I have, praise God, prospered to the extent that you can
observe with your own eyes.'—'You have acquitted yourself
well,' said the pagan, 'you will never be hanged on the
gallows.'   [1246]

A Saracen—called Barré by those who knew him—who was
the king's seneschal left the scene intending to go and prepare
the meal and light the fire in the kitchen. He found the
doorway to the palace so cluttered up that he could not find
any way of getting in. Seeing this, he nearly went berserk and
swore by Mahomet that somebody would pay for this. He
went and told Harpin, who, with his brother Otrant the
Accursed, was the ruler of the city, all about it, addressing
him courteously: 'My young lord, pay attention to what I have
to say. By Mahomet, this fellow who came in here has brought
trouble upon us. He has so cluttered up the door of the palace
for us that one cannot get in or out. If you take my advice, we
will sting him to anger. Look at his belongings that he has
dumped here in a heap. He will not give you or anybody else
anything. Have all these oxen slaughtered, sire, to be used for
food in the kitchen.'—'Bring me a big mallet,' said Harpin.
'At your command,' answered the rogue, setting off to go and

fetch him an iron mallet. He came back to Harpin and thrust the mallet into his hand and Harpin lifted it in the air and killed Baillet and then Lovel who was next to him (they were the two leading shaft-oxen), and made the young man skin them to prepare them for food in the kitchen. He intended to let his Saracens eat their fill of them, but, to my way of thinking, before they have so much as a taste they will pay dearly for what has happened, for a Frenchman has been watching everything. When he saw all this, he felt sad and went and told William all about it, whispering softly in his ear, so that the Saracens and Slavs did not notice. 'Believe me, my lord, something bad has happened to you. They have killed two of the oxen in your waggon-train, the finest we brought. They belonged to that worthy fellow you met on the way, and they were put in the lead. Do you know who got into that barrel? Count Gilbert of Falaise, Walter of Termes and L'Escot Gilemer. Your nephew Bertrand was in charge of them: you have not looked after them properly.' Hearing this, William nearly went out of his mind, but he replied calmly and quietly. 'Who did this? Take care not to hide anything from me.'—'Indeed, sir, do not refuse to believe me: Harpin, the treacherous scoundrel, did it.'—'What the devil for?' he asked. 'In God's name, I do not know, sir.' Hearing this, William became very angry and said in low voice so that no-one heard: 'By St Denis who watches over me, this will be paid for dearly, and today too!' The Saracens had crowded around him, jeering at him and provoking him. Harpin had ordered them to do so, wanting to pick a quarrel with him, with his brother Agrapart [11] the Slav joining in. [1314]

50. God bless you, my lords. Hear how they provoked William. King Otrant began to say: 'Look here, you wretch, God damn you! Why have you and your men not a single fur coat to wear amongst you? Your men would have been more highly thought of if you had.'—'I care nothing about that: after we have got home, well laden and well supplied, to my wife who is waiting and longing for me, and not before, my men will be properly fitted out by me.' [1326]

51. 'Look here, you wretch, Mahomet curse you!' King

Harpin snapped back at him. 'Why are your cow-hide boots and your tunic and your equipment so dilapidated? You do not look like a man who takes much care of himself.' He stepped forward and tugged at his beard and nearly pulled out a hundred of his whiskers. At this William nearly went berserk and muttered, so that not a soul heard him: 'Though the great cow-hide boots I am now wearing and my tunic and my equipment are so dilapidated, yet my name is William Strongarm, son of Aymeri of Narbonne, the wise, the noble count of such great valour. This Saracen has just provoked me. He did not know who I was when he pulled my beard—that was no way to treat it, by St James!' [1343]

52. William said in a low voice, secretly to himself: 'If my breeches are muddy and my tunic is too long and too loose, yet Aymeri of Narbonne, a man of proven valour, is my father. I whose beard you pulled am William: that was no way to treat it, by St Peter the apostle, and before this evening shall pay you dearly for it.' [1351]

53. Hear my lords, God grant you greater valour, how William reacted. When he felt his moustache plucked and when he had two oxen in his waggon-train killed, you can imagine that he was very angry. He would go out of his mind if he did not take his revenge. He climbed on to a mounting-block and began to shout: 'God damn the lot of you, you treacherous pagans! You have insulted me and mocked me today, calling me a merchant and a peasant. I am no merchant, and my name is not Tiacre. By the apostle whom they seek in Nero's Meadow, you shall find out this very day what kind of goods I have brought with me. And you, Harpin, you arrogant rogue, why did you pull my beard and my moustache? Believe me, I am very angry. I shall not eat until you have paid for this with your own person.' Suddenly he stood up, clouted him on the head with his left fist, pulled him towards him, forced his head down, raised his great square fist and struck him with such fury that he broke his neckbone and threw him down dead at his feet. The pagans saw this and nearly went out of their minds. They began to shout: 'You robber, you traitor, you cannot escape! By Mahomet, our

defender, you shall be tortured for this, hanged, burned, and
your ashes strewn to the wind. You shall regret having touched
King Harpin today.' They rushed at him without waiting any
longer. [1386]

54. The pagans shouted: 'You are wrong, merchant. Why did
you kill King Harpin? It will do you no good: you will never
get out of here.' You would have seen many fists clenched
against the duke: the pagans thought that there were no more
of our men there. Count William put a horn to his lips and
blew it three times, on a high note and on a low note. When
the barons in hiding heard it in the barrels where they were
enclosed, they took the mallets and knocked out the top of the
barrels and leapt out with drawn swords, shouting 'Mount-
joy!' with all their might. Soon there would be men wounded
and killed. When the soldiers were out of the barrels, they
rampaged through the streets. [1402]

55. The battle was fierce and terrible, the fighting heavy and
fearful. When the pagans, the foul mercenaries, saw that the
French were so savage and full of fight, the foul mercenaries
rushed to arms. The pagans, each and every one of them,
equipped themselves in their houses and their strongholds and
prepared to defend themselves. They came out of the houses,
their shields before them, and assembled at the sound of a
trumpet. Then there were there a thousand valiant knights of
mighty William's household. Their fiery steeds were brought
to them and at once they quickly mounted them. They slung
their stout, heavy shields round their necks, seized their strong,
sharp lances, and hurled them at the pagans. 'Mountjoy!'
they cried, before them and behind. The pagans fought for
their lives, for the town was full of their people. There you
would have seen such a mighty battle, so many lances broken
on the heavy shields, so many Algerian hauberks ripped apart,
so many Saracens hurled down dead and covered in blood. No-
one escaped alive, they all died where they were, and the
ground was drenched in blood. Otrant turned away and
stayed no longer. [1430]

56. The battle was fearful and intense. They struck great

blows with their swords and their lances. Otrant fled in terror
of death. Count William followed close behind him, seized him
by the collar, and shouted: 'Do you know over what race of
men I have been given authority? The race that has no trust in
God. If I take them, their life shall be one of shame. Believe
me, the time has come for you to die! [1440]

57. 'God damn you, Otrant, you treacherous king!' said bold-
faced William. 'If you were to put your trust in the Son of
Mary, I tell you truly, your soul would be saved. And if you
will not, I swear to you and give you my oath that you will not
keep your head on your shoulders, despite all that the worth-
less Mahomet can do.'—'There is nothing I can say to that,'
Otrant replied. 'I will do as my heart bids me. By Mahomet,
what I will not do is believe in your God and give up my
religion.' Hearing this, William lost his temper and dragged
him right down the steps. The Franks saw this and began to
speak to him. [1454]

58. 'Otrant!' cried the French. 'Just say the word and your
death will be put off for six days.' Count William shouted with
all his might: 'A hundred curses on anyone who offers him
conditions!' They threw him out through an upper window
and he was dead before he reached the ground. After him they
threw a hundred more who broke their limbs and their necks.
[1462]

59. Then the French delivered the city, the lofty towers and
the paved halls. They found wine and wheat there in abun-
dance: it would take seven years to starve the city into sub-
mission, or capture it or get the better of it. William regretted
that the French—the thousand barons who had stayed behind
in the tents—did not know about it. So they sounded a trumpet
from the top of the palace and our men who had stayed outside
heard it. They mounted their horses without delay and did not
stop until they reached Nîmes. When they arrived, they
rejoiced and so did the peasants who followed them and who
were asking for their carts and oxen. The French were over-
joyed and did not refuse to let them have them. Indeed the
peasants were fully compensated for any slightest loss they may

have suffered and in addition were well rewarded, and then
they went back to their own country. The tidings spread
through France that William had liberated Nîmes. The news
was brought to Louis and, when he heard it, he rejoiced and
worshipped God and Mary His Mother.   [1486]

GLANVILLE PRICE
Aberystwyth

NOTES

This translation is based on Professor Duncan McMillan's edition of
Le Charroi de Nîmes, Paris (Klincksieck), 1972, which supersedes most
earlier editions. The edition provides *inter alia* a study of the eight
existing manuscripts of the poem, a commentary on language and
versification, and (pp. 53–6) an up-to-date bibliography, listing all
earlier editions and important studies, both literary and textual,
relating to the poem. A French translation that appeared too late to
be included in McMillan's bibliography is that by Fabienne Gégou,
Le Charroi de Nîmes: chanson de geste anonyme du XIIe siècle, Paris
(Champion), 1971.

[1] See *laisses* 19 to 28 of *The Crowning of Louis*.
[2] It is not clear what the word *cristal* in the original text refers to.
[3] It is not clear what this sentence refers to.
[4] Literally, 'through fields and through marshes'.
[5] The import of this ironical statement is that the only extra studs one
could win in Louis's service were the heads of enemy lances embedded
in one's shield.
[6] See note 4 to *The Crowning of Louis*.
[7] 'Spain', here as elsewhere in the poem, includes the South of France
—see note 16 to *The Crowning of Louis*.
[8] Line 750 is ambiguous, as it can read as either 'breaking *him* (= the
victim) in two' or 'breaking *it* (= the apple-tree) in two'.
[9] A mark was a medieval weight—usually 8 ounces—for precious
metals.
[10] This speech of the king's is translated from the text of a different
manuscript given in the notes to Professor McMillan's edition. The

text of the manuscript used as the basis of the edition is not wholly clear and it is possible that the scribe has omitted a line or more.

[11] Although, according to the group of manuscripts used as the basis of the edition, Harpin's brother is here named as 'Agrapart', Professor McMillan points out that the introduction of this character, not mentioned elsewhere, seems to be due to the arranger of the version of the text from which these manuscripts derive: certain other manuscripts refer to the brother, here as elsewhere, as 'Otrant'.

The Capture of Orange

1. Hearken, my lords—may God bless you, the glorious God, Son of Blessed Mary—to a fine tale that I will tell you, a tale not of pride and folly, nor taken and drawn from falsehoods, but about the noble men who conquered Spain.[1] Those who go to Saint-Gilles know about it, for they have seen the trophies at Brioude: William's shield and the embossed buckler, and the shield of noble Bertrand his nephew.[2] I do not think there is any learned man who would dispute it with me, nor any version written down in a book. For everyone has told of the city of Nîmes which William rules, with its high ramparts and halls of stone, its palace and many fortifications. But, by God, he did not yet hold Orange. There are few men who will tell the truth about this, but I will tell you, for I learnt it long since, how Orange was damaged and destroyed, for it was William the bold who cast out the heathen, those of Aumaria, Susce and Pincernia, of Baudas and of Tabaria. Orable, the queen, he took to wife; she was born of the pagan race and was wife to Tibalt, king of Africa, but she came to believe in God, Son of Mary, and founded abbeys and churches. There are not many who can tell you this tale. [30]

2. Hearken, lords, noble and valiant knights, would you hear a tale of fine deeds? How Count William conquered Orange and took to wife the wise lady Orable who was the wife of Tibalt, king of Persia? Before he won his love he had to suffer many hardships, many days of fasting and nights of watching. [38]

3. It was the month of May, the beginning of summer when the forests burgeon and the meadows grow green, the gentle waters return to their channels and the birds sing sweet, melodious songs. Count William rose up early in the morning

93

and went to church to hear mass. When it was over he came
out and returned to the palace of the pagan Otrant, which he
had conquered by his cunning and strength. He leant out of
the window gazing over the land, seeing the fresh grass and the
blossoming roses and listening to the song of the thrush and the
blackbird. He remembered the pleasures he used to have when
he lived in France and said to Bertrand: 'Come here, good
nephew. We left France very ill-equipped, for we did not bring
a harper or minstrel or any ladies for our entertainment. We
have good swift chargers, hauberks and gilded helms, sharp
swords and fine embossed shields and lances with stout steel
heads. Bread and wine we have, salt meat and corn. God con-
found all pagans and Slavs that leave us here dozing and
dawdling and have not crossed the sea in arms so that each one
of us may prove his valour! I am bored to death staying here!
We are shut up in this place like a man in prison.' He railed
thus, but it was folly, for before evening and sunset he will hear
news that will anger and appal him.   [73]

4. William stood by the open window and some sixty French-
men were with him there, every one of them wearing fresh
white ermine, silken breeches and shoes of Cordovan leather
and most of them holding young falcons. Count William's
heart was light as he looked down the steep slope and saw the
green grass and blossoming roses and heard the songs of black-
bird and oriole. Then he spoke to Guielin and Bertrand, the
two nephews whom he loved dearly: 'Hearken to me, valiant
knights. It is not very long since we all left France; if only we
had a thousand girls here, girls from France, attractive and
charming, the lords here would be disporting themselves and
I myself would be courting them also, which would please me.
We have plenty of fine swift horses, good hauberks and gleam-
ing helmets, sharp lances and good stout shields and fine
swords with hilts of silver, bread and wine, salt meat and corn.
God confound the Saracens and Persians who do not attack us
from across the sea, for I am bored with hanging around here
and not being able to prove my courage!' He is very foolish to
rail in this way, for before evening comes and the sun has set
he will hear great tidings to anger and appal him.   [104]

5. William was standing by the windows, with him more than a hundred Frenchmen, every one of them dressed in ermine. He was looking down on the flow of the Rhône, towards the road that comes in from the east, when he saw a wretched man coming from the water: it was Gilbert of the town of Lenu. He had been captured during a sudden assault on one of the Rhône bridges and the Turks had carried him off to Orange and kept him prisoner there for three years, until one day at dawn it pleased God to give him his freedom. A Saracen had untied him on his own initiative, and was beating and insulting him; but the knight was angry that he had been captive so long and he seized the pagan by the forelock, dragged him down and gave him such a blow with his great fist on the neck that he broke his spine and back and flung him dead at his feet. Then he dropped down out of the window and nothing could hold him or keep him back for he never stopped till he came to Nîmes. There he will tell such news to the barons who are there discussing festivities, as will cause William more trouble than he would have pleasure in bed naked with his lady-love. [130]

6. Now William the warrior was standing by the window and the prisoner had crossed the Rhône, climbing up hill and down dale, never stopping till he reached Nîmes. He entered the fair city by the gateway and found William under a wide branching pine tree with many a noble knight around him. A minstrel was singing to them, under the pine tree, an old song of great antiquity, a very good song which gave the count much pleasure. Gilbert came up the steps and when William saw him he looked hard at him and saw he was very dark and tanned and dirty, gaunt and thin, unkempt and pallid. He thought it was some Saracen or Slav who had struggled across the sea to tell and hear news. Then the prisoner addressed him: 'May God who created bread and wine, and gives us the light and brightness of Heaven, and makes men and women walk and speak, save William, the short-nosed marquis, the flower of France and the noble throng of warriors whom I see gathered here.'—'Good friend, God give you blessing. Now tell me and do not try to hide it: where did you learn the name of Wil-

liam?'—'Lord,' he said, 'you shall know the truth. I heard it
in Orange where I have been for a long time and I could never
escape from there until early one morning it pleased Lord
Jesus to give me deliverance.' Then said William: 'May God
be praised! Now tell me, and do not seek to hide it, what is
your name and where were you born?'—'Lord,' he said, 'you
shall know all truly, but I am very tired and weary with days
of fasting and nights of watching. I have not eaten for more
than four days.'—'You shall have plenty,' promised William
and the count summoned his steward: 'Bring him plenty of
food, bread and wine and spiced ales and liquors, herons and
cranes and well-peppered peacocks.' And he did as he was
commanded. And when he had been given all that he needed,
he sat down at the count's feet and began to tell his story. [178]

7. William called the newcomer to him and began to question
him: 'Where were you born, my friend, in what country?
What is your name and your dwelling in France?' Then
answered the valiant Gilbert: 'I am the son of Guy, the duke
of Ardennes, who rules over Artois and Vermandois. I was
coming into Burgundy from Germany along Lake Lausanne
when a great gale of wind struck me and drove me to the port
of Geneva. Pagans captured me at Lyons on the Rhône and
took me to the harbour at Orange. There is no greater castle
from here to the Jordan, for the walls are high and the towers
large and spacious, so, too, are the palace and surrounding
buildings. Within are twenty thousand heathens with lances
and seven score Turks with very rich banners who guard the
city of Orange carefully, for they are very much afraid that
Louis will take it, and you, good lord, and all the French
barons. There is Arragon, a mighty Saracen king, who is son
of Tibalt of Spain, and the lady Orable, a noble queen, the
fairest woman from here to the East. She is beautiful, slender
and noble, whiter her skin than the hawthorn blossom. Ah,
God, alas for her youth and beauty for she does not believe in
God, the Father almighty!'—'Truly,' said William, 'it is a
place of great strength, but by Him in whom I trust, may I
never bear lance and shield again if I do not go and make its
acquaintance.' [211]

8. Count William listened to the baron; he sat down beside him on a marble bench and addressed him, saying affectionately: 'Good friend, you talk very well; have you ever been a prisoner of the pagans?'—'Yes, indeed, lord, for three years and fifteen days. I could never manage to break out and escape until the morning of a God-given day when a vile and arrogant Saracen was going to flog me, as he did every day. I seized him by the forelock and gave him such a blow on the neck with my fist that I shattered his neckbone. Then I escaped alone out of the window and not one of them saw me. I came to Beaucaire, the port below Oriflor, where I saw Turks and Persians and King Arragon, the eldest son of Tibalt the Slav. He is big and broad and thickset and tall, with a broad brow and a wrinkled forehead, his nails long and sharply pointed. There is no worse tyrant under the canopy of heaven, for he kills and slaughters our fellow-Christians. Anyone who wins the city and castle and puts to death this wicked traitor will have laboured well.' [238]

9. 'My good friend,' said noble William, 'is Orange such as you have described it?'—'It really is far finer,' said Gilbert. 'If you could just see the main citadel, how high it is and all walled round. It can only be looked up at. If you were there at the beginning of summer, you would hear the little birds singing, the cry of falcons and the goshawks in mew, the horses neighing and the braying mules, the Saracens disporting and amusing themselves. The aromatic spices smell very sweet for there is an abundance of peppers and cinnamon there. There you might see the lady Orable, wife of Sir Tibalt the Slav. You could not find a more beautiful woman in Christendon or among the heathens. She is beautiful in form, slender and soft, her eyes are bright as a moulted falcon. Alas for her great beauty since she does not believe in God and his goodness! A noble man could enjoy himself with her. She could be saved if only she would agree.' Then said William, 'By my faith in St Omer, you know how to sing her praises, my friend. But by the Saviour of all, may I never more bear lance or shield if I do not have the city and the lady. [266]

10. 'My good friend, is Orange so mighty?'—'As God is my

helper, good lord,' said the prisoner, 'could you but see the fortress of the city, with its vaults and jousting grounds! It was built by Grifaigne of Aumaria, a Saracen of very great skill. There is no flower growing from here to Pavia which is not cunningly painted there in gold. Therein lives Orable the queen, she is the wife of king Tibalt of Africa. There is no more beautiful woman in heathendom. Fair is her neck, slender and long, her skin as white as the hawthorn bloom. Her bright, shining eyes smile on all around. Alas indeed for her beauty when she does not believe in God, the Son of Blessed Mary!'— 'Truly,' said William, 'you have praised her highly, but by the faith I owe my beloved, I will not eat bread made from flour, nor salt meat, nor will I drink wine till I have seen what Orange is like and till I see this marble tower and lady Orable, the courteous queen. Love for her goads and drives me so that I can neither imagine nor describe it. If I do not win her, I shall soon lose my life.'—'What you have in mind,' said the captive, 'is madness. If you were now in the city fortress and could see the Saracen race, God damn me if you would not have doubts of ever getting out again alive! Let this be, such thoughts are madness!'   [298]

11. William heard the anxious words spoken and told him by the captive and he called his own people together. 'Give me your advice, noble and honoured men. This captive has sung the praises of this city to me. I have never been there and do not know the region. The tumultuous waters of the Rhône flow there, and but for that I would have put it in an uproar.' The captive replied: 'Such thoughts are madness. If you were a hundred thousand men, well armed with swords and gilded shields and tried to start a fight there, supposing there were no river nor barrier, even before you came to the gates there would be a thousand blows struck with swords, many saddle-girths broken and shields battered and many a warrior laid low on the roadway. Let this be, such thoughts are madness!' [316]

12. 'Truly,' said William, 'you have much disturbed me. You tell me that no king or count has such a city and then you blame me for going to see it! By St Maurice of Amiens, I order

you to come with me. But we will not take with us horses and palfreys, nor bright hauberks nor helmets from Amiens. No shield or lance or spear from Poitou, but hairy garments to disguise us as beggars. You have been in the region and speak Turkish well, and the tongues of African, Bedouin and Basque.' The captive heard him and you can imagine how this distressed him. He wished then he was at Chartres or Blois or Paris in the king's domain, for he could not think how to escape from this predicament. [332]

13. William was angry and full of wrath and his nephew Bertrand began to speak to him: 'Uncle,' he said, 'give up this madness. If you were in the citadel now and saw the pagan race, they would recognize you by your speech and your laughter, and they would know for sure that you were a spy. Then perhaps they will carry you off to Persia. They will eat you without bread or flour. They will not hesitate to kill you; they will throw you into a marble dungeon and you will never get out again in your life until king Tibalt comes from Africa, and Desramed and Golias of Bile, and they will do what they choose to you. If for love's sake you are put to torture then all the people in your land will cry: Alas the day you saw Orable the queen!'—'Truly,' said William, 'I have no fear of this at all but by the apostle who is sought in Galicia I would rather die and lose my life than eat bread made of flour, or salt meat or vintage wine, before I have seen what Orange is like and Gloriette, the marble tower, and the courteous lady, Queen Orable. Love for her overwhelms and drives me and a man in love is ripe for any folly.' [360]

14. Now William was excited by Orange but his nephew Bertrand began to criticize him: 'Uncle,' he said, 'you want to bring shame and disgrace upon yourself and get yourself hacked to pieces!'—'Truly,' said the count, 'I have no fear of that. A man who truly loves is quite beyond reason. Not for fear of being hacked to pieces nor for any man who might entreat me, will I give up the idea of going to see what Orange is like and Lady Orable, who is so highly favoured. Love for her has overwhelmed me so much that I cannot rest or sleep at night, nor can I eat or drink, bear arms or mount a horse,

go to mass or enter a church.' He had dark juice pounded in a
mortar with other herbs known to the baron and Gilbert, who
did not dare to leave him. They stained their bodies both front
and back, and their faces, chests and feet, so they looked
exactly like devils or demons. Guielin exclaimed: 'By St
Richier, you are both marvellously changed. Now you can go
anywhere in the world and never be recognized by a single
person. But by the apostle who is sought at Rome, I am deter-
mined at risk of life and limb that I will go with you and see
what will happen.' He smeared and stained himself with the
unguent, then all three of them were quite ready and took their
leave and set out from the town. 'O God,' said Bertrand,
'great Father of rightousness. How are we betrayed and
beguiled! What madness has been the cause of this business
by which we shall be shamed and dishonoured, unless God
intervenes, who is Judge of all things?'   [396]

15. William set out, the proud-faced marquis, with Gilbert
and Guielin the proud. Count Bertrand turned back again and
they went on without further delay. They came to the Rhône
below Beaucaire and cautiously crossed to the other side,
rowing themselves quietly over; then they crossed the Sorgue
without ship or sloop and went on through Avignon straight
towards Orange with its walls and ditches, lofty halls and
citadel adorned with gilded balls and eagles. Within they
could hear the singing birds, the cry of falcons and goshawks
in mew, the war horses neighing and the bray of the mules and
the Saracens amusing themselves in the tower; they smelt the
aroma of peppers and cinnamon from the great store of sweet-
scented spices. 'By God who created me!' exclaimed William,
'this is a very marvellous city! Whoever rules here has truly
great riches!' They went right up to the gate without pausing
and Gilbert spoke to the porter, addressing him courteously in
his own language: 'Open up, porter, and let us enter; we are
dragomans from beyond the sea, from Africa, and followers of
king Tibalt the Slav!'—'I never heard such a thing!'
answered the porter. 'What sort of people are you, calling to
me out there? King Arragon has not yet risen and I dare not
unfasten the gate, for we are very much afraid of William

Shortnose who has taken Nîmes by a daring trick. You stay there and I will go and tell the king and if he gives permission, I will let you in.'—'Go at once then,' said noble William, 'swiftly and be sure not to loiter.' Then he went off without further delay, up the marble steps of the citadel. He found Arragon seated by a pillar surrounded by Saracens and Slavs, and politely addressed him: 'Lord,' he said, 'listen to me. At the gate are three worthy Turks who say that they come from beyond the sea, from Africa.'—'Go, good fellow, and let them enter here. I want to ask them news of what my father is doing, for he has been away a long time.' Then he hastened to open the gates for them. Now William had entered Orange with Gilbert and the valiant Guielin, but they would not get out again, if they should wish to, without great difficulty and trouble. [449]

16. Now William was inside Orange with Guielin and the worthy Gilbert. They were daubed with alum and dark stain so that they looked just like Saracens or heathens. Along the street [3] they met two Saracens who were conversing in their own tongue, saying: 'These men come from Africa. Now we shall have good tidings!' Count William went straight ahead until he came to the palace of king Tibalt the Persian. The pillars and walls were of marble and the windows worked in silver, with a golden eagle which gleamed and glittered. No sun shone there nor breath of wind was stirring. 'God,' said William, 'Father and Saviour, whoever saw such a well-built palace! The lord of this place is passing rich! Would to God, who created all men, that now I had here the paladin Bertrand and with him ten thousand fighting Frenchmen. This would be the start of a bad year for the heathens—I would kill more than a hundred by noon.' He found Arragon sitting by a pillar surrounded by fifteen thousand Persians. William was lost if he did not spin them a story! Now hearken to what he said to them. [475]

'Lord Emir, noble and valiant knight. Mahomet save you and the god Tervagant!'—'Come forward, sir,' answered the emir, 'where do you come from?'—'From the kingdom of Africa, from your father, the mighty King Tibalt. Yesterday

morning, before they rang prime, we were at Nîmes the strong
and powerful city. We expected to find there the mighty King
Otrant and Synagon and Lord Harpin; William and his
Frankish warriors have slain them, he has killed our men in a
bloody carnage. He had the three of us in prison but he has so
many friends and kinsmen that he let us escape for some reason,
I do not know why, the devil take him!' Then Arragon said:
'I am much grieved by this. By Mahomet, in whom I trust, if
I had William here in my power he would soon be put to death
in torment, his bones and ashes scattered in the wind.' When
William heard this, he kept his head down, he would rather
have been in Paris or Sens. Fervently he prayed to God the
Father: [4] 'Glorious Lord, Creator of all men, you who were
born of the Virgin in Bethlehem where the Three Kings came
to visit you, who were hanged on the Cross by the tormentors
and whose side was pierced by the lance of the blind man,
Longinus, so that blood and water flowed down to his hands
and when he touched his eyes he received his sight. As this is
true that I relate, keep our bodies from death and torment that
we be not slain by Saracen or Persian.'   [509]

17. Now William was in the palace of the citadel.[5] He spoke to
his companions, in a low voice because of the pagan race:
'My lords,' he said, 'we are trapped here, unless God helps us
by His most holy name.'—'Uncle William,' said Guielin,
'most noble lord, you are here for love's sake. Behold the tower
and palace of Gloriette, so ask where the ladies are! You can
well act the part of a fool.'—'What you say is true, boy,'
answered the count. Then King Arragon addressed him:
'When were you in Africa, sir?'—'Most honoured lord, not
more than two months ago.'—'Did you see King Tibalt?'—
'Yes, noble lord, in the town of Valdon. He embraced us and
sent a message to you, by us, that you should safeguard his city
and lands. Where is his wife? Will you let us see her?'—'Yes,
lords,' answered Arragon, the king. 'There is no woman more
beautiful from here to the clouds above. I have need of my
father, sirs,' he continued, 'the French are capturing our
citadels and towers. It is the work of William and his two
nephews. But, by my faith in Tervagant and Mahomet, if

I had William in my prison, he would be burnt in coals of fire, his bones and ashes scattered to the winds.' William heard this and bowed his head, wishing he were in Rheims or Laon. He prayed to God and His glorious name: 'Father of Glory, Creator of Lazarus, you who were conceived of the Virgin, keep my body from death and prison that we be not slain by these wicked Saracens.' [544]

18. Now William was in the royal palace. The Saracens and pagans called for water, the tables were set up and they sat down to dinner. William sat there with his nephew, Guielin; they spoke softly and kept their heads down, greatly afraid of being made captive. King Arragon had them well looked after: they had plenty of bread and wine to eat, crane and wild goose and good roast peacock; I cannot tell you all the other dishes but they had as much as they wanted of them. When they had eaten and drunk at leisure, the cup-bearers drew the cloths and the pagans and Saracens played chess. William heard the voices re-echo in the palace carved of green and light-brown marble, he saw the painted birds and lions. 'By God,' said the count, 'who was hanged on the Cross, whoever saw such a splendid palace? Would to God, the ever faithful, that Bertrand the paladin was here now with twenty thousand well-armed Frenchmen. This very day the pagans would come to a bad end and, by my head, I would slay four score.' [568]

19. King Arragon called William to him and sat him down by the pillar beside him, and spoke very softly in his ear: 'Noble Turk,' he said, 'now tell me truly. What sort of man is William Shortnose who captured Nîmes by a daring trick and killed King Harpin and his brother? Did he, indeed, put you in his prison?' Then William answered: 'You shall hear the truth. He is so wealthy, powerful and rich that he cares not at all for pure gold or bright silver, but he let us go free for nothing, except that he made us swear by our religion that we would give you his message, without concealment: you must go away beyond the sea to Africa, for before the month of May is out he will pursue you with twenty thousand armed men. The towers and pillars cannot save you, the wide halls and the

deep ditches, for they will be smashed by rams of iron and if
he takes you, you will be slaughtered, hanged on a gibbet
where you will swing in the wind.'   [590]

'What you say is madness,' retorted Arragon. 'I shall now
send over the sea to Africa and my father will come with his
mighty forces and Golias and Desramed, the king, Corsolt of
Mables and his brother Aceré, and Clarel and King Atriblé,
and Quinzepaumes and King Sorgalé, the king of Egypt and
King Codroé, King Morant and King Anublé, and the caliph
of Sorgremont by the sea, my uncle, Borrel and his well-armed
sons, the thirty kings born in the Spanish kingdom. Each of
them will bring twenty thousand knights and we shall attack
the walls and ditches. William will be slain and meet his end
and his nephews will be hanged on a gibbet.' When William
heard this, his senses reeled, but he muttered between his
teeth: 'By God, you lie, sir scoundrel! Rather will three
thousand Turks be slaughtered before you are prince or ruler
of Nîmes.' If he had had weapons to arm himself with, then the
whole citadel would have been in an uproar for he could not
have controlled himself.   [614]

20. Now William was in the marble hall. He began to speak:
'King Arragon,' he said, 'show me, lord, the queen, who is so
beloved by the emperor of Africa.'—'He is a great fool,' said
Arragon, 'for he is an old man with a white beard and she is a
young and beautiful girl, there is no one so beautiful in all
heathendom. She carries on her love affairs in Gloriette; she
would rather have Sorbant of Venice, a noble youth who has
just entered manhood and takes a leading part in pleasure and
in fighting, than Tibalt of Slavonia. An old man is very foolish
to love a young girl, he is soon cuckolded and made a laughing
stock.' When William heard this he started to laugh: 'Indeed,'
he said, 'do you not love her, then?'—'Not I, truly! may God
curse her. I wish she were in Africa now; or at Baudas in the
realm of Aumaria!'   [634]

21. Noble William was in the palace with Gilbert and the
powerful Guielin. They went out through the hall and Mal-
cuidant, one of the pagans, led them to the queen whom the
king loved so well. It would be better for them to be going back

across the Rhône to the great city of Nîmes, for before vespers comes and the sun has set, unless God intervenes, in his great wisdom, they will hear tidings which will cause them distress. Then they came to Gloriette. The walls and pillars were of marble and the windows worked in silver; the golden eagle gleamed and glittered; the sun did not shine there nor breath of wind enter; it was richly adorned and very pleasing to look at. To one side of the hall there was a very unusual pine-tree, as you shall hear if it pleases you.[6] The branches were long and the foliage abundant and the blossom was most attractive: white and deep blue and crimson; often were the meetings held there. The air was sweetly scented with spices and cinnamon, incense and galingale, hyssop and all-spice. There sat Orable, the lady of Africa, dressed in sumptuous silken stuff, tightly laced over her elegant figure with rich silk embroidery on the panels; Rosiane, the niece of Rubiant, was fanning her with a fan of silver. She was whiter than the gleaming snow, redder than the scented rose. When William saw her, his blood was stirred. Fair and courtly was his greeting: 'May God save you in whom we trust.'—'Come hither, lords,' said the queen. 'Mahomet save you, who rules the world.' She sat them down by her on a bench, all inlaid in gold and silver. Now they could express something of their feelings. 'God,' said William, 'it is Paradise here!' Guielin said: 'I never saw so fair a place. I would like to stay here the rest of my life and would never want to move for anything at all.' [679]

22. Now William was seated in Gloriette, with him Gilbert and the valiant Guielin, beside the maidens in the shade of the pine-tree. There sat Orable, the bright-faced lady. She was wearing a fur-trimmed robe and under it a silken tunic tightly laced over her well-shaped body. When William saw her, his whole body trembled. 'God,' said William, 'it is Paradise here.'—'So help me God,' replied Guielin then, 'I would willingly stay here always, and without ever wanting to eat or sleep.' The noble lady then addressed them: 'Whence do you come, noble and valiant knights?'—'Lady, we are from the kingdom of Persia, from the land of your husband, Tibalt. Yesterday morning, as day was breaking, we came to Nîmes,

the wonderful city, thinking to find there men of our race, King
Synagon, and Otrant and Harpin; but all three have been
slain by Strongarm. The French took us captive at the gates of
the city and led us in to the paladin's presence. But he is so rich
and well endowed with friends that he has no interest in fine
gold or silver. He let us escape on one condition, that we swore
to him, by our religion, to bring you the message he sends you,
as I am now doing: you must flee away to the kingdom of
Persia, or you will see, before April is out, that he will pursue
you with twenty thousand armed warriors; the walls and
ramparts will not protect you, the great halls and strong
palisades, you will be overcome by force of arms. If he can
capture Arragon the Arab, your stepson whom you cherish, he
will put him to a shameful death, hanging or burning or
roasting with fire.' The lady heard this and she sighed deeply.
[718]

23. The lady listened to the strange messengers then spoke to
them without any hesitation: 'My lords, I know your language
very well. What sort of man, then, is William Strongarm who
has captured the citadel and the halls of Nîmes, and killed my
men and still threatens me?'—'Truly,' said the count, 'he has
a very proud spirit, and huge fists and marvellous arms. There
is no man, from here to Arabia, so big that if he struck him
with his sharp-edged sword he would not cut through the
armour and body, and the sharp-edged sword would go
swiftly down into the ground.'—'Truly,' said the lady, 'this is
grievous news. By Mahomet, he must be a good man to safe-
guard the border-lands. Happy is the lady on whom he sets his
heart.' A crowd of evil pagans came up to the place; soon
William will hear such ill-tidings as he never heard in his life
before. God defend him from harm and death! [737]

24. Now William had gone up into the tower with Gilbert and
Guielin the brave. Under the pine-tree, beside the maidens, he
was talking quietly to the queen. The evil pagans came up in a
crowd to see and gaze at the warriors. If God does not inter-
vene, who was hanged on the Cross, William will soon be in an
evil plight. Then there appeared a pagan, Salatré; may he be
damned by the Saviour of all men! The count took him

prisoner in the city of Nîmes and one day at dusk the scoundrel escaped and took flight along a ditch so that he could not be found or captured. He now brought such an accusation against William as you shall hear related hereafter. He came up to stand by Arragon and whispered a long time in his ear. 'By Mahomet, lord, here is your chance to win glory! Now will I be avenged for the great cruelty that I would have suffered in the city of Nîmes. Do you see this great tall fellow? It is William, the short-nosed marquis, and the other young man, here, is his nephew and the one behind, holding that square-cut staff, is the nobleman who escaped from here. They have disguised themselves to deceive you, thinking to capture this good city.' [765]

'Are you telling me the truth?' said Arragon. 'Lord,' he answered, 'disbelieve me at your peril. There is William who had me made captive and wanted to hang me and let me swing in the wind, if Mahomet had not protected me. Now today he will reap his reward.' Hearken now, valiant and noble lords, for the love of God who was hanged on the Cross, how this villain set to work. He took a goblet [7] of pure refined gold and struck William with it on the forehead above the nose. The stain came away and showed his colour: his skin was white as blossom in summer. When William saw this his senses reeled and all the blood in his body turned to water. He prayed to God, the King of Majesty: 'Glorious Father, Saviour of all men, who condescended to be born of the Virgin for the sake of mankind whom you wanted to save, and gave yourself to toil and suffering and on the Cross were beaten and wounded. As this is true, of your goodness keep my body from death and destruction, lest we be slain by the Saracens and Slavs.' [790]

25. When Arragon heard that the heathen recognized all three companions, he rose to his feet and thus addressed them: 'Lord William, your name is well known. In an ill hour did you cross the Rhône, by Mahomet! You will soon die and be killed, your bones and ashes blown through the world. I would not take this castle full of gold not to kill you and burn you to cinders.' William heard him and went red as fire—he wished then he were in Rheims or Laon! Guielin saw that they could

not conceal themselves; he wrung his hands and tore his hair. 'God,' said William, 'by your most holy name, Father of glory, Creator of Lazarus, who were born of the Virgin, who rescued Jonah from the whale's belly and Daniel from the den of lions; who pardoned the Magdalen and set St Peter's body in Nero's Meadow; who converted his companion, St Paul, who was at that time a most cruel man, but then he joined the company of the faithful and followed in their way of life. As this is true, Lord, and we believe it, defend us from both death and prison lest we be slain by the wicked heathen.' He had a long staff, solid and thick; he lifted it up high in his two hands and with it he struck the scoundrel Salatré, who had denounced him to King Arragon, such a great blow on the head with the stick that all his brains were scattered about. 'Mountjoy,' he cried, 'Now smite hard, barons!'   [824]

26. William had set the palace in an uproar and killed a pagan in front of the king. Count William looked and saw a great log brought there to make a fire and running towards it very quickly, he seized it in both hands and raised it on high. He struck Baitaime, the reckless, such a violent blow on the head with the log that he spilt the brains from his head and smashed him down dead in front of the king. Gilbert went and struck at Quarré and gave him such a thrust in the belly with his staff that it went right through him a long way and he was thrown down dead by the pillar. 'Mountjoy,' he cried, 'barons, attack! Since we are thus doomed to die, let us sell ourselves dearly as long as we can survive.' When Arragon heard him he nearly went mad and shouted loudly: 'Now, lords, seize them! By Mahomet, they shall come to a bad end, thrown and cast into the Rhône or burnt with fire and the ashes blown on the wind.' Said Guielin: 'Barons, keep your distance, for by the apostle who is sought in Nero's Meadow, before you take me you shall pay for it dearly.' Full of wrath he brandished his club. Count William struck out then with his log and Gilbert with his sturdy staff. The noble warriors dealt great blows, fourteen Turks were struck down dead and all the others were so frightened that they drove them out through the door with blows; they shot the bolts and locks and raised the drawbridge

on great chains. Now God grant them aid, who was hanged on the Cross, for William is in a dangerous plight and Gilbert and the noble Guielin, in Gloriette where they are immured. The Saracens, the vile pagans, are attacking so hard they cannot hold out very long. [864]

27. The Saracens were proud and arrogant; they pressed them hard in hundreds and thousands, hurling lances and sharp steel spears. But these defended themselves as noble knights should, casting the scoundrels down in the ditches and trenches. Fourteen and more were hurled down, the luckiest one had his neck broken. When Arragon saw this he nearly went mad, wrath and distress drove him out of his mind and he started shouting in a loud voice: 'Are you up there, proud-faced William?' and the count replied: 'I am indeed here, and by my valour I have found this shelter. God grant me aid, who was raised on the Cross!' [878]

28. Now William held Gloriette and began to speak to the Saracens: 'Cursed be anyone who hides the truth from you! I came into this town as a spy and now I have so beguiled and led you on that I have driven you out of Gloriette. Henceforth you will be the shepherds of the tower. Guard it well and you shall have good payment!' Arragon heard this and his mind reeled. He called together the Saracens and pagans: 'Now to arms, noble warriors! Let the assault begin in force. Whoever captures William the warrior for me shall be the standard-bearer of my kingdom and have his choice of all my treasures.' When they heard this they were pleased and delighted. The vile rascals hastily armed themselves and attacked William on every side. When the count saw it, he was quite overcome and called on God, the only true Judge. [898]

29. Now William was very angry and distressed, and Guielin, too, and the worthy Gilbert, all together inside in Gloriette. The pagan hosts pressed them hard, hurling lances and sharp steel spears. When William saw it he went almost demented: 'Nephew Guielin, what will become of us? We shall never get back to France nor see again our cousins and kinsmen, unless it be God's will to help us.' Then retorted Guielin, the hand-

some: 'Uncle William, you are talking nonsense. You came
here in search of love. There is Orable, the lady of Africa: none
so fair in all the world. Go and sit down beside her on this
bench and put both your arms around her body and do not be
behindhand in kissing her. For by the apostle of the penitents,
we shall not have a kiss that is not going to cost us twenty
thousand silver marks and great suffering for all our kinsfolk.'
—'God,' said William, 'I shall go out of my mind if you con-
tinue to mock me!'   [922]

30. Now William was very angry and wrathful and Gilbert
and the noble Guielin, together locked up in Gloriette. The
wild Saracens pressed them hard and they defended themselves
like valiant knights, throwing down sticks and great hewn
beams. Then the queen called to them: 'Lords,' she said,
'surrender, Frenchmen! The wicked pagans hate you. You
will see them swarm up the steps and you will be slain, hacked
to pieces and killed.' When William heard this, he went
demented; he ran into the chamber with the branching pine-
tree and began to harangue the queen: 'Lady,' he said, 'give
me some armour, for the love of God, who suffered on the
Cross; by St Peter, if I live long enough you shall be richly
rewarded for it.' The lady heard him and wept for pity, then
without further delay went swiftly into her chamber and
unfastened a coffer from which she drew a fine yellow hauberk
and a green helmet adorned with gold and ran back to bring
it to William. He took the things he had so much wanted, put
on the hauberk and laced the helmet and the lady Orable hung
at his side a sword which belonged to her husband, Tibalt the
Slav. Hitherto she had refused to give it to any man, not even
Arragon who coveted it greatly, he who was her son by
marriage. Round his neck she hung a strong shield on which
was depicted a gold-crowned lion and in his hand put a stout
square-cut lance whose pennon was fastened with five golden
nails. 'By God,' said William, 'what fine weapons I have now.
I beg you also to think of the others.'   [959]

31. When Guielin saw his uncle was armed he ran into the
chamber to Orable's attendant and spoke to her, beseeching
her gently: 'Lady,' he said, 'by St Peter of Rome, give me

arms in this pressing need.'—'Young man,' she replied, 'you are but a youth. If you live, you will be a most valiant man. The Vavars and Hungarians hate you mortally.' She went into the chamber and brought forth a byrnie forged by Isaac of Barcelona, no sword could cut through a single link. She put it on him to his uncle's great joy, and laced on the helmet of Aufar of Babylon, the first king ever to rule in the city; no sword could ever destroy it, damage a jewel or facet of the carbuncle. She girded him with the sword of Tornemont of Valsone, stolen from him by the thief of Valdon who sold it next to Tibalt at Voirecombe. He paid a thousand besants and a thousand ounces for it, for he thought with its help to win his son a crown. The sword with its long baldric was girt at his side and on his neck she hung a round shield. She gave him the lance of the lady of Valronne, its shaft was stout and its blade was long. He was well armed and Gilbert as well. Now Gloriette will see some fighting today! [986]

32. William was well armed, and his nephew and Gilbert, and all rejoiced and were glad of it. They put on Gilbert's back a strong double hauberk and laced on his head a green chased helmet. Then they girded on him a steel sword and hung round his neck a quartered shield. Before he had received a stout, sharp lance, the wicked pagans had made such efforts that they were on their way up the stairs. Count William went to strike Haucebier, and Gilbert, Maretant the porter, and Guielin in his turn struck at Turfier: these three did not escape death. They broke the shafts of the annealed lances so that the shards flew into the air; now they had to make use of their swords and they would soon be tried and tested. Count William drew out his sword of steel and struck a pagan across from behind cutting him like the branch of an olive tree and the pieces fell up there in the palace. Gilbert went to strike at Gaifier whose head flew off up there in the palace. Guielin was no whit dismayed. Grasping his sword, he set his shield on his arm and whoever he attacked was condemned to death. The pagans saw this and began to retreat; the cowardly rascals took to their heels and the Franks pursued them like noble warriors. Fourteen and more of them were cut down there and the

others were so affrighted that they drove them out through the doors. The Frenchmen swiftly shut and locked them and pulled the drawbridge up on great chains which were attached and made fast to the tower. Now may God, Judge of all men, give them His aid! When Arragon saw it, he nearly went mad. [1023]

33. Now William was angry and troubled, Gilbert also and Guielin the brave, for the pagan hosts were pressing them hard, hurling their lances and darts at the tower, knocking down the walls round them with iron hammers. When William saw it he nearly burst with rage: 'Nephew Guielin,' he said, 'what shall we do? I do not think we shall ever get back to France and embrace again our kinsmen and nephews.'— 'Uncle William, you are talking nonsense. By the apostle who is sought in Nero's Meadow, I intend to sell myself dearly before we go down.' They hurtled down the steps of the tower and struck the pagans on their rounded helmets, hacking them all on the chest and chin, so that some seventeen were laid on the sand: the luckiest of them had his lungs slashed. The pagans saw this and were deeply afraid and shouted aloud to great King Arragon: 'Call a truce, we shall never break in here!' Arragon heard them and nearly burst with rage; he swore by Mahomet that they would pay for it.   [1045]

34. Arragon saw the pagans hang back and spoke to them fairly and quietly: 'Sons of whores, scoundrels, curses on you! Why have you not entered? [8] You shall never have fiefs or border-lands from me! Attack them again yet more fiercely!' And the misbelieving scoundrels obeyed him, hurling lances and darts and spears and knocking down the walls around them with iron hammers. When William saw this he was nigh mad with rage. 'Nephew Guielin, what can we do? We shall all be killed and brought to destruction.'—'Uncle William, such talk is folly. For by the apostle who is sought at the Ark, I will sell myself dearly before the heathen can take me.' The points of their lances were all in splinters and each one armed himself with an axe given them by the noble lady Orable. They sallied forth in all their armour and smote the pagans on their crimson shields, slashing at their feet and faces till more than fourteen

lay on the marble floor. These were dead, the others were
swooning. Never was such havoc wrought by three men.
When Arragon saw it he was nigh mad with rage. [1069]

35. When Arragon saw his men so ill-treated, he was so dis-
tressed he nearly burst with rage. He cried out in a loud voice:
'Are you up there, William, the noble, son of Aymeri of the
great city of Narbonne? Do something as a favour for me:
leave the palace of Gloriette now and depart alive, safe and
well, before you lose your limbs and your blood. If you do not
do this you will have a bad bargain, for, by Mahomet in whom
I trust, I will make such a fire in this place that all of you will
be burnt and consumed in the blaze.' William replied: 'You
are talking nonsense. We have plenty of bread, wine and corn,
salt meat, spiced wines and liquors; bright hauberks and
gleaming green helmets, sharp-edged lances and good stout
shields and fair ladies for our pleasure. I shall never go away,
but the news will travel to the noble King Louis, Bernard, my
brother who is white and hoary, Garin of Anseüne, the fighter,
and the mighty duke, Beuves of Commarchis, and my nephew,
Bertrand, who is valiant and noble, whom we left behind us in
Nîmes. Each of them, when he wants to, can easily summon
twenty thousand fighters. When they learn that the tidings are
true that we are here like this, they will help us, of their good
kindness, with all the followers that they can muster. Then
these walls will not protect you, nor the citadel gleaming
resplendent with gold. You will see it smashed in a thousand
pieces. If they take you, you will have a bad bargain for you
will be hanged and left to swing in the wind.'—'We shall be
sorry for that,' answered Arragon. Pharaon spoke, the king of
Bonivent: 'My lord Emir, you are not worth a glove. By
Mahomet, you have little understanding! Your father was
most valiant and brave; this town, with the palace of Gloriette,
he left in your keeping. These three scoundrels are defying you
here and they are killing your followers and people. By
Mahomet, you are not worth anything if you do not burn
them in stinking Greek fire.' [1118]

36. 'My lord Pharaon,' said King Arragon, 'by Mahomet,
give me good counsel. You see here Gloriette, the tower and

the palace, built of stone right to the top; all the men together from here to Moncontor could not make a hole through it at any level. Where the devil could the firecoals ignite? There is not a stick of wood nor a beam. Through their boldness these three scoundrels are within and it would take seven years for us to get them out.   [1128]

37. 'My lord Pharaon,' said King Arragon, 'by Mahomet who gave us our law, give me good counsel at this time. You see here Gloriette, the principal palace; it is built of stones that are hard as rock. All the men together from here to the pass of Vauquois could not make a hole in it in a month. How the devil could the firecoals ignite, when there is no beam of wood or of laurel? Through their boldness these three have got in and I could not get them out in seven years.' Then came forward a heathen, Orquanois, whose beard was black but his hair and eyebrows were white. He was a judge of their laws. In a loud voice he cried three times: 'My lord Emir, hearken to me. Tell me now if I would be rewarded if I delivered William Strongarm to you so that you could have him in prison?' Arragon answered: 'Yes, indeed, by my faith. I would give you ten mules loaded with pure Spanish gold provided you told me the truth.' Orquanois replied: 'Hearken to me. If you give me your promise on the spot, I will attend to it. I do not care what may happen.' Arragon said: 'I promise you this and swear truly at this time that you shall have the treasure when you want it.' The pagan replied: 'And I pledge myself, too.' [1157]

38. Orquanois said: 'By Mahomet, good lord, I will tell you now how you can capture him by a trick. You see here Gloriette, this marble tower, whose foundation is in the solid rock. It was built by Grifaigne of Aumaria, a Saracen of very great cunning; you do not know the secrets he made there. Underground is a secret vault with a drop-stone door into your citadel. Take a thousand Turks and go that way yourself. Have them attacked also from the front and a great assault from the back. William will be killed and delivered to torment.' Arragon said: 'By Mahomet, you speak truly. You will have your reward, by my lord Apollyon.'   [1172]

39. When Arragon heard the news of the subterranean tunnel in the ground beneath him, he was so delighted his heart was throbbing. He took a thousand Turks who laced on their helmets and left a thousand on the open space in front who were attacking William and Guielin. They set off without delay or hesitation, scarcely stopping till they reached the passage; they carried with them candles and lanterns. In went the vile, infidel race and nothing of this was known to the noble warriors until they had reached the inside of the palace. William was the first to see them. 'Great God,' said the count, 'Majesty in Heaven! Now we are all doomed to death and torment!'—'By St Hilarius,' answered Guielin, 'so help me God, Orable has betrayed us. God damn the whole pagan race!' [1190]

40. Count William saw the palace filling with Saracens who were storming in; he saw the hauberks and helmets gleaming. 'God,' said the count, 'who art always faithful, now we are doomed to death and destruction.'—'In faith, good lord,' Guielin answered him, 'the fair-faced Orable has betrayed us. God damn the Saracens and pagans. This is the day that will see the end of us, so let us help ourselves as long as we can, for we have here neither kinsmen nor friends.' Count William held the tempered steel blade and in his wrath he smote at a pagan, a back-handed stroke which cut him in half. The pagans were astonished at the blow, they rushed at him with fury and anger. The valiant counts gave great blows and defended themselves like noble knights. The attack was fierce and the battle too, and only ended when they were overcome. No struggle ever had such a fine ending for in defending themselves they had slain thirty Turks. Who cares about that? for they will never come to an end of them! Then they were seized by the pagans and Saracens, the Turks and the Persians, the Almoravides, Acoparts, Esclamors and Bedouin. They swore to Mahomet they would wreak their vengeance. Today they will avenge the death of their friends. [1218]

41. By fatal treachery William was captured, with Gilbert and the valiant Guielin. The evil heathens had laid hands on them and swore by Mahomet they would take vengeance on them. They sent twenty retainers into the city and had a great and

deep trench dug and filled with great piles of sticks and
faggots, for they were intending to roast our men there. Fair-
faced Orable came forward and spoke thus to her stepson
Arragon: 'Friend,' she said, 'hand over these prisoners to me
and I will put them in my deepest dungeon where there are
toads and snakes that will devour them, and serpents that will
swallow them.'—'Royal lady,' said King Arragon, 'it is you
who have brought all this trouble upon us by giving these
scoundrels armour up in the tower. Mahomet curse anyone
who would give them up to you!' When the lady heard it she
nearly burst with rage. 'Cursed be such thoughts, you whore-
son scoundrel! By Mahomet, whom I worship and pray to,
were it not for these other lords here, I would give you a punch
on the nose! Out of this tower, immediately! You shall regret
it if you linger!' She called the wicked traitor to her: 'Villain,'
she said, 'put them in your prison, until Tibalt comes back
from Valdon with Desramed and Golias the fair. They will
then wreak the vengeance they want.'—'I agree to that, Lady,'
said King Arragon. They cast William into the deepest
dungeon with Guielin and the worthy Gilbert. Now I shall
stop telling you about our warriors but I shall return to them
when the time comes. Meanwhile I will sing about the pagan
people. [1254]

42. King Arragon did not lose any time, but summoned his
messengers and sent them across the sea. They set off at once
without pause or delay and did not stop till they reached the
Rhône where they took ship in the galley of Maudoine of
Nubia. It was artistically covered in silk and feared neither
north wind nor storm. They pulled up the anchor and un-
furled the sails and put out to sea away from the town. They
voyaged with oars and sails and rudder, fair winds blowing
them on a straight course. They arrived at the port below
Aumaria, dropped anchor and furled their sails. They
mounted their horses without delay and rode without resting
or stopping until they reached the city of Africa. They dis-
mounted in the shade of the olive trees and went up into the
marble hall where they found Tibalt and his heathen court
and greeted them in Saracen fashion: 'May Mahomet, the

ruler of all things, save King Tibalt of Slavonia! Your bold-
faced son sends to you to aid him with your fighting men. He
has captured William, I will not conceal it, the son of Aymeri
of Narbonne the great, inside the splendid city of Orange.
They had entered the town in disguise, thinking to take it as he
had taken Nîmes and win the love of the lady Orable. But this
devilish plot did not succeed. He gave us much trouble with
Gloriette for he held it and her for seven days and but for the
subterranean tunnel whose trapdoor of stone comes out at
the top of the tower, you would never have won back Orable,
your most noble wife. But Mahomet came to your aid and we
have shut him up in a dungeon from which he will never get
out alive and you can take what vengeance you choose.' When
Tibalt heard this he began to laugh and summoned the
warriors in his realm. 'Now quickly to arms, noble and valiant
knights!' [1299]

They obeyed without delay, mounting their horses from
Apulia and Russia. When Tibalt set off from the city of Africa
he took with him the heathen from Aumaria, those from Susce
and from Slavonia. Sixty thousand made up the vanguard.
They rode to the sea without pause or delay and the ships were
very soon loaded, with wine and meat and biscuit and flour.
Then the pagan race all embarked, pulled up the anchors and
unfurled the sails. The winds were blowing them on a straight
course and they put out to sea and started their voyage. Then
you could have heard many trumpets and bugles, the grunting
bears and hounds barking, mules braying and horses neighing
and sparrowhawks crying on their perches, so they could be
heard a full league distant. They sailed eight days and the
ninth day dawned, but, before they reach the great city of
Orange, Tibalt will have such grief and great sorrow as he
never had in his life before, for he will lose his great and
splendid city and his wife, the slender Orable.[9] [1323]

43. William was in the dungeon there with Gilbert and the
noble Guielin. 'God,' said the count, 'fair and loving Father
and King, now we are doomed to death and torment. O God!
why does not Louis the valiant know of this? My brother
Bernard, white-haired and hoary, and master Garin the mighty

from Anseüne; Beuves the fighter from Commarchis, my
nephew Bertrand the noble and valiant whom we left behind
us in Nîmes together with twenty thousand fighting French-
men; we have great need of their assistance.' Guielin spoke, the
fair and handsome, 'Uncle William, you are talking nonsense.
Send for Orable, the lady of Africa, that she should succour her
lover for love's sake.'—'O God,' said William, 'your constant
mockery is nearly breaking my heart.'   [1341]

44. Then William was angry and desolate, with Gilbert and
Guielin the brave, in the dungeon where they were making a
great uproar. While they were lamenting in this way, Orable
appeared coming to the dungeon. When she saw the counts she
spoke to them thus: 'Hearken to me, noble and valiant knights.
The pagans and Saracens hate you mortally, they will hang
you tonight or tomorrow.'—'There is nothing we can do,
lady,' said Guielin, 'now take some action, noble and high-
born lady, so that we may get out of this dungeon! I would be
your man sworn and pledged and serve you very willingly
when it pleased you. Mercy, noble lady.'—'Indeed,' said
William, 'she has betrayed us and because of her we are in this
dungeon.' The lady heard him and sighed deeply.   [1359]

45. 'Noble lords,' said the courtly Orable, 'by Mahomet, you
are wrong to blame me. I gave you arms in this very tower. If
you could have fought in the palace until news reached Louis,
the son of Charles, and master Bernard of Brubant and
Aymeri and the rest of your great kin, if the wretched scoun-
drels had not learned of it until they were in the famous tower,
they could have won the border-lands and the narrows, the
fords and the passes.' Guielin said: 'Lady, you speak well. If
we were now out of this dungeon, I would be your man for the
rest of my life.'—'By my faith,' said Orable the queen, 'if I
thought I should be safe-guarded from trouble and that
William Strongarm would take me, I would bring you out of
the dungeon and would at once become a Christian.' When
William heard her, his heart was lightened. 'Lady,' he said,
'here is my pledge: I give you my promise, by God and St
James and by the apostle who is sought at the Ark.'—'Truly,'
said the lady, 'I seek no other pledge.' She opened all the

gates of the dungeon and these men of great valour all came
out and everyone rejoiced in his heart.   [1386]

46. Now the lady had protected the counts and set them free
from the dungeon and led and conducted them to Gloriette.
When they had been richly apparelled, they sat down to
dinner up there in the palace. The noble lady then addressed
them: 'My lords and barons, hearken to me. I have set you
free from prison and led and taken you up to the palace. I do
not know how you can escape, but I will tell you what I have
in mind. Underneath us is a secret tunnel that is not known by
any man living except my grandfather who had it dug out,
tunnelling through from here to the Rhône. If you could send
out a messenger to Count Bertrand and the other barons, he
could come underground to speak to you, and the mis-
believing pagans would know nothing of it until they had
reached the paved palace up here; and they would strike with
the swords they were wearing and thus could capture all the
city, and the narrows, the fords and the passes.' Then said
William: 'Lady, this is quite true, but I do not know where to
find a messenger.   [1411]

47. 'Nephew Guielin,' said Count William, 'go to Nîmes
without pause or delay and tell this news to your brother,
Bertrand, that he may come to my aid with all the men from
his domain.'—'Really, uncle William,' answered Guielin, 'so
help me God, you must be joking! By St Stephen, I would
rather die in this fine tower than in fair France or at Aix-la-
Chapelle.'   [1420]

48. 'Nephew Guielin,' said noble William, 'you will go into
the secret tunnel here and make your way to Nîmes without
delay and tell the paladin Bertrand that he must speedily and
soon come to my help.'—'Uncle William, you are talking
nonsense, I would not leave you though it cost me my limbs. I
would rather die here in this tower than in fair France or
among my kinsfolk. Send Gilbert the Fleming thither.'—
'Will you go, friend?' said the noble William. And the warrior
replied: 'Truly, I will go and give your message loyally.'—
'Go then, good friend, I commend you to Jesus. Tell the

paladin Bertrand for me that he must aid me and that without
delay, for if he does not, by God, the King of Love, he will
never see again his kinsman, William.'   [1438]

49. When the messenger heard that he must go, he began to
make a great outcry, how he might escape from that place,
'for I was never here before and do not know the way'. And
the lady said: 'I can guide you. You need fear no man alive
save only the Lord Jesus.' Near one of the pillars she moved a
stone slab that was full six feet long and six feet wide. 'Brother,'
she said, 'here is the entrance. At the end you will find three
pillars made and built in arcades.' He set off and began to
make his way under the city, not knowing where. Count
William accompanied him a great distance, with the lady
Orable and the noble Guielin, and they did not pause till they
reached the three pillars. Then he went through the middle of
them and came to the Rhône where he found a boat and
rowed across very quietly. Count William went back again with
Guielin and bright-faced Orable and all three of them entered
Gloriette. It would have been better if they had returned and
gone down into the prison for not one of their words or plots or
actions but was overheard by a Saracen who went and told the
story to King Arragon.   [1466]

50. The Saracen was very cunning and went to tell the tale to
King Arragon. When he saw him he thus addressed him: 'My
lord Emir, be silent and hear how your stepmother has
treated the captives you had in prison: she has released them
from the dungeon and led and taken them up to the palace.
They are sitting in Gloriette, eating.'—'Is this true, mes-
senger?' said Arragon. 'Lord,' he replied, 'I am no liar. I saw
them in close counsel together, kissing and embracing each
other. She loves them, and William in bed, more than your
father or King Haucebier.' When Arragon heard this his
senses reeled; he called together the Saracens and Slavs:
'Lords,' he said, 'now give me your advice how I should act
towards my stepmother who has so degraded me, bringing
shame to me and disgrace to my father.'   [1487]

51. Arragon said: 'Noble and valiant knights, by Mahomet,

now take up your arms. Let everyone who takes part in the distribution of armour know that the capture of the Christians will cost us dear.' And they replied: 'At your command.' Fifteen thousand men hastened to arm themselves. Alas! What a pity William did not know about it, or the lady Orable and the valiant Guielin. They were hidden in Gloriette playing chess quite at their ease. The noble counts knew nothing about it until the Saracens and Slavs fell upon them. [1499]

52. Arragon found William under the pine-tree with the lady Orable and the brave Guielin. The valiant paladins knew nothing until they were seized by the pagans and Saracens, Turks and Persians and wicked Bedouin. They swore by Mahomet that they would have vengeance. Pharaon spoke, who claimed to be the wisest among them: 'Lord Emir, listen to me. Tibalt your father is high-born and valiant; he left you this town to govern and Gloriette, the royal palace. These scoundrels have defied you here, they have slain your men, maimed and killed them. By Mahomet, you are not worth a groat if you do not have them torn limb from limb, and have your stepmother who has so disgraced us condemned to the fire and burned.' Old Esquanor spoke, the grey haired and hoary: 'King Pharaon, what you say is not right.' [1518]

53. Said Esquanor, the old and hoary: 'King Pharaon, your judgement is bad. You should not start an evil course, for what is begun cannot be amended. My lord Emir, be silent and hearken to me. Tibalt your father is very wise; he left you this town to govern, the palace of Gloriette and the fief. If it should befall that you burned his wife, he would soon be very angry with you. Have these lords thrown into prison and cast the lady Orable in with them; summon your messenger and send him across the sea. Your father will come and King Haucebier and they will take vengeance as they see fit.'—'You have given good counsel, and shall have honour for it and lack for nothing. But I have already sent off a messenger to my father, the king, who is ruler of Africa. He will be back again here in a week.' They threw William into the dungeon, with Guielin who was spirited and brave, and they cast the lady Orable in with them. Now may God, Judge of all men, watch over them! [1542]

54. Now William was thrown into the dungeon with Guielin and the courteous Orable who often lamented her sorry plight: 'God,' said the lady, 'dear Father and Spirit, why have I not been baptized, wretched that I am? I thought to receive it and become one of the faithful. Alas the day, Lord William, that I ever saw your valour, your handsome person and great bravery —since for you I am cast into this dungeon in such distress as though I were a whore.' Guielin said: 'You are talking very foolishly. You and my uncle are very well placed and should take great delight in this trouble.' William heard him and went nearly mad with wrath and in his rage he swore by St James: 'Were it not for shame and scorn I would give you a great buffet now.' Guielin said: 'That would be very foolish. Henceforth I shall say, and I care not who knows it, that you used to be called William Strongarm, now they will call you William Sweetheart: you came into this city for love.' When the count heard it, he bowed his head. [1565]

55. William was angry and grieved, there in the dungeon where he had been thrown, with the lady Orable and Guielin his nephew. 'God,' said the count, 'great King of Heaven, we are now doomed to death, tricked and betrayed. It was madness to engage in this enterprise through which we are disgraced and shamed if He who is Judge of all men does not intervene. Alas! Why is it not known to Louis the proud, Bernard my brother, grey haired and aged, and the worthy master Garin of Anseüne, and, in Nîmes itself, Bertrand the mighty? We shall need their succour now.'—'Uncle William,' said the proud Guielin, 'let this be, for it is of no use now. Here is Orable, the courtly lady, and you can truly kiss and embrace her: I ask and seek for no livelier lady!'—'God,' said the count, 'I shall go mad!' The pagans heard them quarrelling in the dungeon, and more than forty of them rushed in and took the pair of them out of the dungeon, leaving there Orable, the courtly lady. They led the uncle and nephew to the palace. Pharaon said with growing anger: 'My lord Emir, be silent and hearken to me. Tibalt, your most praiseworthy father, gave you this city to govern and the palace of Gloriette and the fief. Here is this scoundrel, this young warrior, who cares not a

groat for anything you say. By Mahomet, you are worth less than a nobody if you do not have him torn to pieces, him and his uncle, William the fighter.' Guielin heard him and his senses reeled, he gnashed his teeth and rolled his eyes. Rolling up his sleeves he advanced upon him and setting his left hand on his head, he raised the right and struck him on the neck, breaking his neckbone in pieces and throwing him down dead at his feet.[10] When William saw it he was happy and joyful. 'God,' said the count, 'Judge of all men, now we are doomed to death and destruction.' [1609]

56. William saw the fallen Pharaon: 'God,' said the count, 'fair Lord of Paradise, now we are doomed to death and destruction.'—'Do not worry, uncle,' Guielin answered, 'you are not without friends in this palace.' Then the young Guielin looked around and saw a great axe beside a pillar. He went forward, seized it in both hands and smote a pagan barbarian, cleaving him right down to the chest. When Arragon saw it he lost his temper and shouted loudly: 'Seize them, Saracens! By Mahomet they shall suffer for it and be thrown and hurled into the Rhône.' Guielin said: 'Scoundrel, out of here! You have brought us out of the dungeon, led and guided us up here to the palace; but by the apostle who is blessed in Rome, you have acquired yourselves companions here who will cause you trouble and destruction.' As he was speaking, two Saracens approached bringing with them a barrel of wine which they were going to serve up there in the palace. When they saw these great blows being struck, they dropped everything and took to their heels. Count William went and seized the carrying-stick [11] and, quickly grasping it in both hands, he dealt great blows at the pagans and Saracens: whoever he pursued could no longer use his body. [1639]

57. Now William was in the paved palace with his nephew, the valiant Guielin. One had an axe and the other a cudgel with which the noble lords struck great blows so that fourteen Turks were knocked down dead there. All the others were so terrified that they drove them out through the doors, which they then swiftly bolted and barred, pulling up the drawbridge on its great chains. When Arragon saw it he nearly went out of

his mind and summoned the Saracens and Slavs: 'In the name of Mahomet, my god, give me your counsel! This William has treated me badly, taking away my chief citadel from me and I can see no way of getting back inside it!'   [1654]

Now I shall say no more about the Saracens for henceforth I must sing of Gilbert, the messenger who had crossed the Rhône. He climbed up hill and down dale, never pausing till he came to Nîmes. Count Bertrand had got up early and climbed up to the citadel of the infidel Otrant, which he had conquered by his valour and daring. The count was leaning up by the great windows looking down over the region. He saw the green grass and the bushes of roses, heard the blackbird and oriole singing and was reminded of William Shortnose and his own brother, the valiant Guielin. He began to weep very tenderly and mourn for them as you can now hear: 'Uncle William, you acted very foolishly, when you went to spy out Orange, disguised in such a way, as a rascal. Guielin, my brother, how valiant you were! Now the Saracens and Slavs have slain you and I am left alone in this country, without any man of my great lineage from whom I can seek good counsel. Now the Slavs will come back to these parts, and Golias and King Desramed, Clarel and his brother Aceré, Aguisant and King Giboé and the chieftain of Reaumont by the sea, King Eubron and Borrel and Lorré and Quinzepaumes and his brother Gondré, the thirty kings born in Spain. Each will bring with him thirty thousand knights and they will assail me in the city of Nîmes and capture me by brute force and I shall be slain, killed or slaughtered. But I have made up my mind on one thing: not for the gold of ten cities will I fail to return to the land where I was born and take with me all my followers who were brought here by William Shortnose. When I come to the city of Paris, I shall dismount at the inlaid marble stairway. Then the men at arms and young warriors will come up and ask me about William and my brother Guielin the valiant. Alas! woe is me! I shall have nothing to tell them but that they were slain in Orange by the pagans.' Twice he swooned on the steps of marble and the barons hastened to lift him up.   [1704]

58. Count Bertrand was very grieved and distressed for

Guielin and the noble William. In fair, courtly terms he lamented them: 'Uncle William, it was folly when you went thus to Orange, in a vagabond's disguise. Guielin, my brother, alas for your valour! Now the Saracens and Persians have slain you, I am alone in the pagan kingdom and have no cousin or kinsman with me. Now King Tibalt of Africa will return, with Desramed and the huge Golias, the thirty kings with all their forces. They will assail me here before Nîmes and I shall be slain and delivered to torment. But, by the apostle of the penitents, though it cost me my limbs, yet I will not fail to go to Orange the great city, and avenge the grief and torment that the Saracens have brought on our kinsmen. Alas! wretch that I am! Why do I hesitate and not set out to confront them in person?' [1726]

59. Count Bertrand was full of wrath and despair, but while he was weeping and lamenting, Gilbert entered the town and climbed the steps to the marble hall. When Bertrand saw him, he began to laugh and called out to him in a loud, clear voice: 'You are most welcome, noble and valiant knight. Where is my bold-faced uncle? and where is Guielin? Tell me the truth.' And he replied like a noble warrior: 'Inside Orange, the magnificent city, in the marble tower of Gloriette. The wicked heathen have taken and tormented them and at any moment I expect both to be slain. William has sent for you, I will not hide it from you, to come to his aid with your knights, swiftly and without any delay.' When Bertrand heard him he began to laugh and called on his followers in the hearing of all: 'Now, swiftly to arms, noble, valiant knights.' And they obeyed without hesitation, mounting their Spanish and Syrian horses. When Bertrand set out from the city of Nîmes, he led with him all the host from his domain; fifteen thousand and more were in the vanguard. They rode without pause or delay as far as the Rhône. The French all embarked in the ships and galleys, crossing over with sails and rudder. The proud companies arrived on the great plain outside Orange where they pitched their tents and set up their pavilions. Count Bertrand did not hesitate but called on the messenger and began to address him: 'Gilbert, my lord, tell me the truth. Shall we

attack this town of Orange? Will we break through the walls
and the marble chambers?' Gilbert replied: 'What you say is
madness, for Orange does not fear the whole Frankish empire.
You will never take it.' When Bertrand heard him, he was
nearly mad with anger.   [1766]

60. 'Gilbert, my friend,' said Count Bertrand. 'Shall we make
an assault on Orange the mighty? Shall we break down the
walls and high fortifications?' Gilbert replied: 'You are talking
nonsense. You will never take it.' Bertrand was very angry at
this but the messenger spoke words of comfort: 'Lord,' he said,
'hear my advice. I will get you into the city in such a way that
the Saracens and Persians will know nothing of it.'—'Do so,
good friend. I commend you to Jesus.' He set off, as one who
knew the way, together with thirteen thousand fighting
Frenchmen, leaving the others in the tents and pavilions. They
did not pause till they reached the arcade and went inside
between the pillars. They went in single file through the total
darkness for they had no candle or burning taper. Bertrand
was very disturbed by this and called the messenger and spoke
to him loudly. 'Gilbert, my friend, tell me the truth! I believe
my uncle is dead and you have sold us to the unbelievers.'
Gilbert replied: 'This is foolish talk! I would not do that,
though it cost me my limbs. You will arrive inside Gloriette.
In God's name I beg you, do so nobly.'—'Carry on then, good
friend, by the grace of God.' Even while they were speaking,
they came at that moment into Gloriette and Count William
was the first to see them: 'God,' said the count, 'loving Father,
great King, now I see the band of men I have so much longed
for!' The noble knights took off their helmets and kissed each
other, with tears of joy. Count Bertrand spoke to him first:
'How are you, uncle? Tell me the truth.'—'Very well, fair
nephew, by the grace of Almighty God. I have suffered great
torment and great pain and thought I would never see you
again, for the Persians and Saracens have given me such
trouble.'—'Uncle William, you will soon be avenged.'
[1808]
   They sounded a horn up in the palace. Those in the tents
and pavilions outside seized their arms. Count William was

both daring and valiant. They lowered the drawbridges and went down to the gates of the magnificent city and swiftly and speedily they were opened. Those outside entered in and 'Mountjoy' sounded on every side. The pagans were astonished at the rejoicings and the infamous traitors ran for their weapons and immediately they came out of their lodgings, having swiftly armed to defend themselves. But it availed them not a jot for the French host was too numerous and Bertrand took possession of the whole city. Then you might have seen a fierce struggle to capture the strongly fortified citadel, many shafts splintered and shields shattered, the mail links broken on the hauberks from Algiers, and many a pagan cast down dead and bleeding. When Arragon saw his people slaughtered he was so distressed he nearly went out of his mind. He leapt into the saddle of a swift charger, and took a shield he had seized from a Frenchman. He looked on the ground and saw a sharp lance and, bending down, grasped it in both hands. He pricked his horse with the sharp spurs and thrust into the middle of the fiercest fighting. He killed Foucher of Meliant and then a second of our men and a third also. When Bertrand saw it, he nearly went mad. He drew his sword with its good cutting blade and struck Arragon and did not spare him. In his fierce wrath he gave him such a blow that he cleft him in the front down to the chest and struck him down off his swift charger, dead. The pagans lost their strength and their daring. Why should I prolong the narration? Cursed be he who might have escaped, for on the ground ran a stream of blood! Count William did not delay but hastened at once towards the dungeon and freed Orable, the valiant lady. He called Bertrand and spoke to him loudly: 'Fair nephew,' he said, 'hear my opinion about this fair and lovely lady who has truly saved me from death. I pledged her my faith, loyally, that I would truly make her my wife.' And Bertrand answered, 'What are you waiting for? Keep your promise to her faithfully and marry her with great rejoicing.'—'Just as you say, nephew,' answered William. [1861]

61. Count William was very noble and brave. When he had conquered the city by force, he had a great basin prepared and

clean water poured into it. In the presence of the bishop of the
city of Nîmes, they made Orable disrobe and baptized her to
the glory of God and took away her heathen name. Bertrand
was her sponsor and the valiant Guielin and the wise and
worthy Gilbert: they named her Guibourg in our religion.
Then William went and was married to her in a church they
had consecrated, where Mahomet was worshipped before.
Bishop Guimer sang mass for them and after the mass they left
the church and led the lady up to Gloriette. Great was the
wedding feast up there in the marble palace. Count Bertrand
waited on them at dinner with Gilbert and valiant Guielin.
The feast and rejoicing lasted for a week, and the harpers and
minstrels received many robes of silk with ermine collars,
Spanish mules and sturdy chargers.   [1885]

62. So Count William married the lady and stayed thirty
years in Orange, but not one single day passed without
fighting.[12]   [1888]

LYNETTE R. MUIR
Leeds

NOTES

The *Prise d'Orange* has survived in nine manuscripts which are
described in detail by Claude Régnier in his edition of the poem, *Les
rédactions en vers de la Prise d'Orange*, Paris, 1966. Régnier distinguishes
five versions of the story which he labels from A to E. The earliest
version, A, found in four manuscripts, is closely followed in subject
matter and order of events by the later group, B (two manuscripts),
which is written in a considerably more expanded style. The single
manuscript of C has been extensively revised and rearranged: it
shows also many linguistic peculiarities. Closely linked with it is the
manuscript of E, which has, however, a unique concluding section
telling of Tibalt's siege of Orange. The manuscript of D presents yet
another independent revision of the material. Régnier has printed
three versions of the poem, AB, CE and D, plus the *Siege of Orange*
from the end of E. In this translation the text of AB has been followed

throughout except for an occasional modification where the sense is not clear. These changes are indicated in the notes. Régnier gives a full bibliography for both the cycle and this poem in particular.

1 'Spain', here and elsewhere in the poem, includes the south of France—see note 16 to *The Crowning of Louis*.

2 Saint-Gilles and the church of St Julien at Brioude were important stages in the medieval pilgrim route to Compostella through central and southern France. William bequeaths his shield to the church of St Julien when he becomes a monk (see Introduction, p. ix, *William the Monk*). Bertrand's shield is not referred to elsewhere in the poems, but Bédier suggests that he may well have been venerated also at Brioude.

3 The French text AB has *el pales*, 'in the palace', but this has been amended according to another manuscript as the Frenchmen do not reach the palace for several more lines.

4 For William's prayers, here and in other texts, see note 7 to *The Crowning of Louis*.

5 The author is rather confusing in his description of the palace. It seems that he uses the term both for the whole palace, where Arragon lives, and for Gloriette, the separate tower or palace of Orable. There are a number of references to 'up there in the palace' which suggest that Gloriette or at least Orable's apartments are on a higher level than the rest of the citadel.

6 It is not clear whether the pine-tree is *in* the hall or, as has been suggested, in a sort of enclosed garden or terrace to one side of the hall.

7 The AB redaction has *cote*, 'mantle' or 'coat', but it seems probable that the *coupe*, 'goblet', found in another manuscript is correct here.

8 The text suggests that Arragon curses his men because they *had* entered the tower. As they had not in fact done so, the translation has been modified accordingly.

9 Only manuscript E recounts the arrival of Tibalt at Orange, and his many vain attempts to recapture it. All the other manuscripts ignore him from here onwards, though his attacks are hinted at in the closing lines of the poem.

10 Guielin is here using William's favourite blow which kills many men in the *Crowning* and the *Waggon-train*.

11 The word translated as 'carrying-stick' is *tinel* which is used in the *Song of William* for Rainouart's cudgel (see *The Song of William*, note 19).

12 The ending of the poem is abrupt, but it leads effectively on to *The Song of William*, so I have not tried to make it less sudden by adding the account of the siege of Orange from manuscript E.

The Song of William

1. Would it please you to hear of great battles and mighty skirmishes? How Desramed, a Saracen king, made war against our emperor Louis? Lord William fought back against him vigorously and finally slew him gloriously on the field of the Archamp. Many times he strove against the pagan hosts and lost the flower of his men and the valiant Lord Vivien his nephew. Long did he grieve for them in his heart. Monday in the evening. Now begins the song of William.   [11]

2. King Desramed set out from Cordova, and sailed over the high seas with his fleet. He sailed up the Gironde in force, and pillaged as he went, laying waste the borders and seizing the frontier territories. He seized and carried off the sacred relics from the kingdom, leading off the noble knights in chains. Today it is the Archamp which is the scene of destruction. One knight made his escape from the pagans and carried the news to Thibaut of Bourges.[1] There indeed, at that time, he found Thibaut in Bourges with his nephew Esturmi and the noble Count Vivien, and seven hundred young knights were with them: every one of them had both hauberk and byrnie. Here comes the messenger bringing the news.   [27]

3. Count Thibaut was on his way back from vespers, with his nephew Esturmi at his side; Vivien was there too, William's noble nephew, and with him seven hundred knights from his lands. Thibaut was just as drunk as he could be and Esturmi, his nephew, supported him by the right hand. Then entered the messenger bringing the news: 'God save Thibaut on his way back from vespers! I bring you dire tidings of Desramed. There is bitter warfare in the Archamp.   [37]

4. 'King Desramed has set out from Cordova, and sailed with

his fleet over the high seas. He has sailed up the Gironde in force and in your lands is sacking and pillaging, laying waste the borders and seizing the frontier territories. He has seized and carried off the sacred relics from the kingdom and is leading away your knights in chains. Take heed, Thibaut, lest the pagans carry them off.'   [45]

5. 'Noble lords,' said Thibaut, 'what shall we do?'—'Let us fight them now,' said the messenger. 'What shall we do, Lord Vivien?' asked Thibaut. 'We cannot rightly do anything else, Lord Thibaut,' replied the worthy Vivien. 'You are the count and highly honoured by all the great men along the coastlands. Trust me and you will not be blamed. Call for your messengers, summon your friends. Do not forget William Hooknose for he is a man very experienced in warfare; he can well maintain and fight a battle. If he comes we shall defeat Desramed.' [58]

6. 'Do not believe it, Thibaut,' then said Esturmi. 'In any part of this kingdom, wherever pagans or Arabs appear, they send for William, the marquis. If there are twenty thousand of your men and William comes with only five of his followers, or three or four, or any small number, you may fight and conquer the Arabs but everyone will say that Lord William did it. Whoever earns it, he always gets the credit. Let us fight, lord, and I promise you we shall win! Then you will be rated as highly as William.'—'I beg you, noble lords,' said Vivien, 'with a small host we cannot defeat the Arabs. Let us send for William the marquis, my lords; he is skilled in ordering a battle. If he comes we shall conquer the Arabs.' And Esturmi said: 'This is bad advice. Strangers praise him so much every day that he causes our people to be held in disdain.' Thibaut replied: 'He said it for no other reason, but he will not dare to come to the battle.'   [79]

7. Then said Vivien: 'Now you are talking slander, for there is no man born of woman, beyond the sea or beyond the Rhine, neither in Christendom nor among the Arabs, who is readier than I am to uphold a battle, except for William Hooknose,[2] the marquis. He is my uncle, and I do not claim to be his

equal. Monday in the evening.[3] I do not claim to have William's valour.' [88]

8. Then Thibaut said: 'Bring me the wine and give it me and I will drink to Esturmi. Before prime tomorrow we shall seek out the Arabs. Their cries will be heard seven leagues away with the splintering of lances and the clashing of stout shields.' Then the butler brought them the wine and Thibaut drank and gave some to Esturmi. Vivien went away to his lodging to sleep. [96]

9. Then all the men from their lands assembled and by dawn there were ten thousand with helmets. Thibaut stood up in the morning by a window and opened a casement towards the wind. He looked at the sky but could not see the ground, for wherever he looked it was all covered with byrnies and helmets and Saracens, the vile, infidel race. 'God,' said Thibaut, 'what can this mean?[4] [104]

10. 'Lords, my noble friends, for love of God, I implore you! It is now eighteen years and more since first I held sway over this region, and never did I see so many armed knights that they did not know which way to turn. If you attack either fortress or stronghold they will be grieved whom you have challenged, and grieved too will be the lands that you will lay waste.' Said Vivien: 'I can understand this business very well. Thibaut was drunk with wine last evening, but now he has slept long and is sensible. Now we shall wait for William Hooknose.' Then he who had spoken that evening was ashamed, and more ashamed were those who had boasted. [118]

11. Then said Vivien, the worthy knight: 'I can understand this business; last night, by my head, Thibaut was drunk when he came back from vespers. Now he has slept long. We shall wait for William.' Then came Esturmi through the throng; he came to Thibaut and seized his right hand. 'Lord, do you not remember when you came back from vespers, about Desramed and the dire tidings?' Thibaut replied: 'Have I sent for William?'—'No, good lord, for he cannot get here in time. [128]

12. 'You will have the devil round your neck ere evening if you send for William Hooknose.' Thibaut answered, 'Let it be then.' He called for his arms and they brought them, and dressed him in a fine, bright byrnie and laced a green helmet on his head. Then he girded on his sword with the bright blade hanging down and took a great shield by the arm-straps. In his right hand he held a sharp lance with a white pennon winding round it to the ground. Then they brought him a Castilian steed and Thibaut mounted by the left stirrup and rode out through one of the postern gates. Ten thousand helmeted men followed behind him: they were going to seek King Desramed in the Archamp. Thus Thibault set off from his fine city, ten thousand armed men following behind him. They sought the pagan Desramed in the Archamp, but they had a bad lord to lead them. Monday in the evening. They came into the Archamp on the right hand by the sea.   [149]

13. Thibaut looked at the open seas and saw the rigging of twenty thousand ships. Then Thibaut said: 'I can see their lodgings.'—'No, that cannot be they,' said Vivien. 'Those are ships coming in towards land; if they have disembarked, they will prepare dwellings.' He moved forward and saw the tops of five hundred tents, the turrets and the shelters. 'This may well be they,' said Vivien. Then said Thibaut, lord of the Berry: 'Noble Vivien, climb up this hill and survey the infidel horde, see how many men they have by land and sea.'—'You must not ask that of me,' said Vivien. 'Rather should I carry my helmet down there to the field and strike out with my right hand, for so my Lord William taught me. Never, please God, shall I survey a camp.   [167]

14. 'Lord Thibaut,' said the noble Vivien, 'you are the very honoured lord of the finest men along the coast. Climb the hill, for you should look out and see how many men they have by land and sea. If you have men enough in whom you can trust, then ride against them and attack. By God's mercy we shall defeat them. If you have but few men for an open battle, assemble your followers here in this valley, appoint your messengers and send for your friends. Do not forget William Hooknose, for he is experienced in open fighting, well knowing

how to maintain and keep it. If he comes we shall vanquish Desramed.'—'You give me good counsel,' answered Thibaut, and spurred his horse to the top of the hill. Thibaut looked at the coastal water and saw it covered with barges and ships, boats and great armoured galleys. He looked at the sky but could not see the ground. Quite forgetting himself in his fear he rushed back down the hill and came to tell the Frenchmen what he had seen: [191]

15. 'Noble household, what will become of us? For every one of us there are a thousand of them. If we do not flee at once we shall soon all be killed. Let us be off quickly to save our lives. [195]

16. 'My lord Vivien, lead the way round this rock and guide our army down through the valley, so that the Saracen fleet does not see you. I will send for William, let him fight if he dare. Monday in the evening. I shall certainly not fight without William.' [201]

17. 'This is bad advice,' said Vivien, 'you have seen them and they have seen you. If you leave now, you are running away. Christianity will be for ever degraded and paganism will be more exalted. Fight on bravely, and I guarantee we shall win. You must make yourself as famous as William. Yesterday evening, you claimed to be the count's equal. Monday in the evening. You must make yourself as famous as William.' [211]

18. There were a hundred thousand of Desramed's men in the transports and ships, who saw Thibaut up on the mound. They recognized him by the great embossed shield, and knew that he had left in the valley many of his friends and his followers. [217]

19. Monday in the evening. The Saracens were from the land of Saragossa, a hundred thousand of the vile race, and everyone armed himself in a bright hauberk, and put a green Saragossan helm on his head with golden frontals and flowers and trimmings. They girded on their swords with the bright blades hanging down and took their stout shields by the arm-straps;

in their right hands were sharp spears and lances; their
saddles were set on swift Arab horses. They disembarked on
the sand and the shingle, and began to occupy the firm ground.
They were preparing a mighty attack on Count Thibaut.
Grievous were the tidings they heard. [231]

20. The day was clear and the morning fair, the sun shone and
day became brighter. The pagans rode down through an
ancient wood, the whole earth shaking as they passed, and the
wood glittered with the strong gilded helmets they wore above
their shoulders. Whoever saw them disembark and set out
could tell that they were men of might. Then Vivien pointed
them out to Esturmi. [240]

21. 'Brother Esturmi, I see the pagans advancing. Their
horses are so swift, that even after being spurred for fifteen
leagues they would run on without heaving flanks. This day
the cowards will die in the Archamp. Already the advance
guard are approaching; the great will not be able to save the
small, nor the father to protect his child. Let us trust in
almighty God, for He is greater than all the pagans. Let us
fight for we shall win the day.' [251]

22. Then said Thibaut: 'What do you advise, Lord Vivien,
for the approaching battle?' Then he said: 'What do you
advise, Esturmi? How may each of us save his life?'—'Anyone
who does not flee will soon be dead. Let us away to save our
lives.' Then Vivien said: 'That is a cur's counsel.' Thibaut
replied: 'From my close kin I want no counsel that may
shame my person, or trick me and bring me harm. [261]

23. 'Nephew Esturmi, break this banner that no one may
recognize us as we flee, for the cursed heathen will flock to this
ensign.'—'Blessed be God,' exclaimed Esturmi. Then the
scoundrel held up the shaft and, putting the spear-head on the
pommel before him, with both hands he tore off the white
pennon and trampled it underfoot in the mud. [269]

24. Count Thibaut was holding a great spear: he turned the
butt up towards the sky and put the spear-head on the saddle
behind him. Tearing the pennon from the shaft of applewood,

he trampled it underfoot in the mud. 'I would rather, pennon, that you were struck by lightning, than that the pagans should recognize me in battle.'—'These are grievous tidings,' said Count Vivien, 'now we shall have no standard-bearer on the field. [278]

25. 'Noble followers, what will become of us? We have no banners on the field of battle. Thibaut and Esturmi have deserted us. Look at the pagans who are very near at hand. When we have five or ten men and the pagans a hundred or a thousand, we shall have no one whom we can follow, no standard round which to rally: men with no leader are in a sad plight. Go your ways, fair, noble knights, for I cannot endure and suffer such noble men to be evilly led. I will ride into the grievous peril and never turn back for I have made an oath to God that never will I flee for fear of death.' Then the French spoke, now hear what they said to him! [294]

26. 'Lord Vivien, you are of this kin and may well lead us in the great battle, for you are the son of Marquis Beuves Cornebut, born of the daughter of good Count Aymeri, nephew to Marquis William Hooknose. You may well lead us in this great battle.'—'Now my lords, great thanks in God's name. But there is one great impediment. You are not my liege men, I was never your lord; you could desert me without any oath-breaking.' 5 Then as one man they all cried out: 'Silence, lord, never speak thus. We will have sworn to you, by the law God gave to men, to His apostles when He dwelt among them, that we will never fail you while you still live.' [309]

27. 'And I pledge you, by God, the great King and by the spirit He had in His body when He died for sinners, that never will I fail you for any physical weakness.' At these words he set up his standard. He put his hand in his crimson hose, drew out a silken pennon and fastened it to the lance with three golden nails. Then he flourished the shaft high in his right hand, the tongues of the pennon hung down to his fist. He spurred on his horse, that could not turn aside, and struck a pagan on his double shield, split it across from one side to the other, cut the

arm that was thrust through the straps, pierced the chest and cut through the heart, so that his great spear thrust through the spine and brought him down dead on the ground. 'Mount-joy,' he shouted, the war-cry of Charles.   [327]

28. As gold divides itself from silver, so all the good men set themselves apart: the cowards fled away with Thibaut, all the valiant knights remained with Vivien; all together they struck straight ahead. Just as gold separates from silver, so all the good knights set themselves apart, and immediately they struck with their lances, all the worthy knights together, so that none could tell which was most valiant. At the first blow Count Thibaut turned and fled along the road leading to Bourges. At a crossroads where four ways met, there hung four robbers, face to face. The beam was low, the gallows-tree was short. Pulling on its reins, the horse carried him beneath it, and one of the corpses struck him on the mouth. When Thibaut saw this he was grieved and ashamed, for fear he shit all over his saddle-cloth and when he felt it was covered in filth, he raised his leg and dragged it out from under him. He called to Gerard who followed close behind: 'Friend Gerard, take this saddle cloth, it is worked with fine gold and precious stones, you would get a hundred pounds for it in Bourges.' But Gerard retorted: 'What should I do with it, covered with filth!'   [354]

29. Then spoke Gerard, the valiant youth: 'Lord Thibaut, listen to me a moment, and you shall tell them in the kingdom of Berry that I have stayed behind while you took to flight. I do not say that you will see me again alive, for I shall try to aid bold Vivien. He is my kinsman and I have little renown for that! I have buried a treasure deep in the earth, and I will tell you where it may be found, that after my death there may not be any quarrel about it.'   [364]

30. Then Thibaut did a very foolish thing: he pulled up his horse as Gerard had said. When the latter reached him he seized him by the neck with his hand and thrust him out of the saddle on the other side so that his helmet was sunk into the ground as far as the lacing. Then he put his hand to Thibaut's neck and took from him the great double shield. The golden

border was exceeding wide, the boss was made of Arabian gold. Vivien himself had won it from a Hungarian in the battle beside the Gironde when he killed the pagan Alderufe, and beheaded all the twelve sons of Burel. This great double shield he took from the king and gave it to Lord William, his uncle, who gave it to Thibaut the cowardly count. But now, today, a very worthy man will hang it round his neck! He took his hauberk which was strong and of double mail, and the good sword with cutting edge and point. [383]

31. Gerard armed himself with the weapons in the roadway. He abandoned the hackney and mounted the good horse. And Thibaut sat up like a man in a daze, saw the hackney in front of him and with the help of the stirrup pulled himself into the saddle. When he was mounted he remembered his flight. In front of him he saw a great fence, made of stout stakes, so that he could not pull one out, and so high he could not shake it. He did not dare venture into the valley for he could hear the cries of the Saracens. Up above on the hill he saw a flock of ewes and tried to make his way through the middle, so that a grey sheep caught on his stirrup. [397]

32. A grey sheep was stuck fast in his stirrup. He trailed it over hill and dale so that when Thibaut came to the bridge at Bourges there was only a sheep's head left in his stirrup. Never did gentleman bear such a strange trophy. Monday in the evening. The poor wretch had less to lose by it. [404]

33. Now I will tell you about young Gerard. As he returned along his way he saw Esturmi in front of him. He had treated his good horse so badly that it could hardly keep on its feet. Esturmi was trying to get a great speed out of it. When Gerard saw him he addressed him thus: 'What is the matter, Sir Esturmi?' He replied: 'Take heed and flee.'—'Turn again and renew the attack; if you do not return, you will soon lie dead.'—'That will I not,' said Esturmi. 'You shall not go like this,' replied Gerard. He spurred his horse and attacked him in fine style, breaking his shield, piercing the hauberk and damaging three of the ribs in his side. On the end of the lance he was hurled down from the horse. When he had him down

on the ground he addressed him politely: 'Vile wretch, you are now mortally shamed. You will never boast now to Thibaut, your uncle, that if you flee no worthy men will stay behind. You will never have Count William or his nephew, Vivien, or any other worthy man. Monday in the evening. You will have neither William nor Vivien.'   [429]

34. Gerard went his way as fast as he could. He had a fine shield both inside and out. All the neck strap was plated in gold, so were the arm-straps and the whole front section. No finer man did Jesus ever bring to an army than Gerard appeared when he left Thibaut. He came to the battle as fast as he could, and struck a pagan on the back of his byrnie. His strong lance thrust through the spine, so impaled he threw him down dead. He shouted 'Mountjoy' that is our war-cry. Then he struck another on his double shield, split it across from one edge to the other, cut the arm that was thrust through the straps, pierced the chest and cut through the heart, so that his great spear thrust through the spine and brought him down dead on the ground. He shouted 'Mountjoy', the war-cry of Strongarm. Monday in the evening. In their grievous plight they observed him.   [449]

35. The valiant Vivien summoned his barons: 'Strike, lords, with your five swords! Strike, Frenchmen, break through this throng! I have heard Louis or William. If they have arrived the skirmish will not last long.' The Frenchmen struck out with their good swords and made their way through the grievous throng till they recognized Gerard. Gladly they called to him.   [457]

36. Then the valiant Vivien spoke to him: 'Since when have you been a knight, cousin Gerard?'—'Lord,' he replied, 'quite recently. Not very long since.'—'Do you know what has become of Lord Thibaut, Gerard?' And he told Vivien what he had done to him. 'Silence, Gerard, my friend,' said the count. 'Let not your tongue speak shame of any nobleman.   [464]

37. 'Come over here, Gerard, on my right hand. We will go together. Set forth your standard. If I have you, I fear no misfortune.' They joined battle and fought that day as barons,

two noble companions in arms they were, and they wrought great destruction among the pagans. Monday in the evening. Grievous is the field without Count William. [472]

38. Vivien gazed over the countryside and saw before him the proud company, France's best for fighting a great battle. Many of them he saw stretched on the ground. Then he wrung his hands and tore his hair and beard, tears sprang to his eyes and ran down his face. Greatly did he regret William Strongarm. 'Ah, noble marquis, why are you not in the battle? Sorely have we missed your fair person today and these noble men have suffered much harm from it. [482]

39. 'Noble followers, by the power of our Lord, be not dismayed, my noble lords and brothers. We will wait here for my lord William, for if he comes, we shall win the struggle.' Monday in the evening. Alas for the fight begun without William! [488]

40. On the hill top, thirty horns sounded the alarm. Seven hundred men mounted guard, not one but had a bloodstained sword, with which he had struck great blows in the field. And before they departed they would strike many more. Vivien wandered over the hill top, and saw three hundred men from his domain. Not one but had his bridle bloodstained and a crimson saddle between his thighs. They held up their entrails before them with their hands, that the horses might not trample upon them. When he saw them, he addressed them together. 'My noble brothers, what can I do for you? No man on earth could bring you a surgeon. [502]

41. 'My noble lords, I beg you, for the love of God, why should you go and die in your beds? Who will wreak vengeance for your friends? There is not a man in Louis's kingdom who would be able to make peace, or a truce with your sons, if he had treated you so ill; no mound or palisade, castle, tower or ancient moat would save him from death by their swords. Let us avenge ourselves therefore, while we yet live.' Then they replied: 'As you will, noble marquis!' They took their arms and sallied forth on their horses down the hill to meet the enemy. Then they began to fight vigorously again.[6] [516]

42. The French came down from the height on which they had
been standing, to the grassy meadows, and saw their fellows
dead and wounded. Then you might see the skilful young men
tying up wounds and bandaging their sides.The man with a
wounded arm would cut the shaft of his spear and lash it
together so he could carry it. They drank the wine they found
on the field and those who had none drank muddy water; the
whole men gave it to the wounded, the man without a lord
gave it to his equal. Then they left the living and turned to the
dead.   [528]

43. They found seven hundred of their fellows, their entrails
trailing between their feet, brains coming out of their mouths
and running down the shields on to the grass; their faces were
contorted and their cheeks pale, their eyes turning back in
their heads, they moaned and cried as their souls departed
from them. When they saw them they addressed them thus:
'Noble lords, what will become of you? No man on earth
could bring you a surgeon.'   [538]

44. 'Now my lords, I beg you for the love of God,' said Vivien.
'You see there the wicked Arabs who have killed your sons and
your brothers, your dear friends and nephews. They do not ask
for peace or seek a truce. Let us avenge the dead while we yet
live. For St Stephen and the other martyrs were no better than
all these who have died for God in the Archamp.' And they
replied: 'Forward, then, noble marquis.' They went back to
their horses, remounted and rode to the field. They attacked
again, striking with great vigour. They slew fifteen thousand
Saracens.   [552]

45. The pagans assailed them in a fearful battle, of ten
thousand men they left but a hundred. Well may the noble
knight lament who led ten thousand men into battle and of the
ten thousand has now but a hundred knights, full half of them
wounded. Such a man is the warrior, Vivien.   [559]

46. 'Lord Vivien, what shall we do, in God's name?' And he
replied: 'We shall defeat them indeed. Let us call on God to
send us aid, that He may send me William, my lord, or that
Louis the emperor may come.' And they replied: 'By the

grace of God.' Vivien struck straight ahead of them, casting down a thousand Saracens dead in the skirmish. The pagans troubled him very sorely, so that of the hundred only a score remained and they went aside to the cleft of a mountain. [570]

47. 'Lord Vivien, in God's name what shall we do?'—'I can say nothing else but fight on, for we may well defeat them with the help of God.' And they replied: 'He has quite forgotten us.' Some of them said that he was mad to lead twenty men into a battle against five hundred thousand fully-armed pagans. 'If they were pigs or wild boars we could not kill them all in a whole month.' But Vivien said: 'I know your views, you are thinking of the vineyards and fields, castles and cities, and your wives at home. A man who is thinking so will never fight boldly. Go your ways, lords, with my good will. I shall remain here on the bitter field and never turn back, for I have promised God that I will never flee from the field of battle. I shall truly conquer with the help of God. [589]

48. 'Now, lords, I beg you, in God's name. Why should you go to die in your beds? Behold there the maimed and noble knights. As long as they were safe and sound and living, they held the field with us. You know very well what you have promised them, and no-one should be forsworn to the dead. Go your way and I will remain; I shall not depart, for I promised God never to flee for fear of death.' At his words the French all left him except Gerard alone who stayed by him. Thus they remain in grievous peril to continue the battle with only two shields. Monday in the evening. Two shields alone were left on the field. [605]

49. The French went away round the spur of a hill and gazed before them at the fair open plains: nowhere could they see a patch of ground that was not covered with the vile enemy; everywhere swords and helmets gleamed. When the French saw that the way was blocked so that they would never pass through the great host, they rode back to Vivien and when they reached the count they cried out to him: 'Lord Vivien, do you know what we are going to do?'—'I will hear what you

have to say,' replied the count. 'If you turn to flee, then we will
flee, and if you fight we also will fight. Whatever you do, that
will we do also.'—'Great thanks to you, my lords,' said Vivien,
then he turned to his brother-in-arms, Gerard, and spoke to
him in French: [622]

50. 'Gerard, my friend, are you free from all wounds?'—
'Yes,' he answered, 'within and without.'—'Tell me, Gerard,
what is the state of your weapons?'—'In faith, lord, they are
good and sound, like the armour of a man who has fought hard
and, if need be, will fight again.' [628]

51. 'Tell me, then, Gerard, do you feel quite strong?' And he
replied he had never been better. 'Tell me, then, Gerard,
what of your horse?'—'He is fresh and fit and strong.'—
'Gerard, my friend, could I dare to ask you to go by night to
William for me? Go and say to my uncle, William, that he
should remember the field of Saragossa when he fought the
pagan Alderufe. As he well knows, the Hungarians had
defeated him when I arrived on the scene with three hundred
followers, and with a cry of "Mountjoy" I broke through the
press and won the battle for my uncle. I killed the pagan,
Alderufe, and slew all twelve of the sons of Burel. From the
king I took the great double shield, from a Hungarian I took it
that day and gave it to my uncle William, and he gave it to
Thibaut, the cowardly count. But now a worthy man has it
round his neck. By these signs, let him come to my aid. [649]

52. 'Cousin Gerard, tell him all without concealment, and
remind him of the city of Lympne, and the great port on the
edge of the sea and Fleury which I captured by force. Let him
come to my aid on this field of battle. [654]

53. 'Do you know what you must say to William the faithful?
Remind him of the campaign against King Turlen when I
made three and thirty sorties for him, and defeated more than
a hundred and fifty of the most powerful of the Saracen faith.
When Louis took to his heels and fled away, I came to the
mound with two hundred of my followers, and shouting
"Mountjoy" won the field for him. That day I lost my liege-
man Raher. Whenever I remember him, every hour of the day

weighs heavily upon me. Let him come to my help in this grievous plight. [665]

54. 'Do you know what to say to William, the good Frenchman? Remind him of the great battle at Orange, with Tibalt the pagan.' When the French vanquished him in the battle I came to the mound with Bernard of Brubant, he is my uncle, a most valiant lord, and as a companion I had Count Bertrand, one of the best of our great family. I cried "God help us", the Norman war-cry, and won this battle for him on the field and there I killed Tibalt the pagan. Let him come to my help in the Archamp and aid me in this grievous plight. [678]

55. 'Do you know what to say to my young brother, Guy? Until he is fifteen he should not gird on a sword, but now he may gird it on for his mother's son's sake. Let him come to my aid in this foreign land. [682]

56. 'Do you know what to say to my dear lady Guibourg? Remind her of the care with which she nurtured me for fifteen years and more. Let not that care for God's sake be wasted. Let her send me her lord to help me, for if she does not send the count there is no-one I want.' [688]

57. 'Alas!' said Gerard, 'I leave you most unwillingly.'—'Do not speak thus, for it is to save me.' Then the two dear friends were parted, with great sorrow, and no smile or jest, but tenderly weeping, both of them. Monday in the evening. God, why did they part on this grievous field? [695]

58. Gerard set off round the curve of the hill. For five leagues there was such a thronging mass that he could not proceed a single yard without unhorsing a Saracen, and cutting off a foot, a hand or a head. And when he came through the grievous throng, his good horse foundered beneath his saddle. [702]

59. When Gerard set off from the grievous field, his horse foundered and fell beneath him. For fifteen leagues the countryside was ravaged by fear and he found no-one to speak to, no horse that he could ride. On foot he set off from the grievous field. The day was as hot as a summer's day in May, with long hours of light. For three days he had not eaten and

his thirst was almost unendurable, yet for fifteen leagues he found no stream or ford, nothing but the salt water of the nearby sea. Then his arms began to weigh on him and Gerard began to rebuke them severely.   [715]

60. 'How you weigh on my arm, great lance. This will be no help to Vivien who is fighting a hopeless battle in the Archamp.' Then Gerard threw it away in a field.   [719]

61. 'How you weigh on my neck, great shield. This will not save Vivien from death.' He unslung it from his back and flung it in the field.   [722]

62. 'How you make my head ache, good helmet. This will not help Vivien who is fighting the hosts on the grass of the Archamp.' He cast it from him and threw it to the ground. [726]

63. 'How you weigh me down, great byrnie. This will be no help to Vivien who is fighting a hopeless battle in the Archamp.' He took it off and threw it away. The noble man threw away all his arms except the steel-bladed sword, which was all crimson from pommel to point, while the scabbard was filled with liver and blood. He carried it unsheathed, leaning upon it with the point on the ground. All day he wandered across the plain running heavily down the great valleys, climbing nimbly up the high hills with his naked sword held in his right hand, leaning as he went on the pointed blade. He would bring William news from the Archamp, where Vivien was fighting a grievous battle, left in the Archamp with a mere score of men. Vivien attacked straight before him, and slew a thousand Saracens on the field.   [746]

64. Count Vivien had lost ten men of his score, and the rest asked him, 'Comrade, what shall we do?'—'Fight on, my lords, in God's name. You know that I have sent Gerard for help. Soon William will come, or Louis. Whichever it is, we shall conquer the Arabs.' Then they replied: 'That is good tidings, noble marquis.' With his ten men he returned to the attack, but the pagans overwhelmed him so mightily that not one of his ten men was left alive, and he had but his own shield

left in the battle. Monday in the evening. With his own shield alone, he was left in the throng.   [759]

65. When he was left with only one shield, he rushed at them repeatedly, and with his lance alone he struck down a hundred. Then the pagans said, 'He will never be beaten while his horse still bears him. We shall never conquer this noble warrior while we leave his horse alive.' Then they hunted him over the valleys and hills like any wild beast brought to bay. A company of men attacked him in an open place and hurled sharp darts and javelins at him. So many struck his horse's body that the shafts alone would have filled a cart. A knight from Barbary rode out of a valley, a swift horse between his thighs, bearing a sharp spear in his right hand. Three times he brandished it, the fourth time he flung it, striking his hauberk on the left side so that thirty links fell from the mail. The spear made a great wound in his body and the white banner fell from his right hand. The time never came when he could retrieve it. Monday in the evening. The time never came when he picked it up from the ground.   [783]

66. He put his hand to his side and pulled the spear out of his body; he struck the pagan on the back of his byrnie, thrust the spearhead right through his spine and with the blow cast him down dead. 'Ha! villain, evil Berber,' said the young Vivien, 'you will never go back again to your kingdom, never boast on any occasion that you have slain the warriors of Louis.' Then he drew his sword and began to strike out. Whether the blow fell on hauberk or helmet it carried through to the ground without stopping. 'Holy Mary, Virgin and Maiden, send me, Lady, Louis or William.' This was Vivien's prayer in the battle.[8]   [799]

67. 'O Lord, King of Glory, who gave me life and were, yourself, born of the Holy Virgin. In three Persons was your Being made. You suffered on the holy Cross for sinners. You made the heaven and earth, the land and sea, sun and moon, all was your commandment. You made Adam and Eve also, to people the world. As truly, Lord, as you are true God, defend me by your holy goodness, that it may never enter my heart to flee

even one foot though I lose my life. Grant that I may be
faithful even unto death, O Lord, by your holy goodness.
[812]

68. 'Holy Mary, Mother of God, as truly as you bore God as
your Son, save me by your holy mercy that these evil Saracens
may not kill me!' When he had spoken thus, the knight
repeated: 'Truly that was a stupid, foolish thought, to seek to
save myself from death, when the Lord God Himself did not,
who suffered death upon the Cross to save us from our deadly
foe. I do not ask you, Lord, to save me from death, since you
did not save yourself from it. Send me then, Lord, William
Hooknose, or Louis who has all France to care for, with his aid
we will win the battle. O God, in how many ways may one
man resemble another! Not that I am thinking of William
Hooknose. I am very strong and bold and may well be his
equal as a warrior, yet he has won renown further afield and if
he had been at the Archamp by the sea he would have won the
battle. Alas! sinner that I am, I can do no more. Monday in
the evening. What do these infidels ask of me now?' [837]

69. The heat was as great as on a summer's day in May. The
hours were long and he had not eaten for three days, so that he
suffered greatly from hunger and unbearable thirst. Bright
blood ran from his mouth and from the wound in his left side.
The streams were far off and he could not find them; for fifteen
leagues there was no spring or stream except the salt water
which came from the sea, but through the plain there ran a
muddy trickle which flowed from a rock beside the sea. The
Saracens had fouled it with their horses, and blood and brains
were mingled with it. That way Vivien the noble came run-
ning, and bending down to the brackish water he drank deeply
from it as he wished. As he crouched there on the shingle they
hurled their sharp lances at him. Their great blows could not
pierce his hauberk, whose strength protected most of his body,
but he received more than twenty wounds in his legs and arms
and the rest of his body. Then he rose up like a fierce boar, and
drawing his sword that hung at his left side, Vivien defended
himself very valiantly, while they harassed him like hounds at
a fierce boar. The water he had drunk was salt from the sea

and he could not keep it down but vomited it out through mouth and nose. Great was his anguish and his sight was troubled so that he could not see his way clearly. The pagans began to press him hard, then warriors attacked him from every side, casting spears and sharp steel javelins. They broke off so many bits of his shield that he could not raise it to cover his head but let it fall to the ground at his feet. Then the pagans pressed him more fiercely and his valour was sorely tried. [876]

70. They threw at him darts and sharp spears which beat on every side of the count's hauberk. The sharp steel cut through the slender iron rings of the mail that covered his body. His entrails hung down to the ground. There is no man who could longer endure it. Then he prayed to God to have mercy upon him. [883]

71. Vivien wandered over the plain, his helmet falling over the nosepiece and his entrails dropping at his feet. With his left arm he held them up while in his right hand was a steel sword, crimson stained from pommel to point. The scabbard was filled with liver and blood. He leant upon it, with the point to the ground. His death was now close upon him and still he held himself upright on his sword. Earnestly he prayed to almighty Jesus to send him William the noble warrior, or Louis, the king strong in battle: [896]

72. 'True God of Glory, reigning in Trinity, you who were made flesh of the Virgin. In three Persons was your Being ordained and you let yourself suffer on the holy Cross. Defend me, Father, by your holy goodness, that it may never enter my heart to flee a foot from the field of battle. Grant I may be faithful unto death, let me not weaken, God, of your goodness. Send to me, Lord, William Hooknose. He is experienced on the field of battle and well knows how to maintain and keep it. [908]

73. 'Lord God, mighty and glorious Father, never let it come to pass that it should enter my heart to flee even a foot for fear of death.' A man from Barbary came along a valley, riding a swift horse on a loose rein. He struck the valiant warrior on the

head so that his brains were spilled. The man from Barbary came up at a gallop, a great warhorse between his thighs, and in his right hand a sharp steel dart. He struck the noble knight on the head so that his brains ran down to the ground, and the knight fell on his knees. A shameful thing it was when such a warrior fell. The pagans rushed at him from all sides and cut him down so that he fell on the shingle. They carried him away with them and laid him under a tree near the path. They did not want to leave him where the Christians could find him. Now I shall tell of Gerard the squire who went to carry the news to William. Monday in the evening. At Barcelona he will tell it to Count William. [932]

74. Count William was at Barcelona, having just returned from a long campaign at Bordeaux on the Gironde, where he had lost the greater part of his men. Then Gerard arrived to tell him the news.[9] [937]

75. The noble William had come back from vespers and was standing by a window in the solar with the lady Guibourg at his right hand. He looked up the slope of a hill and saw Gerard returning from the Archamp. In his right hand was his blood-stained sword with the point to the ground, he leaned on it as he walked. [944]

76. 'Sweet lady,' said William Hooknose, 'it was a good day when I took you to wife and a better day when you became a Christian. I see a man coming down the hill with a blood-stained sword in his hand. I can tell you for certain that he has been in a great fight and is coming to me for help. Let us go and meet him and hear his news.' Then Guibourg and William Hooknose hurried down the steps and met Gerard at the bottom. When William saw him he recognized him at once and began to question him, saying: [958]

77. 'Come hither, Gerard, and tell us your tidings.' Then said Gerard: 'They are very evil. King Desramed has set out from Cordova and put to sea with his fleet. He has landed in France and is pillaging everywhere, laying waste the border lands and overrunning the marches, using the whole region as he likes. He is taking your knights prisoner wherever he finds them and

leading them off, raging and lamenting, to his ships. Take steps, William, to aid your men.   [968]

78. 'King Desramed has left his own country and come to this land which he is now laying waste. Thibaut and Esturmi went there to meet him and with them the valiant Vivien. Two of them fled but one is still fighting.'—'God,' said William, 'that is valiant Vivien.'—'Indeed, you speak truly,' answered Gerard, 'and he has sent to you, as I tell you, to ask for your aid in this grievous need.   [977]

79. 'Do you know what message Vivien, your liegeman, sends you? That you should recall the campaign against King Turlen, when he made three and thirty sorties for you, defeating more than a hundred and fifty men. When Louis took to his heels and fled away, he came to the mound with two hundred Frenchmen, shouting "Mountjoy" and won the day for you. That day he lost his liegeman, Raher. Whenever he recalls him, every hour of the day weighs heavily upon him. Go to his aid in his grievous plight.   [987]

80. 'Do you know what message noble Vivien has sent you? That you should remember the city of Lympne and Breher the great sea port and Fleury which he captured by force. Come to his aid in the Archamp by the sea.   [992]

81. 'Do you know what message he sends to his dear lady, Guibourg? That she should recall how carefully she nurtured him for fifteen years and more. Let not that care, for God's sake, be wasted but send him her lord to help him now. For if she does not send him, there is no-one he wants.   [998]

82. 'Do you know what message he sends to Guy, his young brother? Until he is fifteen, he should not bear a sword. But let him now gird one on for his mother's son's sake and come to his aid in a foreign land.'   [1002]

83. 'O God,' said William, 'shall I find him alive?' But Guibourg replied: 'Such talk is useless. Go to his help, my lord, without asking questions. If you lose him, you will have no friend left but God.' When William heard this, he bowed

his head and wept soft and piteously. The warm tears trickled
down past his nose, and wet his white beard right through to
his baldric. He spoke to Guibourg, pretending to remonstrate
with her for the baron wanted to test her feeling and see how
much she loved him and his kin. Then he spoke as a sensible
man: 'Sweet lady, for God's sake, it is not yet three days since
I came back from the fierce battle which I fought at Bordeaux
by the sea. There I lost my noble warriors. The lands under
my rule are far away, and mighty the host I would have to
muster. What is more I could not endure it myself, steel and
iron could be used in vain there. Vivien the noble is a valiant
fighter; I cannot heed his call this time, but he is quite able to
win without me.' Then Guibourg began to weep sorely, she
bowed down and kissed his shoe. She spoke to William and
remonstrated with him. 'Help him, lord. You must not tarry,
and I will commend my nephew Guischard to you. Thanks to
you he has been knighted.   [1032]

84. 'William, my lord, I put Guischard in your care. He is my
nephew, and very close kinsman. Thanks to you he was
knighted the day before yesterday. If you do not restore him to
me you will never lie in my arms again.' He promised her, but
greatly repented it, that he would bring back her nephew,
dead or alive. In the battle Guischard renounced God.
Monday in the evening. In the battle he renounced the God of
Heaven.   [1041]

85. Guibourg herself brought water to Gerard and afterwards
offered him a towel. Then sat him down at the top table and
brought him a shoulder of boar. The count took it and ate it
quickly, she brought him a great bread-cake made of fine flour
and after that a great mazer of wine. Gerard ate the great leg
of pork and in two draughts emptied the mazer, without
offering any to Guibourg, or looking up or lifting his head.
When Guibourg saw this she said to William, 'By God, my
lord, he is one of your kinsmen! He has eaten a great leg of
pork and in two draughts drunk a gallon of wine. He should
certainly give his neighbour a hard fight and never basely
desert the field!'—'For God's sake, Guibourg,' retorted
William, 'he was in great need of all he has taken, for more

than three days he has eaten nothing.' The bed was ready and
they made Gerard rest. Monday in the evening. The bed was
ready and they made Gerard rest. [1064]

86. Gerard stood up and rose from the table. The bed was
ready and he went to lie down. The noble Guibourg willingly
attended on him and stayed at his side until he was sleeping,
then commended him to the care of almighty God. Gerard
slept until it was evening, then the worthy man leapt from bed,
crying 'Mountjoy' and 'Knights, to horse!' He asked for
arms and they were brought to him and before anything else
Gerard was knighted. [1074]

87. They dressed him in a splendid hauberk and laced a green
helm on his head. William girded on the sword on his left side,
and he took a great shield by the arm-straps. He had a good
horse, of the best in the land, and Gerard mounted by the left
hand stirrup while the lady Guibourg held the right one for
him and then commended him to God, the great Father.
[1082]

88. As evening drew on in the fair city, then William Hook-
nose set out with thirty thousand armed knights, to seek the
pagan Desramed in the Archamp. They rode all night in the
cool darkness and came next morning as day was breaking to
the Archamp beside the sea. Desramed had won the battle,
taken the booty and stripped the armour from the dead. The
Saracens had embarked in their ships, in their galleys and
armoured transports. The wind had dropped and they could not
set sail, so the lords and the leaders and peers went to survey
the dry land a great league beyond the coastal shingle. Behold
now, William, the wise in counsel, with thirty thousand
knights in arms. Fifteen thousand of them were already pre-
pared to fight in a field of battle. They shouted 'Mountjoy'
and went to attack them but the pagans could not stand against
them for they had no armour to protect their bodies. They all
fled towards the high seas and swarmed into the ships and
barges and boats; they took their arms and made themselves
ready. [1106]

89. These Saracens from the land of Segune were more than

a hundred thousand all furnished for war: not one but had both hauberk and helmet, with gilded visor and golden adornments. They girded on their swords with the polished blades hanging down and took the shields by the arm-straps. In their right hands they held sharp lances and their saddles were set on swift Arab coursers. They disembarked on the sandy shingle and set off towards the dry land beyond. Evil will be the tales told of them and the great war they made against Count William. The battle lasted all day Monday and the next day, and on Wednesday, without ever ceasing or an hour's respite; almost until prime on Thursday the French never stopped their fighting, nor did those from Arabia stop fighting. Not one of William's men was left alive on Thursday evening,[10] except for the three shields left in the battle.   [1128]

90. Three shields alone remained on the battle ground. One was Gerard, the valiant fighter, the other Guischard, Guibourg's nephew. Would you hear about these noble warriors and how they were separated from their worthy companions? [1133]

91. Would you hear of these noble fighters, how they were separated from the worthy knights? Gerard turned away on the left hand, his horse fell dead on a patch of sand, his hauberk adhering to his shoulders. Thirty pagans came down the valley, in thirty places they wounded the warrior, with darts and lances through his body, so that he cried out as death came to him. Then William came up to them there; ten he slew, and twenty fled the place. He came to Gerard and gently addressed him: [1145]

92. 'Gerard, my friend, if you were borne hence and your great wounds all bound up, do you think, noble friend, that you would be healed? Or do you think you are already on the threshold of Paradise?' Then Gerard answered: 'Lord, let me be. I do not want to be carried hence and have the great wounds in my body tended, for I cannot be healed by any mortal man. But if someone could help me on to my horse and fasten my green helmet for me again, hang round my neck my great bossed shield and put in my hand my keen-edged sword,

and then give me a draught of wine, or muddy water if wine is
lacking, then I will not die, by my faith in God, until they have
dearly paid for the wounds they gave me.' Then the blood
gushed forth in torrents and William said: 'You will not
linger.' Thursday in the evening. Count William dismounted
and stretched out his hand; taking Gerard's right hand he sat
him up on the grass, but his face was convulsed and his cheek
was pale, his eyes were rolling in their sockets and his head
lolled to the left as his helmet fell forward on to his chin. He
could not hold up his head for his soul had left him. And
William said: 'So must it be, Gerard!' O God, what grief
when such warriors are parted! There is no-one who would
not pity William.[11] [1175]

93. Would it please you to hear of Guibourg's nephew, who on
that day parted from William? His horse fell dead on a patch
of sand: his hauberk adhering to his shoulders. Thirty pagans
came down a hill and wounded the warrior in thirty places. He
cried out for help, like any fighter. Then the noble William
arrived, and slew ten pagans, while twenty fled from the hill.
He came to Guischard and thus addressed him: [1185]

94. 'Guischard, my friend, if you were borne hence and had
the great wounds in your body tended, do you think you would
enter Paradise?' Guischard replied, 'Lord, let me be. I do not
want to be carried hence to have the wounds in my body
tended. But if someone will help me on to my horse, I do not
want to bear your arms any longer. But give me a single
draught of wine or, if you have none, of muddy water. Then I
will go back to my birthplace, Cordova, and never more
believe in your God. I cannot worship what I have not seen,
and if I had implored Mahomet's favour I would never have
seen these wounds in my body.' Then the blood gushed forth
in a torrent, and William said: 'Dog, you were born in an evil
hour! While you yet had faith and goodness you followed holy
Christianity. Now you are slain and brought to destruction
and cannot move for very weakness. You will never be carried
from the field by me.' Thursday in the evening. Then Count
William bent down and stretching out his hand took his right
arm and pulled him up sitting next to the saddle. [1211]

95. A man from Barbary came galloping up the valley, a swift courser was between his thighs and in his right hand a cutting lance. Thrice he brandished it, the fourth time threw it and it struck in his left hip, a full span deep, so that Guischard fell dead against the count. His heavy body fell to the side but William pulled him up with his left arm and set him before him on the horse's neck. With his right hand he drew the lance from the body and struck the pagan on the shield, so hard that the force of the blow brought him down. William did not flee but went his way, with the dead Guischard before him. Thursday in the evening. Good Count William did not flee. [1228]

96. The lady Guibourg did not forget him. She knew that William Hooknose was fighting in the Archamp against the pagan Desramed. She sent out her messengers and summoned her liegemen until she had gathered thirty thousand. Fifteen thousand were all prepared, ready to fight on the battlefield. Guibourg selected all the overlords and sat them down to dine in the upper apartments; songs were sung to them and stories told to them, and Guibourg herself brought them wine. Then she leaned against a marble pillar and began to gaze out of the window. She saw William coming down the hill, carrying a dead man before him. Then she remembered Vivien the noble and from being happy she began to weep. 'By God, my lords, I have much to do. I see my lord coming down the hill, carrying a dead man before him leaning against his saddle-bow. It is Vivien. I know it well.'—'Hush, lady, do not say it is he.' Thus spake the lords of the kingdom. [1252]

97. 'For God's sake, my lords, whom else would William bring back from the fray, unless it were Louis, his lord, or Vivien the bold, his nephew?'—'Silence, lady, we will not say it is they, but rather that my lord William has a minstrel: in all France there is no better singer nor more bold warrior in the battle. He can declaim songs of the deeds of Clovis, the first emperor of fair France who believed in our Lord God, and of his son, Flovent the fighter, who renounced the fief of fair France; of all the kings worthy of note, up to the fighting Pepin the Short, of Charlemagne and his nephew Roland, Girard of Vienne and

the valiant Oliver. These were his forefathers and his kinsmen. He is very valiant, therefore my lord loves him, and just because he is so good a singer and in battle so valiant a fighter my lord has carried him back from the fray.' [1274]

98. 'Lords and noble vassals, for the love of God, I would beg you give me leave to go. He is my lord and I must go and attend to him.' She hastened down the steps to the door; she unbarred and opened it so that the count could enter. He looked at her and asked: 'My lady Guibourg, since when have you kept my door?'—'In truth, my lord, only now have I begun to do so. Indeed, my lord William, you have but a small company!'—'Sweet lady, since when have you been my porter?'—'In truth, my lord, quite recently, not for long. Lord William, you have few knights left!' [1287]

99. 'My lady Guibourg, this is your nephew Guischard, take him. You will never again see Count Vivien alive.' The noble woman held out her arms and he laid the dead warrior on them. The body was heavy and her arms gave way, for she was a woman and her body was weak, so that the corpse crashed to the ground and the tongue lolled out to one side. Thursday in the evening. Guibourg looked at him lying there on the ground. The face was convulsed and the cheeks were pale. The eyes were rolling in their sockets, the tongue hung right out to the left and the helmet had slipped down over his chin. Guibourg wept and William consoled her. [1302]

100. 'By God, Guibourg, you are right to weep. They used to say in the court of my lord the king, that you were the wife of William, a powerful man, bold count and valiant fighter. Now you are wife to a wretched runaway, a coward count, a miserable fugitive, who brings not one man home from the battle. Henceforth you will do your own cooking and baking, and never share the company of the proud barons. Never again will you see my nephew, Vivien. My joy is all gone, whatever others may feel, never again shall I have honour in this world!' Then William wept and Guibourg's tears flowed. When the lady heard her lord's lament, she put aside a part of her grief and spoke to him very lovingly. [1318]

101. 'Marquis William, I beg you, for the love of God. It is
grievous when a man must weep and piteous when he must
lament. It has been a custom in your great lineage that they
have often died in the field of battle seeking to conquer other
lands. It would be better for you to die in the Archamp by the
sea than for your kindred to be abased by you or your heirs to
be ashamed of you after your death.' When William heard
this, he hung his head and wept soft and gently. He spoke to
Guibourg, his wife and his love, and thus addressed her in his
French tongue: 'Sweet lady, I beg you, for the love of God.
Whatever others may feel, I have much cause to weep, for
more than three hundred and fifty years have passed since my
mother bore me. I am old and weak and cannot bear arms; the
long youth which God granted me has now all passed and will
not return. The pagans received me in most evil fashion: they
would neither flee nor give way before me. Desramed has won
the battle, taken the booty and stripped the armour from the
dead. The pagans have all embarked on their ships. The lands
which I rule are far away and mighty the host I would have to
muster, so that, if I returned to the Archamp by the sea, all the
pagans would have sailed away. Whatever others may suffer,
I am left alone, never again in this life to have honour.' [1349]

William wept and Guibourg consoled him: 'Now lord
marquis, I beg you, for the love of God! Give me your leave to
tell a lie, and I will have thirty thousand such men, fifteen
thousand fully fit and ready to fight in the field.'—'Where are
they, Guibourg, this you must tell me? Sweet lady, tell me the
truth in this matter.'—'Up there in the palace, sitting at
dinner!' Then the count laughed and left off weeping. 'Now
go, then, Guibourg, and tell your lie with my good will.' Then
she hastened back up the steps; she was weeping before but
now starts to sing. The knights looked at her and began to ask
questions: 'Guibourg, my lady, what did you find outside'?—
'By God, my lords, much to please me. For now has William
Hooknose returned, safe and sound by the mercy of God. He
has won the battle and killed the heathen Desramed! But one
matter has turned out badly: he has lost his valiant fighters, the
flower and beauty of fair France. They have slain the noble
Vivien—not in heathendom nor Christendom could be born a

better warrior, to uphold and maintain the law and exalt holy
Christianity. I beg you, in God's name, to go to the Archamp.
The barges are broken and the ships are shattered. The wind
has dropped and they cannot set sail. In a rocky place beside a
creek are ten thousand Saracens gathered together and with
them all the gold and silver, for they took the booty and
stripped the armour from the dead. My lord was alone and
could stay no longer. Everyone who goes to the Archamp by
the sea will be able to take these things of which I have told
you, and my lord has also many a broad fief, which he will
willingly and gladly give you.   [1389]

102. 'If anyone does not want lands without a wife, I have yet
a hundred and sixty maidens, all kings' daughters and the
fairest in the land. I have cared for them, thanks to William,
they work fine needlework for me, silk cloth embroidered with
flowers and circles. Come with me and choose the fairest. I will
give you a wife and my lord will give you land if you fight well
and are worthy of praise.' Then the one who hastened to choose
the fairest, later lost his life in the Archamp. Thursday in the
evening. Guibourg herself brought water for her lord.   [1401]

103. Then she seated him at one of the lower tables—because
of his grief he would not go to the top one—and brought him a
haunch of boar meat. The baron took it and began to eat
quickly, as he could do for it was tender. She brought a great
loaf of fine bread and in addition two baked bread-cakes; then
she brought him a great roasted peacock and also brought him
a great bowl of wine which she could scarcely carry with both
hands. William ate the fine bread and afterwards the two
baked bread-cakes. He ate the whole of the great leg of pork
and drank a gallon of wine in two draughts and finished off the
two baked bread-cakes without offering Guibourg even a
crumb or looking up or raising his head. When Guibourg saw
this she bowed her head and smiled though tears still flowed
from her eyes. She spoke to William in the French tongue and
said: 'Now by the glorious God who converted me and to
whom I, a sinner, will render my soul when comes the day of
the great Judgement, anyone who eats a loaf of fine bread and
yet does not leave the two baked bread-cakes and eats the

whole of a great leg of pork and after that a great roasted pea-
cock and in two draughts swallows a gallon of wine, should
certainly give his neighbour a hard fight; never will he shame-
fully run from the battlefield and his lineage will never be
shamed by him.'—'Sweet lady,' said William, 'for pity's sake.
If I should die who would defend my lands, for I have no heir
who could defend them?' [1435]

One of his nephews rose from his place by the fire, master
Guy, son of Lord Beuves Cornebut, and his mother was
daughter to the great Count Aymeri. He was nephew to
William, the good lord marquis and was brother to Vivien the
bold. He was very young, not yet fifteen, and had no beard, not
a single hair, except on his head that he was born with. He
stood up and came to his uncle and addressed him in the
following terms. 'By my faith, uncle,' said the young Guy, 'if
you should die I would defend your lands and faithfully serve
my lady Guibourg. She would never suffer anything I could
prevent, for she has brought me up most kindly.' When
William heard this he scolded the boy and replied to him very
harshly, saying: 'Scoundrel, you are better suited to sit among
the cinders than you are to rule my domain. [1454]

104. 'You are better suited, scoundrel, to stay by the fireside
than to try to rule my domain. You shall never have the care
of my wife, Guibourg.' When Guy heard this he answered
prudently: 'In faith, uncle, I never heard such a thing!'—
'Scoundrel,' said William, 'why do you blame me?'—'I will
tell you, but I want to think carefully; for the man is not wise
who gives free rein to his anger. Why should you criticize me
for being young? There is no great man who was not born
small. And by the Cross of God the most high, there is no man
in Christendom, I believe, nor in God's army, who might seize
your domain after your death, now the noble Vivien is dead,
whom I would not kill in open battle and then take possession
of your inheritance and I would take good care of my lady
Guibourg.' When William heard this he bowed his head and
wept soft and tenderly. He called the child to him and em-
braced him, thrice he kissed him and then said to him: 'In
faith, nephew, you have spoken wisely. You have a child's

body but the speech of a fighter. After my death, my fief will be yours. Take him, Guibourg, to your chimney corner.' Thursday in the evening. He was only fifteen but William gave him great lands. [1483]

105. Count William got up from the table and went to rest, for the bed was ready. The noble Guibourg gently caressed him. In all Christendom there was no wife fitter to serve and honour her lord, nor exalt holy Christianity nor uphold and maintain the rule of law. She stayed by his side till he was sleeping quietly and commended him to God the most high. Then she went back to the hall to talk to the warriors. William slept until it was evening then leapt from the bed like the lusty boar and cried: 'Mountjoy! To horse, brave warriors!' He demanded arms and they were brought him. [1492]

106. Then they armed him in a very fine byrnie and laced a green helm on his head. His sword was girt on with the blade hanging down and he took a great shield by the arm-straps and in his right hand a keen-edged lance. Then bowing down to the ground, Guibourg kissed his foot [12] and commended him to the great king of Heaven. [1504]

107. When evening had come to the fair city, William Hook-nose set off with thirty thousand armed knights to seek the heathen Desramed in the Archamp. Guibourg was left alone in the fair city. She took Guy with her into the solar, and Guy and Guibourg commended William Hooknose to the care of God as long as they could see him. When he was out of sight, Guy began weeping and when Guibourg saw it she asked him: 'Why are you weeping, Guy, my friend?'—'In faith, lady, I have good reason. I am only fifteen and so I am shamed and kept away from the battlefield. Who will give me a fief or domain unless I win it with a sword at my side? I see my lord going off over the hill, riding off to mortal battle so bereft he has with him not a single close friend, save God almighty, the Saviour of the world.' Then Guibourg replied: 'For God's sake, Guy! You are but a child of tender years. You could not undergo the hardships, watching by night and fasting by day, nor endure and suffer the fierce fighting. Also the count has

put you in my charge here, and not for any plea will I let you
go for fear of losing his love and favour.'—'I never heard such
a thing,' retorted Guy. 'I can tell lies and could tell him I had
escaped from you by force. And I tell you by my faith in God
and myself, unless I go to the Archamp by the sea, you will
never see William Hooknose again. But if I go, I will bring him
back with me.'—'Then I will let you go,' said Guibourg.
[1540]

108. Then they put on him a little byrnie and laced a little
helmet above it. The sword they girt on him was little but
good. Round his neck they hung a stout little shield and
brought him also a little lance with a good blade and sturdy
shaft; its pennant flowed down to his hand. Then Guibourg
brought him Balzan, her own palfrey, which she had never
lent to a warrior. The saddle was good but the leathers were
short and Guibourg held the stirrup while Guy mounted, and
commended him to God the Creator.   [1552]

109. Guy was small and the horse was large. He sat only a
foot and a half above the pommel and his spurs but three
inches below the saddle cloth, yet he bore arms better than a
man of thirty. Guy spurred Balzan and gave him his head. He
sat only a foot and a half above the saddle, his spurs but three
inches below the cloth. She commended him to God, the great
Father of Heaven. Guy spurred his horse towards the battle-
field.   [1561]

110. All night he rode, spurring his horse until the morning
dawned bright and clear. As soon as William came to the
Archamp by the sea he addressed his warriors; drawing the
leaders on one side to a council, he spoke to them in the French
tongue: 'My noble lords, now you must help me. I do not take
from you your hounds or hunting-dogs—rather if you want
them, I will give you mine. I do not ask for hawk nor falcon,
nor seek to do harm to any person. If the father is dead, I
cherish the son and do not allow anyone to distress the mother
nor any man-at-arms to seize her possessions. Rather I have
gladly brought up the son and kept him till I made him a
knight, and then restored to him the whole estate without

keeping any. Indeed, if it were small I have added to it from my own lands. Cursed be William if he ever had a penny from it. Now then today, succour your standard-bearer.' And all replied, 'Lord, most willingly; while we can still stand we will never fail you.' Monday in the evening. This is a lord from whom to hold land and, if need be, to die for in the battle. [1587]

111. Then William left the barons when they had pledged themselves and came next to the other leaders. He took them aside to a council and then addressed them in his French tongue: 'My noble lords and honoured vassals. Desramed has challenged us in this land; his pride must not triumph long nor must we allow or see him do so. For this reason, I tell you, noble and trusted warriors, that they have killed a man whom I mourn deeply, for they have slain the noble Vivien. From here to the Rhine or beyond the sea, in heathendom or Christendom, nowhere could a better warrior be found to uphold holy Christianity and support and maintain the rule of law. Therefore I tell you, noble and illustrious warriors, there is no man in Christendom could assemble so many and such fighters, save only Louis, the noble and honoured, who rules all France as rightful lord. I do not boast myself equal to him. [1609]

112. 'Now listen, noble and well-tried knights. No great battle can be well fought unless by the endurance of the warriors and the staying power of the young fighters, the strong and vigorous, the bold and famous.' Then he saw Guy standing among them and asked: 'Who is this little warrior I see sitting on his horse among you? Whoever brought him was very short of men!'—'Why do you ask us?' they replied. 'You ought to know your own nephew, Guy!' When William heard this he bowed his head and wept softly and tenderly, but then he began to criticize Guibourg harshly: 'May God curse my wife today. It is obvious, nephew, that you are nothing to her.' Hearing this, Guy replied prudently: 'In faith, my lord, you are wrong to blame her. You gave me into a woman's keeping and I escaped from her by force!'—'Wretch,' said the count, 'why do you blame me?'—'I will tell you, but let that wait a

little. Look at the heathen in the barges and ships there. They
have slain a man whom you must deeply mourn, for they have
killed the valiant Vivien. Let us turn your ill-will against
them!'—'In faith, nephew, you speak wisely; you have a
child's body but the speech of a valiant man. When I am dead
you shall have my fief. But one thing greatly troubles me; you
are but a child of tender years and cannot undergo the hard-
ships of watching by night and fasting by day, nor endure and
suffer the fierce fighting. But I will send you up on the hill
there with twenty of my men to guard you; thus I shall lose
them and gain nothing for they would have helped me on the
field of battle.'—'I never heard such a thing,' said master
Guy.   [1648]

'What are you blaming me for, nephew?' asked William. 'I
will tell you since you have asked me. Do you think God is so
forgetful that He can protect and guard the great man and not
do the same also for the weak? There is no man however great
who was not born weak. This very day I will strike so hard with
the sword at my side that my valour will be proved and my
honour and lineage kept from shame!' Then William said:
'You speak very wisely. Spur your horse and make him
gallop, so that I can see how you manage your arms.' Guy set
spurs to Balzan and gave him his head. His body rose only a
foot and a half above the saddle and his spurs were but three
inches below the saddle-cloth; he swept the lance over his left
arm so that the banner hung down to the ground then raised it
up, fluttering in the breeze. He brought Balzan up standing in
a distance of four feet with his tail dropping on the ground,
then turned his head straight towards his lord. William said:
'You certainly ought to be a knight, for so were your father
and your other kinsmen.   [1671]

113. 'Come, nephew Guy, on my right hand and carry your
standard next to mine, if I have you I fear no ill fortune.'
They joined battle and fought that day boldly, two noble
companions in arms in the battle, causing great dismay to the
pagans. Monday in the evening. If Guy had not gone there,
William would not have returned.   [1679]

114. Desramed had won the day when William Hooknose

was there before. He had taken the booty and stripped the corpses. The Saracens had embarked in their ships but the wind had dropped and they could not set sail. Twenty thousand of the pagans, the lords and the captains of Desramed's host had gone to survey the firm ground, a full league away from the shingle beach. They had taken their food with them and were seated in order at dinner when William came up to the meal with thirty thousand armed warriors, bringing them a cold collation. With a shout of 'Mountjoy' they charged against them and the pagans yelled 'To horse, brave warriors!' They leapt up from the tables and the battle was general. There only remained that which could not depart: a great supply of bread and meat and wine was left, with cloths and cushions and plate of gold. But the pagans could not sustain the attack and fled towards the deep water where they embarked on the ships and transports. Then they armed themselves and made ready for battle and returned to the dry land to fight them. [1704]

115. Count William had done very well then, and God had raised him to great honour, when Desramed leapt out on him from ambush with fifteen kings. I can tell you their names: Encas from Egypt and king Ostramai, Butifer the bold and Garmais the strong, Turlen of Dosturges and his nephew Alfais, Nubles of India and Ander the Persian, Aristragot, Cabuel and Morant, Clamador, Salvain and Variant, and the king of Nubia and the warrior Tornas. Each of them had a thousand men in his train, eaters of men, like dragons or leopards. They fought in battle without any concern; if one was struck down, another would lead them. Henceforth the French were in a grievous plight. Bertrand, William's nephew, was captured, and Guielin and the valiant count Giscard, Walter of Termes and Rainier the fighter. The Saracens and Persians bound them tightly and carried them off to the sloops before the count's very eyes, and he could do nothing to help them. All the French were taken or lay dead on the field, excepting William, who still fought boldly, and at his right hand was Guy his nephew. [1729]

116. Clear was the day and bright the morning, the sun's rays

flashing on the armour and striking the shield of master Guy, while the tears ran down his face. When William saw this, he began to question him: 'What is the matter, good nephew, Sir Guy?'—'I can soon tell you,' replied the youth. 'I rue the time when Guibourg brought me up so kindly and gave me food so early in the day. Now is the hour when she used to serve me and I am so hungry I shall die of it. I cannot hold or wield my arms, flourish my lance or control Balzan. I can neither help myself nor do harm to another. I shall soon die, which is grief and danger. God, how my friends will miss me! I am so ravenous it is driving me mad. I would like to be in my lady's service now! My heart fails and my valour has gone. I can neither help myself nor do harm to another. I cannot carry or handle my weapons. I shall soon die, which is grief and peril. [1751]

117. 'My eyes, uncle, are growing weak, my arms are failing so I cannot help myself, for I am so ravenous I shall soon go mad. Alas! that Guibourg, your noble wife, used to give me food so early in the day. Soon I shall die, it is grief and peril. God, how the knights will miss me! I would live if I could but eat something.'—'God, where can I find something?' William replied. Monday in the evening. Would to God that William had bread and wine then! 'Uncle William, what shall I do? My heart fails me. I pledge you my word, that I cannot hold and wield my weapons nor spur on or rein my horse. If I die it is grief and peril, for scarcely one of my kin will be left.'— 'Nephew,' said William, 'I am much beset. Could you find your way to the farmland, where we found the pagans on Monday, where they were sitting eating? What could not run away is still there!'—'What is that, uncle?'—'Bread and meat and wine! Go there, nephew,' said the marquis, 'eat some bread and drink a little wine. Then come to my help in this grievous plight. Do not forget me, for I am relying on you.' Then William and Guy parted. [1779]

118. Then it was Wednesday. When young Guy turned aside across the fields to the farm for food, the pagans pursued him on their horses but he soon outdistanced them and was beyond their reach. When the pagans saw that they could not catch

him, they let him go, with the curse of Mahomet: 'He is on the
same errand that Gerard was on when he brought William
against us here. This one is going to France, for King Louis.
Let us turn back to the fearful struggle, nobody there will
come back alive.' Then they galloped towards Lord William,
but Guy went straight towards the farmland, then dismounted
from the saddle. He ate some bread, but only a little and
quickly drank a great gallon of wine. Then he remounted and
set off on his way back. The pagans came, both Turks and
Saracens, and attacked the Marquis William. When Count
William saw them coming, he cried: 'Mountjoy!' and attacked
them swiftly, slaying sixty of them with his lance alone. The
pagans hemmed him in on all sides and hurled their lances at
him, darts and javelins and keen-edged spears, so that his
horse, Liard, fell dead beneath him. Now the noble warrior
was on foot but he drew his sword and fought back valiantly.
[1808]

119. When the pagans had surrounded him, they hurled
lances at him and keen-edged spears; so many struck on the
edge of his quartered shield that he could not raise it above his
head. They forced the knight down on to the ground so that
his whole body was on the beach. They gave him great blows
with spears and lances but could not break the links of his
stout byrnie. The blood was running down his neck and he
cried out and shouted: 'Guy, fair nephew, come and aid me as
you are a knight.' The youth was on his way back from eating
and clearly heard the cry below him.   [1821]

120. As young Guy was coming down the hill he heard
William cry out in the struggle; he struck a pagan on his new
double shield and split it through, breaking it to pieces, then he
rent and tore the good hauberk and brought him down dead
from his horse. Guy cried: 'Mountjoy! Are you alive, uncle
William?' then he struck another on his new shield and split it
through, breaking it to pieces. Then he rent and broke the
hauberk, pierced the breast under the full surcoat and hurled
him down dead from the saddle. He cried: 'Mountjoy! Are you
alive, uncle William?' Then he struck a third on the double
shield splitting it as far as the boss so that the pieces struck on

his throat; he put his great spear through to the ground beyond so that the backbone was broken and splintered and the pennon appeared between his shoulders behind, so that when the wretch fell, the shaft was broken. By this blow he showed his good lance. [1842]

121. Guy drew his sword, then he was a knight. He raised the point high in the air and struck a pagan on his helmeted head, cutting and splitting down to the nose piece, so that he broke the skull. The blow was mighty and Guy was angry. He cleft him further down to the baldric, cut the saddle and the back of the warhorse into four pieces there on the field. The pagans were much dismayed at the blow and said to each other: 'It is a thunderbolt falling. Vivien the warrior has returned.' They took flight and left the battlefield. Then William stood up again on his feet, for Count William had become a foot soldier. [1857]

122. Our Lord wrought a great miracle at this time for twenty thousand men were put to flight by one. The Saracens made straight for the sea and William the marquis got to his feet and they pursued them with sharp-edged swords. [1862]

123. As the pagans fled towards the sea, the noble William got to his feet and they pursued them with naked swords. Guy saw his uncle crossing the field on foot and spurred his horse over to meet him. 'Mount on this horse, my lord,' he said. 'My lady Guibourg freely lent it to me.' Guy got down and William mounted. When he was up he began to speak: 'In faith, nephew, you are acting the fool! The other day you told me you had escaped from her. Now you tell me she lent you her horse! Who bade you accuse my wife?'—'I never heard such a thing!' retorted Guy. 'Spur straight on to the sea or the Saracens will have gone already.' [1879]

124. The noble William rode across the field, with drawn sword and bowed helmet. His feet hung down below the boy's stirrups so that the irons beat against his calves. He held the sword between the blade and the hilt, balancing it flat on the pommel before him, and Balzan carried him along at an easy pace. His nephew, Guy, followed him on foot, sometimes up to

his knees in blood. King Desramed was lying in the midst of
the field covered in blood and sand, but William recognized
him when he saw him. The king thought William had taken
such a wound from a spear that he would not be able to defend
himself against anyone. Then he had a bold idea. He got to his
feet and seizing his courser removed the hobble rein from the
right forefoot. He took his lance which was stout and keen,
leapt from the ground straight on to his courser and spurred
directly towards them. [1899]

125. The noble William saw the pagan approach, covering his
body and brandishing his lance, so he held his sword out before
his face. Then the Saracen king looked at him and slowed
down from a gallop to a walk. 'Uncle William,' said his young
nephew, Guy, 'I beg you of your mercy, lord, give me back
my Arab steed and I will joust against this vile Saracen.
[1908]

126. 'Uncle, lord, do me a favour! Of your goodness give me
back my horse so that I may attack this pagan from beyond
the sea.'—'Nephew,' said William, 'you talk like a fool when
you dare demand the first blow from me. No-one has ever done
that from the first day I ever bore arms. Not even my noble
lord, Louis, would do that to me. If I could give him a blow
with my sword, I would be avenged on this pagan from over
the sea.' Then it was Wednesday. Desramed advanced slowly.
William struck the pagan on the helmet and shore off the right
side of it. The force of the blow bent Desramed forward so that
he clung to the horse's neck and the reins. As good Count
William passed him, he cut through his thigh to the saddle, so
that the trunk fell to the ground on the other side. Then good
Count William stretched out his hand and seizing the swift
charger by the rein he brought him to his nephew, Guy, and
spoke to him. [1929]

127. The Saracen lay on the ground and saw William leading
away his good horse and began to lament for it very greatly:
'Alas! my steed, whom I loved so much! I brought you from
the sea-shore and he who now owns you cannot look after you
properly, nor care for you, bleed you, nor shoe you.'—

'Wretch,' said William, 'leave this harangue and consider
how to heal your thigh and I will consider how to look after
the good horse.' He came to Guy and presented it to him.
[1940]

128. The Saracen was full of bitterness: 'Ah! my steed, my
good warhorse. Alas for your fine body and splendid paces!
You have brought me to the place where I have lost my leg. I
have won so many battles on you; no better horse exists under
these skies. Heathendom will feel the loss bitterly.'—'Wretch,'
said William, 'I care nought for your speeches!'   [1948]

129. The noble William crossed the field leading the good
horse on the right. He called Guy and presented it to him:
'Fair nephew, mount this horse, lend me yours, I pray you,
and you ride the one that belonged to Desramed. For the one
I am riding suits me very well.'—'Good uncle, my lord, do me
a favour, of your kindness give me back my saddle and take
the one on Desramed's horse.'—'That I will do gladly,' said
William, and dismounted to change the saddles.   [1960]

130. While William was changing the saddles, Guy saw the
king struggling on the ground. He drew his sword and cut off
his head. This made William very angry. 'Vile wretch, how
dare you attack a crippled man. You will be blamed for this in
the high court.'—'I never heard such a thing,' retorted Guy.
'Even if he had not got a foot to walk on, he still had eyes to
see and genitals to beget children. He would have had himself
carried back to his country and we would have seen
Desramed's heirs coming thence to work us evil in this land.
One should free oneself completely.'—'Nephew,' said William,
'you speak very wisely. You have a child's body but a warrior's
sense. After my death you will hold my lands.' Then it was
Wednesday. Now William had won his battle.   [1980]

131. Count William rode across the field, very angry and full
of bitterness. He broke the laces of his gleaming helmet and
rode bowed towards the ground, with his fair pennon stained
with blood. Guy rode on his right hand, at a distance. He
found many of his people slain and by a pool he found Vivien.
He lay by a spring of noisy waters under the shade of a very

great olive tree, his white hands crossed on his side. He smelled more sweetly than any balm or spices. Fifteen great wounds were in his body, the least of which would have slain an emir, a count or a king, however mighty. Then he lamented very sadly: 'Ah! Vivien, my lord, alas for your boldness, your valour and might and your wise counsel! Since you are dead, I have no good kinsman, nor will not have in the whole of my life. [2000]

132. 'Vivien, lord, alas for your fair youth, your noble body and tender cheek! I dubbed you knight in my palace at Termes. For love of you, I gave away a hundred swords, a hundred helmets and a hundred new shields. Now I see you here dead in the battle in the Archamp with wounds in your body and in your white breast, and with you those others who died in the battle. May the true Father have mercy upon them, he who dwells on high and rules us here below.' [2010]

133. The noble William found Count Vivien beside the spring with its clear flow of water, under the shade of a very great olive tree. Fifteen great wounds were in his body, the least of which would have slain an emir. Then he lamented him sweetly and softly. 'Vivien, lord, alas for your boldness, and the great valour which God had given you! It is but a short time since you were knighted. You swore then an oath to the Lord God that you would never flee on the field of battle and you did not want to break your word to God. Now therefore you are dead, hacked and slaughtered. Tell me, fair lord, can you speak and recognize the Body of the most high God? If you believe that He was slain on the Cross, I have consecrated bread in my wallet, the same that God has blessed with His hand. If you could manage to swallow it, you would have no cause to fear the attacks of the devil.' The count regained his understanding and power; he opened his eyes and looked at his uncle and began to speak with his fair lips: 'Hearken, fair lord,' said noble Vivien, 'I truly know that God is Life and Truth, who came to earth to save His people. He was born in Bethlehem of the Virgin. He let himself be hanged on the Holy Cross and was pierced by the spear of Longinus, so that blood and water flowed from His side. He touched his eyes and

at once they were opened. "Mercy," he cried and God forgave
him. God, I accuse myself of all the evil I have done since the
hour I was born, all the sins and all the omissions. Uncle
William, give me some of it.'—'Ah!' exclaimed the count,
'you were born in a good hour! Whoever believes in this shall
never be damned.' He ran to the spring to wash his white
hands then took the holy bread from his wallet. He put a little
into his mouth and the count contrived to swallow it; the soul
departed, the corpse was left.   [2052]

   When William saw this he began to weep and lifted him up
on Balzan's withers, intending to carry him back to Orange.[13]
Then the Saracens and Slavs attacked him. Fifteen kings
whose names I can tell you: King Mathamar and a king of the
Avars; Bassumet and King Desramed; Eaduel the strong and
the soldan of Africa, and Aelran with Aelred his son; King
Sacealme, Alfamé and Desturbed; Golias and Andafle and
Wanibled. The whole fifteen struck him on his embossed
buckler, and very nearly overwhelmed him. When William
saw that he could not hold on, he laid Vivien down and com-
mended him to God. Then very valiantly he turned against
them and all fifteen rained so many blows on him that they
forced them apart and separated the uncle from his beloved
nephew. Then the Saracens surrounded Guy and brought his
horse down dead beneath him so that the youth was over-
whelmed on the ground. Alas, what a grievous blow when the
warrior falls! Three hundred rushed upon him with swords;
they took the youth and bound him tightly, before William's
eyes, who greatly mourned him. 'Oh God!' he said, 'who
dwells in Trinity and rules the earth and the starry heavens,
what a decline in my great noble family and what destruction
of my mighty kindred! Guy, my friend, now you are a
prisoner! may He deliver you, who suffered on Good Friday
to save Christians!' They carried him off to the ships before
the count's eyes and he was much grieved; and turned on the
Saracens in all his wrath; fifteen of them he slaughtered and
wounded sixty, not one of whom could stay on his feet.   [2090]

134. Monday in the evening. The French were dead or carried
off captives. Not a horse remained, not a man in the saddle,

and William was left alone in the Archamp, with no mortal man, but only God. Then came Alderufe who rode up on his right and when he was before him gazed in his face: 'You are not William, nor Bertrand, nor Guielin, nor Walter of Termes, nor Giscard, nor Gerard who leads them. You do not look like one of that proud kindred!'—'In faith,' said the count, 'I must be one of them!'—'I care not, by my right hand,' said Alderufe. 'Whoever you are you will soon lose your head. Not all the gold of Palermo could save you.'—'It is as God wills,' answered Count William.   [2106]

135. 'Tell me, brother Saracen, what do you blame me for that you wish to fight me? If I have done you wrong, I will make amends, and here is my gage, if you will take it.'—'This is what I accuse you of, William,' Alderufe answered. 'There should be no Christian man or woman, nor any baptism in this land. Whoever receives the water on his head does wrong, for this baptism is not worth a bean. God is in the sky and Mahomet on earth, God gives the heat and Mahomet the cold weather, and when God sends rain, Mahomet makes the grass grow. Whoever would go on living should ask leave of us and of Mahomet who governs the world.'—'You do not know what you are saying,' answered Count William. 'Wretched heathen, you are talking blasphemy. I deny that things are so, for God is greater than any earthly power.' Alderufe pricked his horse, then William spurred forward and they struck each other on their fresh shields, smashing and shattering them from one side to the other, piercing and breaking the mail of the hauberks. William the marquis fell with his legs in the air and Alderufe tumbled down on the grass. Saddle and surcingle could not prevent their visors from sticking into the ground and the soles of their feet from turning towards the heavens.   [2133]

136. The Saracen Alderufe was valiant and bold, a good warrior of mighty strength, but he did not know God and so was quite lost, for he believed in Pilate and Beelzebub, Antichrist, Bagot and Tartarin and old Astaroth of Hell. He leapt first to his feet, and Count William rushed upon him, drawing Joyous, his sword, which had belonged to Charlemagne. The

Saracen was big and heavy, his body was long and his head
was high up, so, not being able to reach it, William struck
lower and cut through his leg at the thigh. Then the foot fell on
the ground on one side and the trunk toppled over on the
other. 'Brother,' said William, 'why should I strike again?
You are crippled and can make no more use of your strength.'
He came to Florescele's stirrup and, seizing the pommel, the
warrior mounted and pricked the horse with sharp spurs so
that it reared up with power and might. 'Ah!' said William,
'my God has been good to me. His champion must be
sustained and whoever believes in Him will never be defeated.
I do not think this horse will be given back today!' Monday in
the evening. 'God has looked favourably on me,' said William.
'This horse is worth all the gold of the lord of Palermo.' He
went to Balzan and cut off his head, but when he had slain him
he sadly lamented: [2163]

137. 'Alas! Balzan, I have wrongfully killed you. As God is
my help, you never deserved it, night or day you never did
anything wrong. But I killed you lest a Saracen should ride
you and be the cause of shame to good knights.' He went his
way, changing his language for he spoke in Hebrew, German
and Berber, Greek and Dutch, Aleis and Armenian, and other
tongues that the warrior had learnt. 'Vile pagans, may
Mahomet fail you!' The valiant William slew many of them,
more than seven score before he departed.   [2175]

138. Count William rode away proudly, like a noble and most
valiant count. Alderufe lay upon the ground and looked at his
steed. 'Ah! Florescele, good worthy charger, never shall I find
your equal. Once you belonged to the great king Desramed
and I brought you to the Archamp by the sea to take my ease
and strike a fine blow. William has taken you and my heart is
full of shame. If I had my way, six devils would take him. Ah!
William, what a horse you have taken. If only you were a man
who could care for him! There is none so good in all Christen-
dom nor in heathendom could you find his equal. Give him
back to me, lord, of your goodness, and I will give you four
times his weight in gold, the finest and brightest gold in
Arabia.' When William heard him, he laughed under his

visor: 'Foolish king, see about getting your thigh mended, having a crutch so you can walk and fitting an iron peg-leg on to your stump! I will see to having the horse cared for, like a man who knows what he is doing, for thanks be to God I have had many a good one.' [14]   [2200]

139. 'Oh! Florescele, sweet-tempered horse. Never was there such a charger. The wind is not as swift as your paces, nor bird in flight. You brought me to this place where I have lost my leg. Now William takes you hence for I am defeated.' Then the count dismounted from the good horse and took the armour from the dead pagan's body. Hastily the count armed himself: he looked more like a Turk than any man alive. [15]   [2205]

140. Monday in the evening. At these words William turned back. He went to the pagan and cut off his head. Then came up swiftly the pagans from Palermo, from Nicodemia, Africa and Superbia. The pagans of the land pursued good Count William right up to Orange. He came to the gate but it was not open so without delay he called on the porter: 'Hi! good porter, let me come in!'—'Who are you?'—'William Hook-nose!'—'You shall not come in here,' said the porter, 'until I have told my lady about it.'—'Go then, good fellow, but do not delay.' Then he climbed the marble steps. 'Now, noble Guibourg, by my faith in God, there is a knight at the gate, big and thickset and strong; he is so fierce I dare not look at him. He says he is William Hooknose, but I do not want to open the gate to him for he is all alone, not a soul with him. He is riding an Arab steed, whose equal could not be found in Christendom nor the heathen lands. Pagan weapons, too, hang at his side.' Then said the lady: 'I shall recognize him easily. If it is he, we will let him enter.'   [2234]

Then she went swiftly down the steps and came to speak to the count. 'Who are you, who call at the gate?'—'Lady,' he said, 'you know me well. I am William the hook-nosed marquis.'—'You are lying,' retorted Guibourg, 'vile pagan, full of deceit, you will not get in by these tricks, for I am all alone, without any warriors. If you were William Hooknose there would be seven thousand knights with you, Franks of France, true-born barons, and all around you minstrels would

be singing and we would hear the sounds of rote and harp.'—
'Ah! woe is me!' said William. 'I used indeed to travel with
such array. Lady, you know well,' he continued, 'that as long
as God wills, a man may be rich and then, if it please God, he
will be poor again. I have returned from the Archamp by the
sea where I have lost the noble Vivien. My nephew Bertrand,
son of Bernard of Brubant, is a prisoner there, with Guielin
and the noble Giscard.'   [2258]

Guibourg gazed along the well-beaten track and saw seven
thousand pagans approaching; they were returning from
pillaging in fair France. They had laid waste St Martin of
Tours and destroyed the main tower. With them were a
hundred captives in chains, who were being beaten with sticks
and clubs, scourges and whips. When Guibourg saw it, she
began to lament: 'If you were truly William Hooknose, you
would defend holy Christianity and the victims that these
wretches are carrying off.'—'Ah!' said the count, 'I never
heard such a thing! Truly you are seeking to test me! Whether
I live or die, I shall have to go there!' Then he spurred and
urged on the swift charger, which galloped faster than a bird
in flight. When the pagans saw him they were very glad. One
said to another: 'This is our liege, King Alderufe of Palermo
by the sea who went to attack the city of Orange. God is good
who has brought him back to us and not let him be slain by
William Hooknose. Truly we must give thanks to Mahomet
and Apollyon, Bagot and Macabeu!' During the time they
were giving thanks, Count William did not delay a moment,
for the first man he met he sent his head flying and the next
ones too, and the fate of the fourth was not any different.
Fifteen of them William slew in one sortie. Said one to another:
'This is a devil,' but the other replied: 'You are much to
blame, for our lord is angry with you because of the battle at
the Archamp by the sea where we were with him.' Then
Saracens and Slavs turned to flee and abandoned all the booty
to him. When William saw this he gave thanks to God and
handed over all the booty to the prisoners from that district.
[2298]

141. Count William urged his horse to a gallop and went to

attack Corberan of Oliferne. He smashed the shield and cut through the hauberk, and brought him down dead to the ground on the end of his lance. The lady Guibourg looked on from a window and when she spoke it was a true word: 'That stroke looks like William's! Come back here and the door will be opened.' [2305]

142. The noble count returned to the city. 'Now, Lady Guibourg, will you let me in?'—'No, by God,' she said, 'not unless you show me on your nose the scar that William, the hook-nosed marquis, received in battle from King Tibalt the Slav.[16] There are many men who are very alike in prowess and valour. And I am alone with not one man except the porter you see here.'—'I never heard such a thing,' said the count, 'this enemy today has caused me much toil!' He undid the laces on his jewelled helmet and let it fall back on his shoulders so that his whole face was visible to her. When the lady saw him she knew him well. With a heartfelt sigh she began to weep: 'Good friend, open the gate for him, for this is William, my true lord.' Monday in the evening. They opened the door and welcomed William. He had been trying to get in for a long time. [2328]

143. Count William dismounted by the step and the lady Guibourg took his horse and led it down into a stall. First she took off the saddle and bridle, then gave it hay and oats to eat and covered it with a thick folded cloth. Then she went to kiss and embrace the count and asked him fair and courteously: 'What have you done with the men, my lord,' she said, 'the four thousand seven hundred you took with you?'—'In faith, lady, the heathens defeated them, and they lie, bloody-mouthed, there on the Archamp.'—'Lord,' she said, 'what have you done with Vivien?'—'In faith, lady, he lies dead and bleeding.' When Guibourg heard this she was very grieved. 'What have you done, my lord,' she said, 'with Bertrand, the son of Bernard of Brubant?'—'Sweet lady, he fought for a long time. Fifteen encounters in the heart of the battle. At the sixteenth they attacked him so fiercely that they slew his swift warhorse beneath him. He drew his sword and held his shield before him, as he slashed at their legs and sides. Then the vile

heathen race took him captive. They bound him hand and
foot and put him in a barge before my very eyes. I could
neither help nor save him.'—'Alas!' said the lady, 'what ill
news of Bertrand! It grieves me for I loved him dearly. [2357]

144. 'What have you done, my lord,' she said, 'with little Guy,
the fair youth with courteous manners? I gave him King
Mabun's banner, the warhorse of Oliver the Gascon, the
hauberk and helmet of Tibalt the Slav.'—'In faith, lady, he
bore them worthily. He bore the standard in the midst of the
battle and did well until the sixteenth attack. Then the vile
Saracens captured him. They bound him hand and foot and
bore him to the galley before my very eyes. No help nor
succour did he get from me.'—'Alas!' said the lady, 'for such
anguish and suffering! It grieves me for I loved him dearly.
[2371]

145. 'My lord, what have you done with Walter, with
Guielin and Count Rainier?'—'In faith, lady, the pagans
overcame them and hold them prisoner in their barges.'—
'Alas!' said the lady, 'for such grief and evil! From what you
say, not one has returned. Wash your hands, my lord, and
come and eat, I have had it ready for you since this morning.
You can have enough for four thousand knights, the men-at-
arms and all the squires.'—'Woe is me,' said noble William,
'It is not yet quite two days since I had nigh on fifteen thou-
sand and now I am here one of but three people. In a short
time I have had a great disaster.' [2386]

146. Then he took hold of his lady's silken sleeves and together
they went up the marble stair-case. No man was there to wait
upon them; the lady Guibourg hastened to bring him water
and afterwards offered him the towel. Then they sat down at
the bottom table, for they were too sad to sit at the highest.
William saw the benches, forms and tables where his great
household used to sit. No-one was amusing himself in the hall,
nor playing at chess nor backgammon. Then he began to
lament, as a noble lord should do. [2398]

147. 'Oh, great hall, how broad and long you are! On all
sides I see you fairly adorned. Blessed be the lady who has thus

prepared you. Oh! high tables, how well you are set up, I see the linen cloths laid over you, the dishes filled and overflowing with haunches and shoulders, cakes and dainties. They will not be eaten by the noble mothers' sons who had their heads cut off on the Archamp.' Then William wept and Guibourg fainted. He lifted her up and thus he consoled her: [2409]

148. 'Guibourg, my lady, you have no need to weep, for you have not lost your dearest kinsmen. I must grieve and make lamentation for I have lost my noble lineage. Now I will flee to foreign lands, to Mont-Saint-Michel, or to Saint Peter's in Rome, or to a waste land where no-one can find me. There I shall take the vows of a hermit, and you will take the veil and become a nun.'—'Lord,' she said, 'it will be time to do this when we have finished our lives in the world. [2421]

149. 'Lord William, go forth in the name of God. Tomorrow at dawn, mount your warhorse and set off to ride straight to Laon, to the emperor who should hold us dear, and ask him to come and bring us help. If he will not, then give your fief back to him, for it would be ill-doing to hold even a span of it for a day. Let him provide for you and your wife or, for God's sake, allow us to eat daily two quartern loaves from his own table.' [17] Then said William: 'I shall go very reluctantly, but I must heed your advice: on many occasions it has been of great service to me.' With these words William went to his rest and next morning at dawn he mounted his good warhorse. [2436]

150. 'My sweet lady, I have accepted your advice and will go to the emperor in his hall and ask him to send us his aid. But if the pagans observe it, they will soon come and take my fortress from me; who will defend these walls and this land against the Almoravides, Saracens and Turks?'—'Lord,' she said, 'the power of Jesus, and seven hundred ladies and more whom I have here. They will cover their bodies with the bright hauberks and their heads with pointed green helmets. If it comes to a battle up there, they will hurl lances, stones and sharp stakes. This will not take long. Then, if God wills, help will arrive.'—'May God help you,' said William, 'God who dwells above but works marvels here below.' [2453]

151. William set off and left Guibourg weeping. He took a
squire, a mere boy who was not even fifteen years old. The
spear was big and weighed him down and the shield dragged
almost on the ground so that he kept nearly falling from the
saddle. When William saw it he was greatly distressed and
took the boy's weapons from him. Whenever they met a
pilgrim or a merchant or journeyed by a castle or township,
William gave the boy back his weapons, but when they were
past he took them again on his own shoulders. The whole day
he wept for his nephew, Bertrand, for Guielin and for Count
Vivien and thus he went on his way lamenting until he reached
Laon and dismounted at the entrance steps. It was William's
custom to take them much Spanish gold and in their folly
many now turned to him. Thirty of them did not get enough,
nor sixty acquire anything from which between them they
could have bought a glove.   [2474]

152. William saw the gay young knights coming to ask him for
Spanish gold, for he was accustomed to give them rings. 'My
lords, you must not blame me. I have still much gold and silver
in my famous city of Orange. But, so God help me, I could not
bring it, for I have returned from the Archamp by the sea
where I have lost the noble Vivien. My nephew Bertrand is
imprisoned there, Walter of Termes, and Rainier the wise,
Guielin and bright-faced Giscard. Guibourg is left alone in the
fair city. For God's sake she begs that you will aid her.' When
they heard speak of misfortunes, they let drop the reins of the
fiery warhorse and left the count alone there on the square.
They went back to the palace and sat down to eat. Now
William Hooknose will learn how a poor man addresses a rich
one, and how small a reward one gets for giving counsel.
[2495]

153. 'Where then is William?' asked the king and they
replied: 'He is still at the foot of the steps. It is the devil him-
self who has brought him here, for he says he has met with
disaster.' Then said the king: 'Let that be. It is not for you to
mock the noble count. Go out at once and bring him to me.'—
'Willingly, lord, since you command it.' William climbed the
marble staircase; the king embraced him and sat him down at

table. When he had eaten, the king began to question him. 'Lord William, how fares it with you? It is more than seven years since I saw you, nor would you seek me now, I know, but for some need.'—'Lord,' he said, 'you shall soon know it all. I had subdued Spain so thoroughly that I feared no man born of woman. Then the noble Vivien sent to me to lead out the warriors from Orange. He was my nephew, I could not refuse him and seven thousand of us set out, all armed knights. Not one of them is left to me. I have lost the noble Vivien, my nephew Bertrand is imprisoned there, the son of Bernard from the city of Brubant, with Guielin and bright-faced Giscard. Guibourg is left alone in the fair city; she implores you, in the name of God, to aid her.' The king never deigned to look at him but he began to weep for Bertrand. [2525]

154. 'Louis, my lord, I have toiled much and striven in many battles. Guibourg is alone in the town of Orange; she implores you in the name of God to aid her.' Then said the king: 'I am not happy about this. I will not set foot there on this occasion.' Said William then: 'A thousand curses on the promise-breaker!' He took off his gold-embroidered glove and threw it at the emperor's feet. 'Louis, my lord, herewith I give you back your fief. I will not keep even half a foot of it. You can give it away to whomsoever you like.' In the hall there were some fifteen knights, brothers, uncles, kinsmen, cousins, nephews, who would not fail William though it cost them their heads. On one side was Reynold of Poitiers, one of his nephews, by his eldest sister, who began to shout in a loud voice: 'Do not do it, uncle, by the powers of Heaven! Keep your fief, baron's son! So help me God who succours all men, I will not be stopped by any man on earth from bringing you four thousand knights with bright armour and swift chargers.'—'By God,' said William, 'you want to help me! Cursed be the uncle who does not cherish a good nephew.' [2551]

155. On the other side was Ernald of Gironde and his father, Aymeri of Narbonne, and Count Garin of the city of Anseüne. They said to each other: 'It would be great shame to our friend if we let him be destroyed.' Then said his father, Aymeri of Narbonne: 'No king or count will prevent me from bringing

him seven thousand of my men.'—'And I, four thousand,' said
Garin of Anseüne.   [2560]

156. Then spoke Beuves of the city of Commarchis. 'I am his
brother and may not fail him. No man alive will prevent me
from bringing him four thousand knights.'—'And I, three,'
said white-haired Ernald. 'And I, two,' said the youthful
Guibelin. 'My lords,' then said Baldwin of Flanders, 'Count
William is noble and valiant. He has loved his peers and his
neighbours and succoured them then whey were attacked. No
man shall prevent me from bringing him a thousand knights.
Let us go to the king and cry him mercy, that he may help us
bring aid to William.'   [2574]

157. All these barons came to the king and Baldwin began to
speak: 'Great emperor, by the Son of Mary, look on William
who is weeping and sighing. His flesh is bruised under his
Syrian tunic: that was never the result of cowardice. Guibourg
is alone in the town of Orange and being attacked by the
pagans of Syria, those from Palermo and from Tabaria. If they
take Orange, then they will hold Spain.[18] They will cross the
passes above Saint-Gilles. When they hold Paris they will have
Saint-Denis. Cursed be the man who then would serve you!'
Then said the king: 'I will go myself, and thirty thousand
knights in my train.'—'That you shall not, my lord,' said the
queen. 'Lady Guibourg was born a heathen and knows many
arts and evil tricks. She is skilled in herbs and compounding
potions. She would soon have you enchanted or killed. Then
William would be king and Guibourg queen, and I would be
left alone and wretched.' When William heard this he was
nearly mad with rage. 'May God curse you, for what you say,
vile queen. You were drunk last night. He knows very well I
have never deceived him. They are only too true, these deeds
of violence which you have heard of down at the Archamp.
[2602]

158. 'Vile queen! You filthy babbler! Thibaut laid you, the
cowardly lecher, and the ill-faced Esturmi. They were sup-
posed to protect the Archamp against the pagans but they ran
away and Vivien stayed behind. More than a hundred priests

have had you and vigorously mounted you, but you never wanted to call for a chamber-maid. Vile queen! You filthy babbler! It would have been better if he had cut off your head, seeing that all France is brought to shame through you. You sit by a warm fireside, eating your well-spiced chicken and drinking your wine from covered goblets, and when you go to bed you are well covered and you get yourself laid with your legs in the air. These lechers assault you in fine fashion, while for us the days dawn grimly as we suffer the buffets and assaults with many a bloody blow to the head in the Archamp! If I draw this sword from its sheath, I shall very soon have your head off!' He drew it a foot and a half out of the scabbard but Aymeri of Narbonne, his father, came forward and spoke to him wisely. 'Lord William, leave this affair alone. She is your sister, cursed be the hour she was born!' And the king said: 'Well spoken, by God, father, for she speaks like a mad woman. If I do not go, I will send my army. Tomorrow before daybreak he shall have twenty thousand men with drawn swords.'—'My thanks to you, Emperor,' said William. [2635]

159. Our emperor had his barons summoned and set his seal to letters and charters and sent them out through all the kingdom. Within a week there were twenty thousand armed men in addition to the host of William Hooknose entrusted to him by his kinsfolk in the kingdom. The emperor sent for William: 'Lord William,' said valiant Louis, 'I have summoned the whole realm for you.'—'Lord,' said William, 'God bless you for it. Noble Emperor, give me leave to depart.' He had his tent pitched on the hill of Laon. A young man came out of the king's kitchen, ragged, barelegged and without any shoes. He had big feet and bow legs and carried a great cudgel [19] on his shoulders. There is no man today who could carry its like. He came to William and thus addressed him: 'Lord William, I want to go with you to the battle at the Archamp by the sea. I will kill the Slavs and the Saracens.' And William answered: 'That would be too much. You look like a man who likes to dine early and does not care for getting up in the mornings.' But Rainouart said: 'You are talking nonsense! If you take me to the Archamp by the sea I will be worth more than

fifteen of your peers, of the very best you have gathered there.'
Then said William: 'Spoken like a fighter. If you want
weapons, I will have you armed.'—'So please God,' said
Rainouart, 'I will never carry any other weapon than my
cudgel and I have no desire to mount a horse!'   [2668]

He went to his master to ask his leave to go: 'Master,' he
said, 'I have lingered with you but now comes the time for me
to better myself. Count William wants to take me with him to
the battle at the Archamp by the sea.'—'Wretch,' said his
master, 'do not do it! For you cannot endure great hunger or
the toils and troubles you will have. You will miss the wines
and liquors, the bread and meat and great plenty; you will die
there in misery and wretchedness. I grieve for it, for I have
reared you softly.'—'You are talking nonsense,' said Rain-
ouart. 'I shall not stay behind for anything you possess, but
rather I will go to the fierce field of battle.' When the master
went towards him, thinking to hold him back by force,
Rainouart struck him such a blow with his cudgel that he
knocked him flat in the fire. Before he could get up, his mous-
taches were singed off. Then he said: 'Lie there, master!
Henceforth you will look after the house and if anything is
missing they will ask you for it.' He came running up to
William Hooknose's tent on the hill top near Laon. He kept on
asking for it until it was pointed out to him.   [2694]

Rainouart went into the kitchen and began to build the fire
and carry water. They made a fuss of him, for he was very
skilled at it, and they gave him wine and spiced ale and
liquors, so much that they got him completely drunk and then
the wretches stole his cudgel. When he awoke, he could not
find it and began to lament. 'Unhappy wretch, alas! woe is
me that ever I was born!' Then the scullions began to mock
him and Rainouart looked at them and said: 'Sons of whores,
have you stolen it from me!' He seized the two nearest, one in
each hand and crashed them together so that the four eyes
started from their heads. 'I'll give you back the cudgel,' said
the third. 'You'll get no thanks for it,' retorted Rainouart.
They took him with them into the hayloft; two of them
together could not lift it, but Rainouart went over to it and
with one hand put it up on his shoulder. Then he challenged

the Slavs and the Saracens: 'Not one of you will escape, now I have my cudgel.' [2717]

160. William rose early as soon as day dawned and had a trumpet blown loudly. More than sixty answered him across the field. Rainouart heard the blaring noise and staggered out of his lodging in a daze, quite forgetting his cudgel in the kitchen. He only remembered it when he came to the ford and began to try the depth in front of the French. He washed his face in the cold water and began to clear his head from the fumes of the wine. Then for the first time he remembered his cudgel and began to retrace his steps. Count William called to him, 'Rainouart, my friend, do you want to go back to the kitchen and look after the cooking-spits? Before you set out I told you clearly you would not be able to endure and survive it.'—'No, good lord, it never entered my head; I just left my cudgel behind in the lodgings.'—'Stupid wretch, let the stick go! I will have one cut for you in the wood, long and stout and just your size.'—'Never, please God!' retorted Rainouart. 'There is no wood on earth where it could be replaced. I've had this cudgel full seven years in the kitchen at the city of Laon and never has it been broken or splintered.' [2744]

Then said William: 'I will have someone fetch it.'—'Now you are talking like a gentleman,' answered Rainouart. He looked around him and saw a Fleming, a fine man, slender and well formed, riding a swift horse, and ordered him to fetch the cudgel. 'Willingly, lord, since you command it.' He set spurs to his horse and rode as far as the meadow where he dismounted and tried to lift it. Then he consigned the club to the devil and remounting his horse rode back again, never stopping till he reached William. 'Tell me, good sir, have you brought the cudgel?'—'No, truly, lord, I could not budge it. Cursed be the beard of the man who forgot it, and his mother, too, for I could not budge it.' Then Rainouart said: 'I shall have to go myself. It will never get here by mortal hands if it is not carried in my own arms.'—'I do not want to wait any longer,' said William. 'What does it matter to me if you go? But be back at the lodgings by nightfall.' Rainouart set off back again with rapid steps, a swift-moving Gascon could not have got there more quickly. When he saw the cudgel he laughed delightedly and lifted it on to his shoulder one-handed. However much the French hurried, Rainouart was back again on the field before they had all passed through the ford. Count William spoke to him: 'Have you got your cudgel, my friend?'—'Yes, good lord, thanks be to God. It was brought to me by Our Lady. The Saracens and Slavs will soon pay for this; not one will escape now I have retrieved it. Monday in the evening. Now, ride out in search of the battle or when we come to the fighting at the Archamp the pagans will have fled from there, those from Palermo, or from Africa, from Nicodemia and Superbia.'—'This fool is going out of his mind,' said the French, 'he is looking for a fight and God give him a fierce one.' For the cowards' bowels were turned to water, but the valiant warriors settled firmly in their saddles on the swift Castilian chargers. [2789]

161. William rode over hill and valley, over the mountains without delaying until he reached Orange which he had longed for. At the foot of the steps he dismounted and the lady Guibourg came swiftly down and kissed his face very lovingly and said: 'How have you fared in France?'—'Very well, so please you, lady. I have brought more than twenty thousand men with me, put under my command by the emperor, in addition to the forces provided by my loyal kinsmen. Thanks be to God, I have more than forty thousand.'—'Is he not coming, then?'—'No, lady.'—'I do not like that.'—'He is lying sick at Aix-la-Chapelle.' Then said Guibourg: 'You are making that up. If he is now stricken, may he never get up again!'—'Now may God the Maker of all things not grant that!' William went up into the marble palace and Rainouart followed him with his cudgel. Those who saw him thought he was the devil and were very frightened lest he should kill them. [2810]

162. William went up the marble steps, followed by Rainouart with his cudgel. The lady Guibourg stared at him, then went to William and spoke to him quietly: 'My lord,' she said, 'who is this gentleman carrying this thick balk of wood on his shoulder?'—'Lady,' he answered, 'this gentleman is a youth

sent me by God,'—'My lord,' she said, 'is he to be feared?'—
'No, indeed, you can safely speak to him.' She drew him aside
for a private conversation. 'Friend,' she said, 'in what country
were you born? Who were your parents and your people?'—
'I am from the kingdom of Spain, lady,' he replied. 'I am the
son of the great king Desramed and my mother was Oriabel
from across the sea.'—'What is your name?'—'Call me
Rainouart.' When Guibourg heard this, she recognized him
for certain. With a heartfelt sigh she began to weep as she
said: 'The name is very well known to me: I had a brother
who was called by it. For love of him, I will have you dubbed
knight and give you a horse and armour.'—'And it please
God,' said Rainouart, 'I shall never carry any weapon but my
cudgel! And I have no wish to mount a horse.'   [2836]

163. 'Good friend, I will dub you knight and give you arms
and a horse in the morning.'—'No, in God's name, lady,' said
Rainouart, 'there is nothing on earth I hate like horses.'—
'Friend,' she said, 'you shall carry a sword, so that whatever
may happen to your cudgel, if it should be broken or splin-
tered you will have it hanging at your side.'—'Lady,' he said,
'give me my sword!'   [2845]

164. The lady Guibourg brought him the sword: its pommel
was of gold and annealed silver. She girded it on him and he
looked at it closely. He did not know that they were brother
and sister, nor will he learn it until the army is beaten and the
forces lost and destroyed.   [2851]

165. Count William ordered supper so that the household
should be well provided for, and Rainouart went into the
kitchen, and wearing his sword began to turn the spit. They
were pleased for he was very skilled at it and gave him so much
spiced wine and liquors that he was completely drunk. The
lady Guibourg did not forget him, but had his bed prepared in
the hall the same as for William Hooknose. She summoned her
brother, Rainouart, very kindly: 'Good friend, lie here in this
bed.' Guibourg went to lie down by William, and Rainouart
looked at the bed but he scorned it as not worth a penny and
went off to sleep in the kitchen. The scullions set his bedding

on fire and singed his hair. When he awoke he smelt the burning and leapt to his feet in a rage, shouting in a loud voice: 'Woe is me, who has scalded me? It was an ill hour when I was born, son of the great king Desramed and Oriabel, my mother from beyond the sea! An ill hour, too, when I met William Hooknose who brought me here from the city of Laon and the kitchens of noble Louis. His scoundrels hold me very cheaply since they have scorched my beard and moustaches.' The scoundrels began to mock him and Rainouart looked at them. 'Sons of whores, have you been scorching me? By the God in whom I trust, you will regret ever starting it, for you shall never get out alive if I can help it!' With his club he killed four of them and chased another out of the lodging, giving him such a blow across the back that it broke him in two and then he kicked him so that he died. Then he went back to sleep in the kitchen. He fastened both the doors securely and pillowed his head on one of the bodies, with his cudgel tucked beneath him. He who lies on a feather bed does not sleep so soundly.   [2895]

166. Rainouart rose up before daybreak and went out of the kitchen to the palace. 'Mountjoy,' he cried. 'To horse, noble warriors! When we get to the Archamp by the sea, the Saracens and the Slavs will have fled. We can never recapture this opportunity.' The French replied: 'Let us be, scoundrel. Cursed be the day you were born! The cocks have only crowed twice so far.' Rainouart answered: 'I have given the order! I must be bold, for I am a king's son. If you do not get up at once, by God in whom I trust, I will make you all pay for it dearly!' He raised the club and struck one of the roof-beams so that he cut through a length of it and made the whole hall shake above them; he very nearly brought the whole thing down in ruins. The French were so scared they got up quickly. A thousand of them lost their shoes in the rush and could not find their clothing. They saddled up the swift warhorses and went a good fifteen leagues in the darkness, for it was still night with no sign of daylight. Everyone cursed Rainouart and his cudgel. 'Cursed be he by the powers of God, this scoundrel, this vile wretch who has us travelling at this hour. He should

be given a good beating.' But William said: 'Leave him be! If he is mad, you should not mock him. There is not one of you so bold or daring, who if he laid a finger on him would not be dead or slain.' [2928]

167. William led the French army until they reached the field of the Archamp. Then spoke his brother, Count Beuves of Commarchis, and his father, Aymeri of Narbonne: 'Noble warriors, fellow-countrymen, the best war is the soonest finished!' The Frenchmen said: 'By the souls of our fathers, we shall strike such blows with lance and sword that France will still be feared when we are dead.' At these words they shouted 'Mountjoy', the war-cry of Charlemagne, emperor of France. Then they lowered their lances and charged the pagans. [2940]

168. William led the French army until they reached the Archamp by the sea, and he saw the ships and barges. 'Noble lords,' said William Hooknose, 'we have now travelled far enough and can see the Slavs and the Saracens. Let us attack and overwhelm them, for they shame our holy Christianity. If anyone is going to disgrace me in the fighting at the Archamp by the sea, I give him my permission, and God's, to return to fair France.' When they heard this they gave thanks to God, and all the cowards turned aside so that the strength and courage of the army was much increased. These wanted to go back to sweet France and they sought William's permission which he granted them, scorning to deny it. [2958]

But do not think they got away like that! For Rainouart met them at a ford, a narrow place where they had to cross, and on his shoulder he bore his great cudgel! 'Lords,' he said, 'where are you going?'—'Count William has given us permission. Come back with us, Rainouart, with your cudgel. You can see that there are so many Slavs and Saracens that not one of us will escape.'—'Scoundrels, you lie,' said Rainouart. 'By the God in whom I trust, you will regret starting this!' Then he rushed at them and changed their minds for them. He killed more than fourteen with the balk of wood and made them all return with him. He went up to William and spoke to him: 'Listen to me, Lord William. These cowards you see here

are my crowd, my people, my followers. Let them and me be
the spearhead against the sharp lances of the Slavs.'—'That
will I do!' said the valiant William. 'So help me God, there
will be no turning back.' These cowards of whom I have
spoken behaved valiantly thereafter in the Archamp and did
great service to William Hooknose.   [2983]

169. Then William Hooknose fought most valiantly and the
God of Glory inspired his followers: the noble Count Beuves
of Commarchis and Aymeri and bearded Ernald and Rainou-
art who bore the cudgel. At the first assault he slew three
hundred. All that day the fierce struggle lasted and all night
they fought the battle until the next day dawned bright and
clear. Such a stream of blood flowed through the Archamp it
would have set a mill-wheel turning. Rainouart looked up,
near noon, and saw the sun high in the sky. 'What the devil is
this! Shall we never do anything but attack and kill pagans!
Indeed there seem to be now three times as many! If I were in
the city of Laon in the kitchen where I used to be, I would
already have had dinner by now and drunk plenty of good
clear wine and I would go to sleep comfortably by the fire. The
Slavs and Saracens shall pay for this!   [3005]

170. 'Lord William, I beg you to wait for me here, and I will
go to the sea over there where the galleys are anchored and
smash and splinter the ships. For when we have won the battle
on the field, the Saracens and Slavs will embark on their ships
and flee over the waters of the high seas. Then, in God's name,
we shall never catch up with them!' The French said: 'Rainou-
art is very valiant, blessed be the day that he was born!' He
began to walk down that way and looking ahead saw a king
riding; Aildré was his name, born in Cordova, and he was
riding a swift warhorse. Rainouart struck him with his cudgel
and smashed him down dead and his horse was split in two.
Entering the ship of the mighty King Aildré, Rainouart found
there seven hundred armed pagans and killed and slew and
smote them all. Count Bertrand was a prisoner there who saw
him and looked at him: 'Lord and knight,' said the valiant
Bertrand, 'baron's son, you who carry this club, blessed be the
day that you were born! Are you a heathen or a Christian?'

Rainouart answered: 'I believe truly in God. What is your name? Do not hide it from me.'—'I am called Bertrand, nephew of William Hooknose.' [3034]

'I know him well,' said Rainouart. 'He brought me here from the city of Laon, from the kitchen where I had been working.'—'Rainouart, my lord, release me! Count William will thank you for it.'—'Wait a little,' said Rainouart. 'I can see some pagans down in the bowels of the ship hiding behind a partition for fear of my cudgel. I'll just go and meet them with my club!' He set off down and pursued them to the deck of the ship and with one blow he broke all their backs. Then he came back and freed the count, breaking the great chain off his neck, and carried him to the fresh grass in the meadow. Count Bertrand then addressed him: 'Rainouart, my lord, you have freed me. Now, for God's sake I beg you to take care of the others.'—'Are there more, then?' said the valiant Rainouart. 'Yes, indeed, four whom you should hold dear. Walter of Termes, and Rainier the wise and Guielin and bright-faced Giscard.' [3056]

'Bertrand, my lord, can you steer a ship?'—'Yes, my friend, I used to be skilled at it, but this galley is so heavy I do not think we could move it with seven hundred people to help.'—'Wait a little,' said Rainouart. 'No-one will speak well of a slowcoach or sing the praises of a bad action.' He thrust his club into the sand, then pushed out from the place, making the ship quiver as he almost sent it flying; Bertrand went to the steering oar. The pagans saw them and were not pleased; they hurled spears at them and stones and sharp stakes. Rainouart came up close to them and jumped, both feet together, into their ship. Then Rainouart laid about him with his cudgel and smote and slew everyone of them but three thousand leapt into the sea in a fright and Rainouart said: 'Now you have chosen a bad way! You would do better to die from my cudgel than drown in the waves of the high seas. Sons of whores, you have come to a bad end.' Then he came to the counts and set them free and Bertrand said to him: 'Rainouart, my lord, you have freed me and these others, God bless you for it! Now, I beg of you to think about horses and good armour such as we were wearing. Then you shall see we know how to fight.'—'You

shall have all you need,' said Rainouart, 'I see the Saracens
have plenty.'   [3087]

   He looked in front of him and saw a king, riding on a swift
steed. With his cudgel he struck him such a blow on the head
he smashed him down dead and the horse was split in two.
'That is a bad blow,' said Bertrand. 'I shall not be mounted
on that horse.'—'Wait a little,' said Rainouart and looking in
the other direction, he saw King Overter. With his cudgel
Rainouart smote him such a blow he smashed him down dead
and the horse was split in two. 'If you go on like this, I shall
not be armed today. You may kill four thousand of them like
this!'—'You are talking nonsense!' retorted Rainouart, 'this
balk of wood is heavy and I cannot control it. These arms of
mine are very strong but when I have lifted it up on high I
cannot possibly restrain it nor give a light blow.' Then said
Bertrand: 'Will you take my advice?'—'Fair lord, you were
born in a good hour!'   [3109]

171. Then said Bertrand: 'Did you ever think that you might
kill them with a thrusting blow?'—'That is true!' said
Rainouart, 'I had not thought of that.' He looked ahead and
saw King Corduel who was riding a swift warhorse. Then
Rainouart charged at him with his cudgel and thrust at his
chest and broke him in pieces so that blood flowed from his
mouth and nose. As soon as he had fallen Bertrand mounted
the charger. Then he equipped the other counts with good
weapons and swift coursers. Then Count Bertrand addressed
him again: 'Rainouart, my lord, you have set us at liberty.
Now for God's sake, I beg you lead us to William.'—'I can
easily show you the way,' answered Rainouart, 'keep close
behind me, my lord Bertrand.' Then he began to deal great
blows and no-one could escape his fists. With his cudgel,
Rainouart cleared a way through the throng of which I have
spoken, so wide that four carts could have passed each other.
[3132]

172. Bertrand was neither poltroon nor coward. He spurred
on the courser and went to attack a pagan, Malagant. He
broke his shield and pierced his hauberk and struck him down
dead from the horse on the end of his lance. 'You have seen

me before!' said Bertrand. 'I know you by your face and
garments. On the boat you often tormented me.'   [3140]

173. They came up to William on the top of a hill and
Bertrand kissed and embraced him. Then William Hooknose
asked: 'Who released you, good nephew Bertrand?'—'In
God's name, uncle,' he replied, 'a warrior bold and proud,
young and valiant. Blessed be the day he was born! He slew
more than three thousand of their men and smashed their
ships and their boats.'—'By God,' said William, 'I would love
him very much if I saw him inclined to good learning.'
Monday in the evening. Then Bertrand and William embraced
each other, and Guielin and Sir Walter of Termes and Giscard
and Gerard who led them. There was great joy among
William's kinsmen.   [3156]

174. Then Gloriant of Palermo appeared, a vile Saracen of
accursed race who brought grief and loss to the Christians.
Then Rainouart struck him such a blow on the helmet that he
broke his head in four places and scattered his brains in
fifteen directions. Then William said: 'You should be a knight.
May I be cursed if I do not give you lands and a noble wife of
good family! Today we shall see, from the first to the last, the
quality of the race of Aymeri of Narbonne.' Not one of them
reposed in the earth or in a crypt, but all of them died fighting
great and fierce battles.[20]   [3169]

175. Then Tabur of Canaloine came along, a Saracen, God
curse him! He was big of body and bent of spine, hairy as a
bear and his teeth were long. He bore no weapons but his
nails and fangs; he saw Guielin and rushed at him with gaping
jaws seeking to gulp him down like a ripe apple! Guielin
struck him in the thigh with his lance and would have slain
him but the shaft broke. Then the noble Count William came
to the rescue and struck him so fiercely with his lance that the
shaft broke in three for his hide was so tough that nothing
could pierce it. Guielin drew his sword and William too, and
they cut and hacked but the Saracen with gaping jaws bit and
snapped at the swords with his great fangs. May God curse
him! He thought he would quite overwhelm William for his

hide was tougher than helmet or hauberk. He will never be slain with a weapon by any man unless he confronts Rainouart and his cudgel! Rainouart came swiftly up the valley. He saw the pagan and rushed at him, and he did the same without hesitation. He opened his jaws thinking to gulp him down but Rainouart struck him with his cudgel on the top of his head. Nine blows he struck and the tenth dispatched him. He cried and howled so that it could be heard four full leagues away. When the pagans and heathens heard it they were much grieved for they knew that Tabur was overthrown.   [3201]

176. When William saw the enemy fall he lifted his hands to Heaven and said to Rainouart: 'A blessing upon you! God keep you from death and danger. Lance and spear are nothing worth: this staff is more use than any weapon in the world.' [3207]

177. The pagans would have been defeated by this loss if the Emir of Balan had not come forward. He bore no arms save a wooden flail and was wearing the hides of four deer; he feared no blows which might fall upon them. The flail was made of a great cleft oak and he rained such a hail of blows on the French that he killed more than would be killed by a wooden mangonel; [21] seven catapults could not have slain so many. When Hugh saw this he was much distressed and spurred on his charger which bore him well. He smote him on the breast with his lance but it made less impression than if it had been a rock. The pagan swung his flail at him and cut right through his shield and slew his horse beneath him, and he had no choice but to flee the battle. 'Alas!' he cried. 'Shame on me, son of Bertrand, cousin of William, the lord of Laon, for a pagan has defeated me today on the field!' The French all cried: 'The end has come! This is Antichrist or Bagot or Tartarin, or old Beelzebub himself from Hell. Ha! Rainouart, where are you with your cudgel? If you do not come, we shall lose all the Christians!' Then Rainouart came down from a hill where he had been fighting against two mighty kings, King Mathamar and King Feragut. But, thanks be to God, he had conquered them both, and his good cudgel was smothered in blood from it. When William saw him, he had never been so glad. 'Good sir,

I thought that we had lost you. Look at the fighting, there has never been such a battle. There is a real devil here with an oaken flail, who is killing us all and smiting and slaying.'— 'Give me seven shields,' said Rainouart and he armed himself with seven hauberks and on his head he set seven spiked helmets. Then he took his cudgel and advanced against him. [3246]

178. When the pagan saw him approach, he spoke to him in his own tongue: 'What the devil! Are you a Christian, who bear such a great club on your shoulder? No mortal man ever bore the like.' Rainouart answered: 'I am truly baptized and if you will not renounce Mahomet and Apollyon and old Tervagant you will soon see who is our God.' He advanced towards him in knightly fashion and with his good cudgel smote him on the head, on the forehead above the eyebrows and made a gash more than a span wide. Devil take it if ever the enemy felt it! For he did not abate his great strength nor change his fierce pride but he attacked him with the flail and cut through six of his shields leaving but one out of seven. Rainouart leapt backwards full fifteen feet, for if it had touched his body he would have been overcome. [3267]

179. Rainouart was both valiant and wise. He made a circle round in French style, and struck him such a blow on the back of the neck that his eyes started from his head, and threw him down dead before all the knights. Then came spurring the mighty King Aildré, who was uncle of Rainouart the cudgeller; he bore an iron mace on his shoulder, and had attacked four hundred of our Frenchmen, but not one could stand against his blows. Now he was seeking William Hooknose when Rainouart thus challenged him: 'Lord,' he said, 'fight with me!'—'Cursed scoundrel, leave me alone! I do not want to talk to such a wretch. Instead, show me William Hooknose and I will attack him with this mace.'—'You are talking nonsense,' answered Rainouart. 'The pagans killed him early this morning. You can see him lying dead there on the field, with the green helmet and embossed buckler.'—'Son of a whore! Are you telling me the truth? Then for love of him I will soon dispatch you!' Rainouart advanced against him with his cudgel lifted and the emir raised his mace; Rainouart

struck him on the head with his cudgel but the helmet was strong and the bright steel shone and the cudgel glanced away from it. Then said Rainouart: 'Now I am shamed—if I do not strike better I have lost my power!'   [3298]

Then Rainouart was angry with the cudgel and with great force he made it strike such a blow that he smashed him to pieces and smote him down dead and the horse was split in two. The staff sank a full yard into the earth and the cudgel was broken into three pieces. If the pagans had been given the whole of Christendom and the length and breadth of heathendom too, you can imagine they would not have been so delighted. They rushed upon him like ravening dogs, seeking to kill him and tear him apart. Then Rainouart braced himself like a warrior; he was not armed with lance or spear but he threatened them with his great fists. If he hit them on the back he snapped their spine; if on the chest, the heart was burst; if on the head, he made their eyes start. The pagans said: 'He is the devil incarnate! He is worse now than he was with his cudgel. Let us hand him over to the devils for no mortal man will ever defeat him!'   [3319]

Then Rainouart unknotted his baldric and came across the hilt of the sword that was given him by bright-faced Guibourg; with great joy he drew it from the scabbard. He looked before him and saw King Foré and gave him a great blow on the helmet and cleft him down to the knotted baldric and his horse was split in two and the sword sank up to the hilt in the meadow. 'By God, this is wonderful,' exclaimed Rainouart, 'that so small a weapon should cut so sweetly. Blessings on the person who girt it on me. Every worthy man should carry four of them, so that if one breaks he can use another.'   [3333]

180. 'We are mad,' said the pagans, 'to let this devil slaughter us in this way. Let us flee out to sea, to the deep waters where our ships are drawn up in order!' But Rainouart had done them such damage that not one was whole and all were crippled. The pagans fled but Rainouart was still fighting; before they got away he had killed two thousand. Then they all took to their heels and not one remained.   [3342]

181. Now the French stopped fighting, for not a Saracen or

Slav was left. They had conquered a vast booty that would make them rich for life. The trumpets were sounded and they all turned back home straight to the splendid city of Orange. They called for water and sat down to dinner, leaving the squires in charge of the booty; stupidly they forgot about Rainouart. Whoever it was will have to pay for it! When they had to bring back the booty he began to lament: 'Unhappy that I am, alas the day that ever I was born! Alas for the son of great king Desramed and Oriabel, my mother from beyond the seas! I was never baptized or christened, nor went to church to pray to God. I have won the battle on the field and Count William rates me so low that he does not think to call me to dinner. Now I shall go to the kingdom of Spain and there I will worship and serve Mahomet. If I choose I can be crowned king and rule over the land as far as Durester, from Babylon to Durazzo by the sea. I shall bear a great cudgel on my shoulder, no other weapon is worth a groat, and I shall come to this country and outside this city I will do to the Christians what today I did to the heathens from beyond the seas! [3372]

182. 'Lords,' he said, 'young knights and squires, I commend you all to God. I am going away to a foreign country; do you go into the fair city and take my challenge to William Hooknose! But, in God's name, I beg you to greet Guibourg for me; there is no-one on earth whom I love so well.'—'At your command,' replied the squires and set off for the city of Orange. 'Lord William, marquis of the hooked nose! The giant is going away who fought with a cudgel!'—'Scoundrels, you are making fun of me!' exclaimed William. 'No, indeed, lord, we are telling the truth: he is going back to Spain. He was never baptized nor christened nor ever entered a church to worship God. If he will, he can be crowned king and rule over the land as far as Durester, from Babylon to Durazzo by the sea. Then he will return to this city with a hundred thousand men, if he wants them, and bearing a great cudgel on his shoulder, and he will do to the Christians what today he did to the pagans from beyond the seas.'—'This is very disturbing,' said William. 'If anyone will go and call him back, I will give

him great presents and anyone who succeeds in bringing Rainouart to me will receive a large part of my lands. Lords, noble barons, be on your way!'—'Willingly, lord, since you command it.' [3403]

Four thousand of them armed themselves with hauberks and helmets and mounted their chargers and they caught up with Rainouart in a meadow as he was about to enter a city. When he saw them riding so swiftly, he did not know what to think or do. He looked around and noticed a cottage, then he went up to it, pulled out the uprights and smashed all the cross-ties and set the roof-tree on his shoulder. Then he turned to face the approaching Frenchmen. 'Lords,' he said, 'where are you going?'—'William has sent for you to come: he pledges you amendment for the wrong he has done you and the dinner at which you have been forgotten.'—'I never heard such a thing,' said Rainouart, 'cursed be he who would take a pledge before I see his people killed and stricken.' [3421]

183. There was a wicked knight among them, named Guinebald, brother of Alealme of Clermont. Like a fool he began to speak: 'By God, you scoundrel, we shall make you come back and hand you over to William in the great keep. You killed Winebold, my nephew, when he burnt you the other day in the kitchen. By the faith I owe to St Simeon, were it not for my lady Guibourg I would put my lance through your lungs.'— 'Hear the fool talking!' answered Rainouart. 'Now as God gives me joy, you shall regret your talking!' He raised the beam and rushed upon him, striking him on the head. He howled like a wolf as his eyes started and his brains were scattered. [3436]

184. Monday in the evening. 'Those were just taps,' said Rainouart. 'I do not know about the others, but the beam has killed you.' The French turned back down the slope of a hill, killing their horses and losing their lances. [3441]

185. Rainouart held the great beam from the cottage; lifting it on high he let it crash down smashing the head of whoever came near him. Count William was beside the doorway—he and Guibourg were embracing and kissing—and William said:

'I can see our men coming and Rainouart is attacking them, in my opinion.'   [3448]

186. Monday in the evening. The French declared: 'Alas the day we went after this devil with his roof-beam! He has killed a hundred men, all unshriven.'—'Now, I will go,' said Count William. With him he took the once pagan queen and Guielin and Sir Walter of Termes and Giscard and Gerard who was the leader, and three hundred French without helmet or hauberk. They found Rainouart on the hill and the lady Guibourg was the first to address him: 'Rainouart, my lord, I beg of you to accept amends from my husband William.'—'Willingly, lady, by my right hand. But had it not been for the beautiful Guibourg, I would strike him on the head with this beam and scatter his brains in all directions. Herewith I pardon you the great wrong you did when you forgot to ask me to sit down to dinner.'—'Then put down your beam,' begged all the Frenchmen. 'Very willingly, in faith,' Rainouart replied. Then he threw it half a league away over the heads of the three hundred Frenchmen, who all rejoiced when he got rid of the beam: more than a hundred of them carried off the weapon.   [3473]

187. Now William and Rainouart were reconciled and with great love made peace between them. They went together to the city of Orange and you may imagine that they soon sat down to eat. The water was brought him by the paladin Bertrand, and Guibourg stood before him with the towel, while Walter of Termes right willingly served him.   [3480]

188. When Rainouart had eaten his fill, the lady Guibourg spoke to him again. 'Rainouart, my lord, tell me in the name of holy charity if you were ever baptized or christened?'— 'Not so,' he answered, 'by the God in whom I trust! I have never been into a church to pray to God.' Then William said: 'I will have you baptized so that you may receive holy Christianity.'—'Thanks be to God,' Rainouart answered and they took him to the church of St Omer and had a great basin brought, big enough for four peasants to bathe in. William was his sponsor and his wife, Guibourg, also, and Count Bertrand also sponsored him willingly, the very flower and cream of fair

France. The gifts were very rich, as you may imagine, for they gave him a thousand pounds in silver, a hundred mules and a hundred chargers. William gave him a fief of seven castles and gave him Ermintrude in marriage, and all the lands of the noble Vivien. Then the lady Guibourg thus addressed him. [3502]

189. The lady Guibourg thus addressed him: 'Rainouart, my lord, in the name of charity, tell me how you left your own country?'—'Lady,' he said, 'I will tell you truly. My father set off to Meliant, together with the emir of Durazzo and left me with a tutor, Apolicant. He went out at break of day and ordered me not to stir until he came back from worshipping Tervagant. I never obeyed him in anything and at once I set off swiftly, playing with my ball, along the shore till I reached the boats and sloops. Full of mischief I boarded a ship and there came a great rushing wind which carried me quickly out to sea where I met with a company of merchants. My little boat hurtled against their ship and broke in more than a hundred pieces. I would have drowned without their assistance, for four of them pulled me into a galley and took me to a great country where they set a wreath upon my head and said I was a slave, a child for sale.   [3528]

'There was no-one, Teuton or Roman, German, Breton or Norman who could afford to buy me there until the king came riding through the fair. He looked at me and when he saw I was a comely child he bought me for a thousand besants. He had me mounted on an ambling mule and took me with him to Paris where he asked if I was nobly born. I told him, without concealment, that I was the son of Desramed and Oriabel was my mother. When he heard I was of high lineage, he greatly feared my father and kinsmen. He handed me over to his cook, Jaceram, and swore by God, the Father almighty, that I would never have a better master in my life. I served seven years in the kitchen and though I was cold I was never hungry. Then William took me with him to the Archamp and there I slew for him thirty of my kinsfolk.' When Guibourg heard this she went up to him and said: 'Embrace me, brother, for I am your true-born sister.' Monday in the evening. 'Are you my brother-in-

law, William? If I had known at the Archamp, though I did
much for you, I would have done even more.' [3553]

LYNETTE R. MUIR
Leeds

NOTES

The *Song of William* is preserved in only one manuscript, which was
published for the first time in 1903. Hitherto, this part of the story of
William had been known only from two later poems (see Introduc-
tion). Even in this manuscript we have a reworking of older material
from two different sources. The first part probably goes back to a very
early poem of the martyrdom of Vivien which some scholars believe
may have been even older than the *Song of Roland*. The scribe who
joined this material with the story of the exploits of Rainouart was a
careless workman and there are a number of contradictions and con-
fusions in the manuscript as we have it. The principal instances are
dealt with in the Notes. The standard edition is that published by D.
McMillan, *La Chanson de Guillaume*, Paris (Picard), 2 vols., 1949–50,
in the *Société des Anciens Textes Français* series: the whole of the text
is included in Vol. 1, with critical studies, notes, glossary, etc., in
Vol. 2. This translation follows McMillan's text, though I have not
always accepted his interpretation of obscure passages.

[1] The geography of this poem is very casual. All the places mentioned
are real ones but the distances are not consistently shown. It has been
suggested that Thibaut's city should be Burgos in Spain rather than
Bourges in France. Both are a long way from the mouth of the
Gironde! I have preferred Bourges as it avoids having the messengers
and armies crossing the Pyrenees.

[2] It is a peculiarity of the manuscript that William is normally called
curb nez 'Hooknose', rather than *court nez* 'Shortnose'. Here, the form
court nez appears for the only time in the manuscript so it has been
translated as 'Hooknose' to match the rest of the references.

[3] The phrase 'Monday in the evening' occurs many times in this text,
generally in a separate short line that does not assonate with the other

lines in the section. No-one has ever found a satisfactory explanation
for this refrain. (See also note 10 below.)

[4] Thibaut seems here to be having a vision of Saracens rather than
seeing the actual forces: a similar scene occurs in *The Waggon-train*,
laisse 23.

[5] Vivien is referring here to the feudal practice by which warriors
were held by oath to their immediate overlord. If he died or fled, they
were free to leave the battle. Thibaut's flight has freed them from any
obligations to continue the battle unless they swear a new oath to
Vivien, as they decide to do.

[6] The text is confused here. Vivien appears to be addressing several
different groups of knights, some more seriously wounded than the
others.

[7] The battle referred to here is not recounted in *The Capture of Orange*,
though it may be one of the many battles foretold at the end of that
poem.

[8] Vivien's prayers in this text are in the same tradition as those of
William in the other poems in this volume. See note 7 to *The Crowning
of Louis*.

[9] William's residence in Barcelona is not explained. Later in the poem
he is back in Orange. If he had just returned from Bordeaux it is
strange that he had not heard of the fighting in the Archamp!

[10] The change from Monday (see note 3) to Thursday (and, in *laisse*
118, Wednesday) only adds to the problem of this refrain. It seems to
hint at an attempt to create a logical time sequence in this part of the
poem. The battle has lasted three days.

[11] Although Gerard dies in this section, Gerard appears as one of the
French prisoners released by Rainouart later in the poem. This is
probably one of the anomalies arising from the clumsy joining up
of the two poems.

[12] The text does not say who kissed William's foot, but it seems likely
that Guibourg is intended.

[13] Here Orange reappears as William's principal city. We seem to
have crossed the no-man's-land between the two poems and this is
emphasized by the return, in the next section, of the refrain ' Monday
in the evening'.

[14] The scene between William and Alderufe is almost a doublet of the
scene with Desramed. Another example of the confused change-over
from one source to another.

[15] The description of William's taking Alderufe's armour is not in *The
Song of William* though it is implied in the next section, where the
porter fails to recognize him. It has been added here from *Aliscans*.

[16] The scar is explained elsewhere in the poems as being the result of a

battle against Corsolt, not Tibalt (see *The Crowning of Louis, laisse* 26).

[17] Guibourg is proposing that William should renounce his status as an enfeoffed vassal and become again a *provendier*, who was directly dependent on the king for his keep, as at the beginning of *The Waggon-train*.

[18] 'Spain', here as elsewhere in the poem, includes the South of France—see note 16 to *The Crowning of Louis*.

[19] It has been suggested that the *tinel*, here translated 'cudgel', was not just a large stick but a yoke or carrying-stick for water-pails (cf. J. Wathelet-Willem, 'Quelle est l'origine du tinel de Rainouart?', in the *Boletín de la Real Academia de Buenas Letras de Barcelona*, XXXI, 1965–6, 355–64). Throughout this poem the term 'cudgel' has been used exclusively for *tinel* and any synonyms have been translated by a different English word (cf. *The Capture of Orange*, note 9).

[20] The meaning of this sentence is obscure. It suggests that their bodies were never buried in ordinary graveyards or crypts as they always died in battle.

[21] A mangonel, like a catapult, was a machine used to hurl stones: it worked on a system of pulleys.

Index of Proper Names

All personal names and geographical terms are listed. The references are to the *laisse* number in each poem: CL (*Crowning of Louis*), WT (*The Waggon-train*), CO (*Capture of Orange*) and SW (*Song of William*).

ABEL   Second son of Adam and Eve, killed by his brother Cain (Genesis 4). CL 22.

ABILANT   Probably ancient Abila, now Nebi-Abil in the Anti-lebanon. CL 59.

ACELIN   Son of Duke Richard of Normandy. CL 43–6. WT 7 (*the arrogant Norman*).

ACERE   Saracen king, brother of Corsolt of Mables and of Clarel of Orange. WT 22. CO 19, 57.

ACOPARTS   A Saracen race or tribe. CO 40.

ADAM   The first man (Genesis 2). CL 22, 26. SW 67.

AELRAN   A Saracen, father of Aelred. SW 133.

AELRED   Saracen king, son of Aelran. SW 133, 160.

Africa   The Roman province of *Africa* = Tunisia and Tripolitania. CO 15, 16, 17, 19, 20, 21, 29, 43, 53. SW 133, 140, 160.

Africa (The city of)   Ancient city in Tunisia, the same as Aumaria. CO 42.

AGRAPART the Slav   Saracen king, brother of Otrant and Harpin of Nîmes. WT 49.

AGUISANT   Saracen king. CO 57.

AILDRÉ   Saracen king, uncle of Rainouart. SW 179.

AÏMER   Brother of William, traditionally known as *li Chétis* (the Captive). CL 22.

Aix   Aix-la-Chapelle, now Aachen; capital of Charlemagne's empire. CL 4. WT 29. CO 47. SW 161.

ALDERUFE   Saracen killed by Vivien. SW 30, 51.

ALDERUFE of Palermo   Saracen king. SW 134–40.

ALEALME of Clermont   French knight, brother of Gunebald. SW 183.

ALELME   A nephew of William. CL 43, 44.

Alemannia   (Text: *Alemaigne* cf. *Germany*). The province of the Alemanni which was a duchy of Charlemagne's empire extending from the Main to Lake Constance and including Alsace. CL 2.

ALFAIS   Saracen king, nephew of Turlen. SW 115.

ALFAMÉ   Saracen king. SW 133.

ALION   Corsolt's charger, taken as a prize by William. CL 21, 29, 51–61.

All Saints (Feast of)   1st November. CL 47.

ALMORAVIDES   Considered a Saracen race; in fact a ruling Berber dynasty of the 11th and 12th centuries. CO 40. SW 150.

206 *Index of Proper Names*

ALORI Ancestor of the traitors including Richard of Normandy. CL 35.

AMARMONDE King whose seat is Bordeaux. CL 48.

Amiens Chief city of Picardy. CO 12.

ANASTASIA (Saint) Historically martyred under Diocletian (3rd century); according to legend she served as midwife at Christ's birth and had her paralysed hands restored in so doing. CL 22.

ANDAFLE Saracen king. SW 133.

ANDER the Persian Moslem king. SW 115.

Andernas *See* GUIBELIN.

Andorra District in the Pyrenees. CL 50.

Anjou County of medieval France, on the Loire. CL 2.

Anseüne *See* GARIN of Anseüne.

ANTICHRIST Considered a Saracen 'god'. SW 136, 177.

ANUBLÉ Saracen king. CO 19.

APOLICANT Saracen, Rainouart's tutor. SW 189.

APOLLYON A Saracen 'god' frequently mentioned in OF epic. Until recently it was thought that his name, *Apolin* (*Apollin/Apollon*), was simply a deformation of *Apollo,* but the name *Apollyon* (= destroyer) given to the Devil in Revelation 9: 11 is a more likely etymology. CO 38. SW 140, 178.

Apulia Province of SE Italy. WT 48. CO 42.

ARAB(S), ARABIAN Of Arabia. CL 15, 58. SW 6–8, 19, 30, 44, 64, 89.

Arabia CO 23. SW 89, 138.

ARAGONESE From Aragon, the kingdom of N Spain. CL 26.

Archamp (The) Battlefield on which Vivien dies and where William and Rainouart avenge his death. The localization of this site is confused: in the first half of SW it appears to be near Barcelona, in the second half, near Orange. SW 1, 2, 3 and *passim.*

ARCHBISHOP (The) Turpin, archbishop of Rheims, a prominent figure in the *Song of Roland* but not there considered one of the Twelve Peers. CL 19.

Ardennes District of the duchy of Lorraine. CO 7.

ARISTRAGOT Saracen king. SW 115.

Ark (The) The Old French word *arche,* used for the Ark of the Covenant and Noah's Ark, is also the regular designation of St Peter's shrine in the Vatican basilica. CL 15, 18, 22, 24. CO 34, 45.

ARNEÏS of Orleans A traitor killed by William. CL 9. WT 6.

ARRAGON (the Arab) Son of Tibalt, stepson of Orable; king in charge of Orange. CO 7, 8, 15 and *passim.*

Artois Medieval county whose chief town was Arras (Pas-de-Calais). CO 7.

Ascension The day Christ rose up to Heaven, celebrated 40 days after Easter. CL 26.

ASTAROTH Saracen 'god'. SW 136.

ATRIBLÉ Saracen king. CO 19.

Brebant/Brabant and is never specifically identified with the province of modern Belgium. CL 13, 22. WT 24, 46. CO 35, 43, 45, 55. SW 54, 140, 143, 153,

Berry　The duchy of medieval France whose capital was Bourges. CL 28. WT 29, 31. SW 13, 29.

BERTRAND the Paladin　William's nephew and most constant companion, son of Bernard of Brubant. CL 9, 15 and *passim.* WT 1, 8 and *passim.* CO 1, 3 and *passim.* SW 54, 115, 134, 140, 143, 151, 152, 153, 170–88.

Bethlehem　Birthplace of Jesus Christ. CL 22. CO 16. SW 133.

BEUVES CORNEBUT　Marquis, deceased brother-in-law of William, father of Vivien and Guy. SW 26, 103.

BEUVES of Commarchis　A brother of William (*Commarchis* is perhaps for Commercy on the Meuse, S of Verdun). CL 22. CO 35, 43. SW 156, 167, 169.

BLANCHEFLEUR　Daughter of Aymeri of Narbonne, sister of William, who marries King Louis. [Not named in these poems.] CL 63. SW *The Queen*: 157, 158.

Blois　City of the medieval county of Touraine, on the Loire. CO 12.

Bonivent　Saracen city. CO 35.

Bordeaux　Capital of the medieval Duchy of Aquitaine. CL 48. SW 74, 83.

BORREL　Saracen king, uncle of Arragon. CO 19, 57.

Bourges　Cathedral city of central France, capital of Berry. SW 2, 28, 32.

Breher　Seaport captured by Vivien. SW 80.

BRETON　Inhabitant of Brittany. SW 189.

Brie　The SE section of the Île-de-France between Paris and the boundary of Champagne. CL 34, 35.

Brioude　Ancient town in the district of Velay, midway between Clermont and Le Puy; sanctuary of St Julian. WT 30. CO 1.

Brittany　Considered part of Charlemagne's empire. CL 2, 51.

Brubant　*See* BERNARD.

BUREL　Saracen king whose twelve sons were killed by Vivien. SW 30, 51.

BURGUNDIAN(s)　Inhabitants of Burgundy. WT 7, 14.

Burgundy　The ancient kingdom of the Burgundians of which the western section became a duchy of France in 843 (capital: Dijon) and the section E of the Saône and Rhône, including French-speaking Switzerland and Provence, composed one or several kingdoms of the Germanic Empire. WT 29. CO 7.

BUTIFER　Saracen king. SW 115.

CABUEL　Saracen king. SW 115.

CAHU　A Saracen 'god' frequently mentioned in OF epic. CL 20, 29.

CAIN　Eldest son of Adam and Eve who killed his brother Abel (Genesis 4). CL 22.

the Ebro. 2. The Kingdom of France (*Francia Occidentalis*) constituted in A.D. 843. 3. The Duchy of France or of Paris, appanage of the Capet monarchs, roughly the Île-de-France and the Orléanais. CL 2, 3, 6 and *passim*. WT 3, 7, 10 and *passim*. CO 3, 4, 6 and *passim*. SW 38, 68, 77 and *passim*.

FRANK(S)   The Germanic race who were overlords of Gaul from the end of the 5th century, their empire reaching its greatest extension under Charlemagne. CL 59, 62. WT 57. CO 32. SW 140.

FRANKISH   Of the Franks. CO 16.

FRENCH, FRENCHMAN   This term is used for all three senses of 'France' (q.v.) often confusingly, thus in CL William is considered a 'Frenchman' by the Saracens (20 etc.) but does not look on himself as 'French' (58). CL 9, 11, 13 and *passim*. WT 6, 7, 20 and *passim*. CO 4, 16, 30 and *passim*. SW 14, 25, 35 and *passim*.

FRISIANS   Inhabitants of Frisia, the islands and coast of the NE Netherlands. WT 7.

GABRIEL (Saint)   The Archangel of the Annunciation (Luke 1 : 26). CL 18.

GAIFIER   A Saracen killed by William. CO 32.

GALAFRE   Saracen king or emir, chief of all the Saracens invading the region of Capua and Rome. CL 15, 17, 18 and *passim*.

Galicia   The province of NW Spain renowned for the sanctuary of St James the Apostle (*Santiago*) at Compostela. WT 48. CO 13.

Gardon (The)   A northern tributary of the river Gard which flows N of Nîmes. WT 40, 42.

GARIN of Anseüne   Brother of William. *Anseüne* is probably the pre-Roman *oppidum* of Ensérune SW of Béziers, Hérault. CL 22. CO 35, 43, 55, SW 155.

GARIN of Rome   Knight in William's army. CL 38.

GARMAIS   Saracen king. SW 115.

GARNIER   French knight of William's army. WT 34.

Geneva   Situated at the outflow of the Rhône from Lake Geneva in the medieval kingdom of Burgundy. CO 7.

GERARD   Vivien's cousin and companion. SW 28–92, 118, 134, 173, 186.

GERIN   One of the Twelve Peers, as in *Roland* (2403 f.). CL 19.

GERMAN(S)   Of the kingdom of Germany. CL 56, 59–61. SW 189.

Germany   OF *Alemaigne* had the extended meaning of 'Kingdom of Germany' from the mid 10th century (cf. *Alemannia*). CL 56–61. WT 48. CO 7.

GIBOÉ   Saracen king. CO 57.

GILBERT of Falaise   A French knight. Falaise is probably the town and castle in W Normandy, birthplace of the Conqueror. WT 40, 49.

GILBERT of Lenu   A Flemish knight, son of Guy, Duke of Ardennes, Artois and Vermandois. CO 5, 6, 15 and *passim*.

GILEMER (*L'Escot*)   A knight in William's army. WT 33, 40, 49.

GILES (Saint)   The 8th-century saint (*Aegidius*) whose sanctuary was at Saint-Gilles-du-Gard. WT 23, 44.

GIRARD of Vienne   Count of Vienne (Dauphiné) who in the poem *Girart de Vienne* is uncle of Aymeri of Narbonne and of Oliver. SW 97.

Gironde   The river on which Bordeaux is situated (cf. ERNALD). CL 8, 22, 48. SW 2, 4, 30, 74, 155.

GISCARD   French count taken prisoner in the Archamp and liberated by Rainouart. SW 115, 134, 140, 152, 153, 170–86.

GLORIANT of Palermo   Saracen knight. SW 174.

Gloriette   Palace of the Saracen rulers of Orange (*see* CO Note 8). CO 13, 17, 20 and *passim*.

GOD   God the Father and God the Son. CL 1, 2, 7 and *passim*. WT 1, 2, 4 and *passim*. CO 1, 3, 4 and *passim*. SW 3, 9, 10 and *passim*.

Golden Gates   One of the Gates of Jerusalem (*Portae Aureae*), not so called in the Gospel accounts of Christ's Entry. CL 22.

GOLIAS of Bile   Saracen king. WT 22. CO 13, 19, 41, 57, 58. SW 133.

GONDRÉ   Saracen king, brother of Quinzepaumes. WT 22. CO 57.

GRIFAIGNE of Aumaria   Saracen responsible for the building of the palace Gloriette in Orange. CO 10, 38.

GUAIFIER of Spoleto   King ruling in Capua. CL 15, 17, 30–2, 56, 57. WT 3, 4.

GUALDIN the Brown   Marquis, nephew of William. CL 35.

GUIBELIN *or* GUIBERT of Andernas   Youngest brother of William. *Andernas* is an unidentified Saracen city in Spain, captured by Guibert. CL 22. SW 156.

GUIBOURG   Name taken by the Saracen queen Orable (q.v.) on her baptism and marriage to William (CO 61). WT 1. CO (= *Orable* 1, 2 and *passim*); 61. SW 56, 75–108, 112, 116, 117, 123, 140–89.

GUIELIN   Nephew of William; brother of Bertrand and son of Bernard of Brubant. CL 15, 18, 28, 29, 30, 59, 61. WT 24, 26, 33, 46. CO 4, 14, 15 and *passim*. SW 115, 134, 140 and *passim*.

GUIMER   Bishop of Nîmes. CO 61.

GUINEBALD   French knight, uncle of Winebold. SW 183.

GUISCHARD   Nephew of Guibourg, killed in the Archamp. SW 83, 84, 90, 93, 94, 95, 99.

GUY   Nephew of William and brother of Vivien; son of Beuves Cornebut. SW 55, 82, 103–33, 144.

GUY   Host of William in Rome (perhaps an error for *Ciquaire* of CL). WT 7.

GUY of Ardennes, Artois and Vermandois   Duke, father of Gilbert of Lenu. CO 7.

GUY of Germany   Pretender to the imperial throne in Rome, killed by William. CL 56–61. WT 7.

HARPIN   Saracen king of Nîmes, brother of Otrant. WT 43–54. CO 16, 19, 22.

Laval on the Cler   Common place-name which the river name does not in this case help to identify. WT 33.

Lavardi   Name given to the quarries near Nîmes, now Barutel. WT 42.

LAZARUS   Brother of Martha and Mary who was raised from the dead by Jesus (John 11). CO 17, 25.

Le Puy   Chief town of the Velay in the Massif Central; famous for its sanctuary of the Virgin. WT 32.

LIARD   Name of William's horse. SW 118.

Lombardy   Kingdom of N Italy conquered by Charlemagne in A.D. 774. CL 2. WT 48.

LONGINUS   Traditional name for the Roman centurion who pierced Christ's side on the Cross (John 19 : 34) and was converted (Mark 15 : 39); according to legend, his blindness was cured when he rubbed his eyes with the blood that ran down to his hand. CL 22, 26. CO 16. SW 133.

LORRÉ   Saracen king. CO 57.

LOT (Saint)   Presumably the O.T. patriarch, nephew of Abraham (Genesis 11 : 27). CL 25.

LOUIS (I, the Pious)   Son and successor of Charlemagne, crowned Emperor at Aix in 813, four months before the death of his father; ruled over the undivided Empire until his death (A.D. 840). CL 1, 7, 8 and *passim*. WT 1–26, 59. CO 7, 35, 43, 55. SW 1, 35, 41, etc.; 153–9.

LOVEL   Name of an ox killed by Harpin. WT 49.

Lympne   Kent, England; site of the Roman shore-fort of *Lemanis*. SW 52, 80.

Lyons   City on the Rhône in the medieval kingdom of Burgundy. CO 7.

Lyons   Name of a forest which surrounded Lyons-la-Forêt (Eure) E of Rouen. CL 51.

Mables   *See* CORSOLT of Mables.

MABUN   Saracen king. SW 144.

MACABEU   A Saracen 'god'. SW 140.

Magdalen (The)   *See* MARY MAGDALENE.

MAHOMET   The Prophet of Islam, frequently considered a 'god' of the Saracens. CL 20, 21, 22 and *passim*. WT 33, 44, 49 and *passim*. CO 16, 17, 21 and *passim*. SW 94, 118, 135 and *passim*.

MALAGANT   Saracen knight. SW 172.

MALCUIDANT   A Saracen (lit. = Ill-intentioned). CO 21.

MANESSIER (the Youth)   Considered one of the Twelve Peers but not in *Song of Roland*. CL 19.

MARETANT   Gatekeeper killed by Gilbert. CO 32.

MARTIN of Tours (Saint)   Roman soldier and bishop of Tours (4th century).   CL 35, 40. SW 140.

MARY (Saint)   The mother of Christ. CL 12, 21, 22, 36, 61. WT 44, 57, 59. CO 1, 10. SW 66, 68, 157, 160.

Pavia Capital of the kingdom of Lombardy. CO 10.

PEPIN the Short Pépin 'le Bref', father of Charlemagne; first Carolingian king of the Franks (751–68). SW 97.

Peralada (Text: *Pierrelate*). The most probable identification of the seat of Dagobert of Carthage is with this town in the province of Gerona (Catalonia). CL 48. WT 6.

Persia Moslem kingdom. CO 2, 13, 22.

PERSIANS Associated with the Saracens as 'pagans'. WT 24. CO 4, 8, 16 and *passim*. SW 115.

PETER (Saint) Leader of Christ's Twelve Apostles martyred in Rome under Nero. CL 13, 18, 19 and *passim*. WT 7, 52. CO 25, 30, 31. SW 148.

Petit Pont (The) Bridge joining the Île de la Cité in Paris to the S Bank of the Seine. WT 1.

PHARAON Saracen king of Bonivent; counsellor of Arragon. CO 35, 36, 37, 52, 53, 55, 56.

PILATE Pontius Pilate of the Gospels, considered a Saracen 'god'. SW 136.

PINCENARS A pagan race, probably the Turco-Tartar Petchenegs who settled near the Black Sea in the 9th century and were exterminated in the 11th–12th. SW 150.

Pincernia Country of the Pincenars. CO 1.

Poitiers Capital of the medieval county of Poitou. CL 39, 46. SW 154.

Poitou County established in the 8th century; a fief of Charlemagne's empire. CL 47, 51. WT 48.

POPE (The) Patriarch of Western Christendom and feudal sovereign of the Papal States. CL 5, 15–33, 56.

Portpaillart Probably Sort in the medieval county of Pallars (*pagus Palliarensis*) in N Lérida, Catalonia. WT 18.

QUARRÉ Saracen killed by Gilbert. CO 26.

QUINZEPAUMES Saracen king, brother of Gondré (lit. = Fifteen hands [tall]). WT 22. CO 19, 57.

RAHER French knight. SW 53, 79.

RAINIER French count. SW 115, 145, 152, 170.

RAINOUART Saracen slave of King Louis; son of King Desramed and Oriabel, brother of Guibourg. SW 159, 160, 162 and *passim*.

Reaumont Saracen city. CO 57.

Red Sea Between Africa and Arabia. CL 15.

Regordane Way (The) The ancient Roman road from Clermont to Nîmes. WT 32, 35, 36.

REYNOLD of Poitiers A nephew of William. SW 154.

Rheims Cathedral city in Champagne. CO 17, 25.

Rhône (The) The river of SE France flowing from Lake Geneva. WT 21. CO 5, 6, 7 and *passim*.

Index of Proper Names

SIMON the Magician   Early Christian convert who sought to buy the gift of the Holy Ghost (Acts 8: 9 f.). CL 26.

SLAV(s)   The pagan Slavonic races, commonly associated with the Saracens in OF epic. CL 22. WT 15, 22, 33, 49. CO 3, 6, 8 and *passim*. SW 133, 140, 142 and *passim*.

Slavonia   Imaginary kingdom of the 'Slavs' (q.v.). CO 20, 42.

SORANT   Pseudonym of Bertrand disguised as a merchant. WT 46.

SORBANT of Venice   A Saracen. CO 20.

SORGALÉ   Saracen king. CO 19.

Sorgremont   Saracen city. CO 19.

Sorgue (The)   East bank tributary which joins the Rhône between Orange and Avignon. CO 15.

Spain, Spanish   The term *Espaigne* usually designates Spain properly speaking, but is sometimes extended to all territory held by the Saracens of Spain which in the 8th and 9th centuries included much of S France, at least sporadically. CL 56. WT 1, 18, 19 and *passim*. CO 1, 7, 19, 57, 59, 61. SW 151, 152, 153, 157, 162, 181, 182.

Spoleto   City of Umbria, Italy; territorial title of King Guaifier. CL 56. WT 3.

STEPHEN (Saint)   First martyr of the Christian faith (Acts 6: 5 f.). CO 47. SW 44.

STRONGARM   Epithet of William. CL 14, 16, 18 and *passim*. WT 42, 45, 51. CO 22, 23, 45, 54. SW 34, 38.

Superbia   Saracen country. SW 140, 160.

Susce   Saracen city. CO 1, 42.

SYNAGON   Saracen king of Nîmes. CO 16, 22.

Syria   Arab kingdom N of Palestine. SW 157.

SYRIAN   Of Syria. CO 59. SW 157.

Tabaria   Saracen district or city, probably Tiberias in Palestine. CO 1. SW 157.

TABUR of Canaloine   A Saracen. SW 175.

TARTARIN   A Saracen 'god'. SW 136, 177.

TENEBRÉ   Saracen king (lit. = Dusky). CL 15.

Termes   Unidentified town considered one of William's seats; also an appanage of Walter of Toulouse. WT 33, 40, 49. SW 115, 132, 187.

TERVAGANT   A Saracen 'god' frequently mentioned in OF epic. WT 44, 49. CO 16, 17. SW 178, 189.

TEUTON   Member of the Germanic race. SW 189.

THIBAUT of Bourges *or* of Berry   Feudatory of King Louis responsible for the Archamp district: uncle of Esturmi. SW 2–36, 51, 78, 158.

THREE KINGS (The)   The three Magi or Wise Men of Matthew 2, called Kings in the medieval tradition. CL 22. CO 16.

TIACRE   Pseudonym adopted by William when disguised as a merchant. WT 46–9, 53.

William's sister. CL 28, 29, 30, 38, 39, 44, 61. WT 26, 33, 40, 49. SW 115, 134, 145, 152, 170, 173, 186, 187.

WANIBLED Saracen king. SW 133.

WILLIAM Son of Aymeri of Narbonne and of Hermengard, one of seven brothers, also brother of Blanchefleur who marries King Louis (CL 63). Captures Nîmes (WT 59) and then Orange, which becomes his main seat on his marriage to Orable (CO 61), but called *count* and *marquis* before these conquests. Nicknamed William *Shortnose* (CL 28); the older form is probably William *Hooknose* as in SW. Also known as *Strongarm*. CL 1, 9, 13 and *passim*. WT 1, 2, 3 and *passim*. CO 1, 2, 3 and *passim*. SW 1, 3, 6 and *passim*.

WINEBOLD Kitchen boy, nephew of Guinebald. SW 183.

YVES One of the Twelve Peers, as in *Song of Roland* (2403 f.), companion of Yvoire. CL 19.

YVOIRE One of the Twelve Peers, as in *Song of Roland* (2403 f.), companion of Yves. CL 19.